The Perilous West

Ramsay Crooks and Robert McClellan
John Hoback, Jacob Reznor, and Edward Robinson
Pierre and Marie Dorion

The Perilous West

*Seven Amazing Explorers and the
Founding of the Oregon Trail*

Larry E. Morris, *1951 -*

ROWMAN & LITTLEFIELD PUBLISHERS, INC.
Lanham • Boulder • New York • Toronto • Plymouth, UK

Published by Rowman & Littlefield Publishers, Inc.
A wholly owned subsidary of The Rowman & Littlefield Publishing Group, Inc.
4501 Forbes Boulevard, Suite 200, Lanham, Maryland 20706
www.rowman.com

10 Thornbury Road, Plymouth PL6 7PP, United Kingdom

British Library Cataloguing in Publication Information Available

Library of Congress Cataloging-in-Publication Data

Morris, Larry E.
The perilous West : seven amazing explorers and the founding of the Oregon Trail / Larry E. Morris.
pages cm.
Includes bibliographical references and index.
ISBN 978-1-4422-1112-4 (cloth : alkaline paper) — ISBN 978-1-4422-1114-8 (ebook)
1. Oregon National Historic Trail—Discovery and exploration. 2. Oregon National Historic Trail—
Description and travel. 3. Explorers—Oregon National Historic Trail—Biography. 4. Explorers—
West (U.S.)—Biography. 5. West (U.S.)—Discovery and exploration. 6. West (U.S.)—Description
and travel. 7. West (U.S.)—History—To 1848. I. Title.
F880.M67 2012
978'.01—dc23
2012032260

Printed in the United States of America

"The feelings of that night were so near that I could reach out and touch them with my hand. I had the sense of coming home to myself, and of having found out what a little circle man's experience is. For Ántonia and for me, this had been the road of Destiny; had taken us to those early accidents of fortune which predetermined for us all that we can ever be. Now I understood that the same road was to bring us together again. Whatever we had missed, we possessed together the precious, the incommunicable past."

—Willa Cather, *My Ántonia*

Contents

Acknowledgments

During my final year of work on this project, I lost three good friends—Matt Brown, Brent Petersen, and Matt Smith. This book is dedicated to their memory.

The editors at Rowman & Littlefield have been great to work with. Thanks to Niels Aaboe, Sarah David, Carrie Broadwell-Tkach, Jon Sisk, Darcy Evans, Benjamin Verdi, and Karen Ackermann.

Thanks to the archivists and staff at the Family History Library, Salt Lake City; Brigham Young University Harold B. Lee Library and L. Tom Perry Special Collections, Provo; the State Historical Society of Missouri, Columbia; the Missouri History Museum, St. Louis; the Filson Historical Society, Louisville; the Kentucky State Archives, Frankfort; the Kentucky Historical Society, Frankfort; the Wisconsin Historical Society, Madison; the Abraham Lincoln Presidential Library and Museum, Springfield; and the Baker Library, Harvard Graduate School of Business Administration.

Thanks to the Charles Redd Center for Western Studies for funding part of the research associated with this book.

Thanks to the many historians who researched these seven remarkable individuals in the past—especially Washington Irving, a tireless researcher and a mighty fine writer.

I appreciate the support of a whole host of folks, particularly Robin Russell, Bill Read, Russ and Cindy Taylor, Rachel and Taeh Osborne, Ron Anglin, Jay Buckley, and Jim Hardee. It has been a particular pleasure to attend the Fur Trade Symposiums held every two years in such historic locations as Three Forks, Montana, and Pinedale, Wyoming. The Museum of the Mountain Man in Pinedale and its parent organization, the Sublette County Historical Society, have done a wonderful job of finding and preserving the history of the Western fur trade.

Most of all, I appreciate the support of my wife, Deborah, and our family—Whitney, Justin, Jen, Elliot, Liam, Courtney, Adam, Isaac, Tahlia, Charles, Tiffani, and Margo. In a series of memorable trips, Deborah and I followed the Astorians along the Wind River, the Teton River, Henry's Fork, the Snake River, the Columbia, Bear River, the south fork of the Snake, the Hoback River, and the Sweetwater, but there was nothing quite like seeing the mouth of the Walla Walla River, where Marie Dorion and her sons were rescued.

Prologue

"The Timely Arrival of This Poor Unfortunate Woman"

On the morning of April 17, 1814, seventy-six well-armed men in ten canoes fought their way up what William Clark called "the great Columbia River," contending with the "strong and rapid" current as they ventured into the Rocky Mountains from the Pacific coast. They had embarked two weeks earlier from Astoria, a trading post at the mouth of the Columbia named after the renowned fur magnate John Jacob Astor, America's first millionaire, who had funded the enterprise—but who would never see the settlement. The War of 1812 and the sale of Astoria to Canada's North West Company had compelled these voyagers, some accompanied by Indian wives and children, to return to their home base in Montreal. They faced the daunting task of ascending the Columbia north into present British Columbia and then winding their way east across the continent, enduring cold, illness, injury, and hunger while infrequently replenishing their supplies at a smattering of trading houses as they paddled the Canoe, Athabasca, North Saskatchewan, Winnipeg, French, and Ottawa Rivers and a host of lakes, including Lake Superior. They would reach their homes early in September, but only after they had made an endless series of troublesome portages—one in neck-high icy water—scaled a series of snowy mountain passes, and lost two of their number to the white water of the Athabasca.[1]

The Astorians were well underway by 8:00 a.m. as they journeyed through the "Great Plains of the Columbia," in present-day southeastern Washington, an area quite unlike the region of lush forests near the coast. They could see "nothing but bare hills" in the distance, with hardly a shrub or a patch of grass visible. Steep cliffs, some two hundred feet high, rose on both sides of the tremendous river, nearly a thousand yards wide at this point.

The barren plains had yielded no game, and the group was subsisting on "extremely lean" horses and dogs purchased from Indians. Then, near the mouth of the "meandering Walla Walla, a beautiful little river, lined with weeping willows," they saw "three canoes, the [Indians] in which were struggling with their paddles to overtake" them. Determined to be on their way—and concluding their pursuers were simply curiosity-seekers—the Astorians "paid little heed," not breaking their resolute rhythm as they plied their oars. But then a child's voice cried out, "*Arretez donc, arretez donc!*" ("Stop, stop!") and the men promptly put ashore and waited. Most of them were French-Canadian, and the sound of a child calling to them in French had sparked their concern.[2]

The landing of the fleet made for a noisy, chaotic scene, with bearded, buckskin-clad boatmen yelling instructions as the oversized canoes—five of birch bark and five of cedar wood, all ten brimming with people and supplies—crowded the rocky shoreline, their sails lowered. The armada totaled ninety passengers, and most of them glanced back for a glimpse of the *enfant* who had called out to them. Then, as the Indians manning the three smaller canoes approached, the Astorians were shocked to see Marie Dorion, the Iowa Indian wife of the well-traveled hunter and interpreter Pierre Dorion Jr., and her two young boys.[3] Seven months earlier, in July of 1813, Marie and her husband and sons had departed Astoria with a small group of trappers bound for Idaho's Snake River country to "join there the hunters left by Messrs. Hunt and Crooks, near Fort Henry, and to secure horses and provisions for [the] journey" back to St. Louis.[4] The hunters they were seeking included three men Marie knew well—John Hoback, Jacob Reznor, and Edward Robinson, three Kentuckians now in the seventh year of their Western sojourn.

As for Dorion and his family, they had plunged westward in 1811 with five score men under the command of twenty-eight-year-old Wilson Price Hunt, a St. Louis merchant singled out by Astor to lead his western fur enterprise. Hunt had been assisted by two of the most fascinating personalities in the history of the early fur trade—Ramsay Crooks and Robert McClellan, unlikely partners whose names will forever be spoken in tandem: Crooks & McClellan. With Hunt's rag-tag collection of savvy North West Company veterans; hard-drinking and hard-driving guides, interpreters, boatmen, and hunters (some French-Canadian, some American, and others Anglo-Indian); and one woman and two children, Crooks and McClellan had made the unforgettable and unforgiving odyssey from the Missouri Territory to the Pacific coast, the second group of Americans to cross from east to west, preceded only by Lewis and Clark. During that journey, Marie had earned a reputation for her impressive stamina, but now she looked wan and feeble.

Several voyagers disembarked to secure a landing spot and check for rattlesnakes among the rocks and wormwood, for they had seen many snakes the previous day. A familiar stench filled the air, both from the "great quantities" of salmon, steelhead trout, and sturgeon drying on Indian scaffolds and from dead fish littering the shore. Marie Dorion's escorts guided their craft to the edge of the water—these were the friendly Walla Walla Indians, described by one Astorian as "tall, raw-boned" men with "strong and masculine" voices, "well dressed; having all buffalo-robes, deer-skin leggings, very white, . . . garnished with porcupine quills."[5]

Someone helped Marie ashore, and her two boys scrambled out of the canoe after her. She undoubtedly hoped to see friends in the group, and she was not disappointed, spotting one man after another who had traveled in Hunt's group, with each familiar face bringing vivid memories of the interminable trek.[6]

Taking full—and normal—advantage of his status as a partner in Astor's Pacific Fur Company, Donald McKenzie sat in the lead canoe as a passenger, not an oarsman. Marie likely remembered him as a strong-willed man who had argued with Hunt as often as he supported him. But perhaps her most memorable image of McKenzie had nothing to do with commerce or status.

Weeks after striking out overland from the upper Missouri River, the caravan had followed a Crow Indian trail that "led them over rough hills, and through broken gullies, during which time they suffered great fatigue from the ruggedness of the country." Traveling in the extreme northeast corner of modern Wyoming, the group found themselves in the badlands lying between the Little Powder and Powder Rivers, their water supply suddenly vanished, the heretofore cool weather suddenly "oppressively warm."[7] Hunt wrote that "the great heat, the bad road and the lack of water caused much suffering," adding that "several persons were on the verge of losing courage."[8] McKenzie's faithful dog, which had struggled so hard to keep up, grew weaker and weaker, its eyes sunken, looking to McKenzie for help, but he had no water to give. Then the dog finally gave out, collapsing on the rocky trail, its heavy panting ceased.

Louis St. Michel, one of a host of French-Canadian oarsmen, sat in another canoe, wielding a paddle and looking right at home. But Marie knew something of what he had endured. Barely a month after forging a tortuous path across the barren ravines, the overlanders fought cold and frostbite as they followed a swift river through a steep, snow-covered canyon. "One of our horses fell with his pack into the river from a height of nearly two hundred feet, but was uninjured," Hunt wrote. The river flowed into a larger, rapid body of water they called "Mad River because of its swiftness. On its banks, and a little above the confluence, [were] situated the three peaks which we had seen [twelve days earlier]."[9] There were signs of beaver everywhere, and Marie and Pierre Dorion had watched as St. Michel and three others prepared to stay behind and trap. Enthusiastic to a man, they checked their Kentucky long rifles and made sure they had sufficient powder and balls. They spread their scalping knives, long English axes, tomahawks, and two-and-a-half-pound steel beaver traps out on the ground and counted them. They packed their buffalo robes and bedrolls, their fishhooks and moccasin awls.[10] They bade farewell to their friends. As Irving wrote, trapping "the upper part of Mad River, and . . . the neighboring streams of the mountains . . . would probably occupy them for some months; and, when they should have collected a sufficient quantity of peltries, they were to pack them upon their horses and make the best of their way to the mouth of the Columbia River, or to any intermediate post which might be established of the company." St. Michel and his companions set out with "stout hearts," determined to strike it rich, but their "lonely cruisings into a wild and hostile wilderness" were like "being cast adrift in the ship's yawl in the midst of the ocean."[11] After being robbed by Crow Indians, they strayed through the Snake River country for more than a year. Three of them somehow survived—they were rescued more than a year later and brought to Astoria.

Marie saw familiar faces in most of the canoes. Joseph Delaunay had barely escaped drowning during the group's winter in the wild, a few weeks before Marie gave birth to her third child. Pierre Brugier had worked with Pierre Dorion for weeks near Astoria, constructing some of the cedar canoes now on the scene. But Marie was likely most relieved to see the Iroquois Indian Ignace Shonowane and his wife and especially their children, the only friends her boys had ever known. Assigned to hunt together, Shonowane and Dorion had grown virtually inseparable, and their families formed their own community at a camp a mile or two from Astoria, along Young's Bay.

Now, as Shonowane and his family, Delaunay, McKenzie, and the others gathered around Marie and her sons, they asked what had become of her husband and his nine companions, knowing full well that whatever his faults, Dorion was not the kind of man who would abandon his wife and children. "This woman informed us, to our no small dismay," reported Gabriel Franchere, "of the tragical fate of all those who composed that party."[12]

When she reached the Pacific Ocean in 1812, Marie Dorion became the second woman known to have crossed the Great Plains and the Rocky Mountains to reach the western coast. The first was Sacagawea, the only member of the Lewis and Clark Expedition destined to become as famous as the captains themselves. Each of these two extraordinary Indian women had been born around 1788, had married a French-Canadian interpreter who would find himself in the employ of Lewis and Clark, had been the sole female member of a historic band of explorers, and had traveled with a young son named Baptiste (Marie with son Paul as well). Not only that, but each woman's final days would be shrouded in controversy. Adding serendipity to coincidence, the two possibly struck up a friendship between 1809 and 1811. Their paths then forever diverged because the noble Sacagawea, praised by Lewis and Clark for her "fortitude and resolution" during the "long, dangerous, and fatiguing route to the Pacific Ocean," fell ill and died of typhus in December of 1812, thirteen months before Marie faced the test of a lifetime.[13]

Given the similarities between Sacagawea and Marie, they had experienced surprisingly different journeys into the West. The former had taken a route sanctioned by Thomas Jefferson and carefully planned by officers under his command. Lewis and Clark had heeded Jefferson's instructions with exactness, exploring the Missouri River as the president requested and even reaching its source at the edge of the Rocky Mountains. They had scaled those mountains and followed the Columbia—one of the western rivers specifically suggested by Jefferson—to the Pacific. The dutiful captains had returned with a remarkable record of the expedition—journals of seven different men comprising close to one million words rife with "careful observations of latitude & longitude"; extensive notes on the "language, traditions, . . . food, clothing, & domestic accomodations" of the Indians; facts and figures on "vegetable productions, . . . animals of the country, . . . mineral productions of every kind, . . . the proportion of rainy, cloudy, & clear days, . . . lightning, hail, snow, [and] ice"; and a host of other details on just about any topic imaginable.[14] Moreover, the expert cartographer Clark, who had sketched a multitude of maps along the way, soon produced a grand map of the West that would prove hugely influential and amazingly accurate. And perhaps most notably, in the year and a half that Sacagawea had "proceeded on" with Lewis and Clark, not a single member of the group had perished. By every indication, this course would guide the next collection of pioneers, and the next.

Marie, by contrast, had traversed the continent with a company of traders forging westward in haphazard fashion. Chancing to meet three vagabonds paddling canoes down the Missouri, they scuttled their plans to retrace Lewis and Clark's eastward course and convinced the trio—who lacked the maps, compasses, sextants, quadrants, and telescopes so carefully transported and used by the Corps of Discovery—to guide them across unchartered territory. They soon lost their bearings in rugged Wyoming mountains never seen by Lewis and Clark. Reaching the Idaho plain just as an early winter set in, the overland Astorians contended with the unforgiving Snake River for three interminable months, forgetting visions of wealth in the face of their harrowing ordeal. Finally defeated—almost destroyed—by the "Mad River," they slaughtered their few remaining horses to stay alive, fragmented into desultory groups, and hobbled across Oregon's Blue Mountains on foot, not reaching the coast until the early months of 1812. By then five men had drowned or disappeared. As the historian Alvin M. Josephy has noted, Marie and her fellow travelers suffered "perhaps the most extreme privations and hardships of any westering expedition in American history."[15] Two diarists kept scant records, understandably concentrating on the privations and hardships, drafting not a single weather log, point of latitude and longitude, or map. This course looked likely to be followed by no one.

The irony was that Sacagawea had taken a path westward that grew obsolete almost immediately, going untrod by the pilgrims who followed her and having little direct impact on the settlement of the West, while Marie's route laid the foundation of the Oregon Trail, a byway destined to link Atlantic and Pacific, spurring national expansion as it carried tens of thousands of explorers, beaver trappers, buffalo hunters, Indian fighters, cowpokes, mule skinners, sheep herders, homesteaders, families of three or four generations, ranchers, schoolmarms, seamstresses, shop owners, blacksmiths, itinerant preachers, missionaries, miners, gold-seekers, snake-oil salesmen, gamblers, hired hands and hired guns, bushwhackers, bartenders, and prostitutes to the Promised Land.

Wars, treaties, trade pacts, explorations, and get-rich-quick schemes were all part of the current that pushed Marie westward, with everyone from Napoleon and Thomas Jefferson to Lewis and Clark and John Jacob Astor taking a role. But the key influence—the brute force—that dictated Marie's future was of course Pierre Dorion Jr., the enigmatic interpreter *par excellence*, who around 1806 took her as a "wife" through barter or wager. Nothing is known about Marie's life prior to that, but Dorion and his father had traded among Iowa Indians near the mouth of the Des Moines River around 1800, and perhaps the son had returned there in search of a second wife. (He had earlier taken a Yankton Sioux wife.)[16]

Born in the late 1770s, and thus a decade older than Marie, Dorion was the son of Pierre Dorion Sr., a French-Canadian from a prominent Quebec family who had abandoned life in the white settlements, learned Indian languages and Indian ways, taken a young Yankton Sioux woman as a wife, and fathered several sons. With their base in the Yankton Sioux country of modern southeast South Dakota, the Dorions became famous—and infamous—up and down the Missouri River. "Father and sons would occasionally get drunk together," wrote Washington Irving, "and then the cabin was a scene of ruffian brawl and fighting, in the course of which the old Frenchman was apt to get soundly belabored by his mongrel offspring." Such widespread rumors hardly deterred traders, explorers, and government officials from hiring the Dorions because Pierre Sr. and his sons were such fluent speakers of Siouan and such skilled negotiators. Gordon Speck hardly exaggerated when he wrote that "three generations of Dorions served the American West. They guided civilization from the Missouri to the Pacific and their lives spanned history from an unexplored wilderness to the State House on the Willamette."[17]

Dorion expertise was not lost on Lewis and Clark, who had hired Dorion the Elder less than a month into the expedition. On June 12, 1804, as they made their way up the Missouri, they met a group of French-Canadian traders transporting trade goods to St. Louis. Several of Lewis and Clark's men bartered for buffalo robes and moccasins, and Lewis purchased three hundred pounds' worth of buffalo fat, useful as both cooking oil and insect repellent. But the captains were most interested in the leader of the group, an "old Frenchman" who spoke several Indian languages—Pierre Dorion Sr., apparently at least in his mid-fifties by this time.

Whether Clark learned or already knew that Dorion had been an associate of his brother George Rogers Clark during the Revolutionary War is uncertain, but he described old Dorion as a "verry Confidential friend" of the Sioux Indians, "he having resided with the nation 20 odd years." The dialogue with Dorion and his fellows was so good that Lewis and Clark, normally quite punctual about getting up the river, spent the rest of the day questioning the traders and no doubt sharing some of the whiskey they had onboard the keelboat. When the Corps of Discovery departed the next morning, Dorion went with them. "Colcluded to take old Durioun back as fur as the Soux nation," wrote Clark, "with a view to get some of their Chiefs to Visit the Presdt. of the United S."[18]

Two and a half months after Dorion signed on, in late August, when the Corps had reached Yankton Sioux country and wanted to council with the chiefs, Lewis and Clark met another member of Dorion's family—Pierre Jr. "At 4 oClock P M. Sergt. Pryor & Mr. Dorion [Sr.] with 5 Chiefs and about 70 men &c. arrived on the opposite Side[.] We Sent over a Perogue & Mr. Dorion & his Son [Pierre Jr.] who was tradeing with the Indians Came over with Sergt. Pryer, and in formed us that the Chiefs were there."[19]

During the key negotiations that followed over the next several days, Pierre Jr. assisted with interpreting and also helped educate Lewis and Clark in Yankton culture as the Indians celebrated the captains' visit with music and dance, demonstrations of the boys' bow-and-arrow skills, and delicacies that included roasted dog. Pierre Jr.'s brief stint with the Corps enhanced his already impressive resumé and also started him on a historic journey: he would be the only person to join in all three of the monumental passages marking the opening of the West—those of Lewis and Clark, Manuel Lisa, and the overland Astorians.

Grateful they had halted their canoes when they did, the voyagers thanked the Indians who had rescued Marie and her boys. "We made them some presents to repay their care and pains," wrote Franchere, "and they returned well satisfied."[20]

The presents, probably wampum—small seashell beads strung together—and tobacco and powder and balls, would all be put to good use. "These

Indians are passionately fond of horse racing," noted Franchere. "The bets they make on these occasions sometimes strip them of all that they possess."[21]

Marie's sons, Baptiste, six, and Paul, four, clung to her as the voyagers offered food and consolation. Some in the party likely proffered clothing to replace the tatters now worn by Marie and her boys. The seating arrangement in the ten canoes—up to this point each canoe had transported six or seven boatmen and two or three passengers—was reorganized to make room for the three new passengers, who were to be taken to a trading post at the mouth of the Okanogan River (in north central Washington).

Before resuming their voyage up the Columbia, however, the Astorians, who had seen their share of hardship and death, had to know the details of what had become of their compatriots and how Marie, Baptiste, and Paul had survived. Marie took up her narrative again and they sat enraptured. As Washington Irving would so aptly put it, "she had a story to tell."[22]

Chapter One

"I Shall Have Two Boats Well Manned and Armed"

Neither Meriwether Lewis nor William Clark left any record of ever meeting Marie Dorion, but as they made their homeward journey they met two men who would figure prominently in her future, two of only five founders of the Oregon Trail to travel the route both west- and eastbound: the middle-aged, mercurial, and famed Robert McClellan and the young, steady, and soon-to-be-acclaimed Ramsay Crooks.

The meeting with McClellan came first, on the morning of September 12, 1806. Traveling in canoes and pirogues—long, flat-bottomed dugouts equipped with sails—Lewis and Clark's party was making good time going downstream when they saw McClellan and his twelve-man crew toiling up the Missouri River in a keelboat overloaded with trade goods. The captains had encountered a drove of traders and trappers in the last few weeks, but McClellan was hardly *any* trader—he was an old army friend of Clark's and a hero of the Ohio Indian wars who "was rejoiced to see" Lewis and Clark and their men.[1]

Both groups docked their boats at a "butifull Prarie" near the present site of St. Joseph, Missouri, and McClellan wasted no time breaking out the liquor. Sergeant John Ordway wrote that he "gave our officers wine and the party as much whiskey as we all could drink." Ordway next reported McClellan's news that "the people in general in the united States were concerned about us as they had heard that we were all killed[.] Then again they heard that the Spanyards has us in the mines &C."[2]

If Lewis and Clark's men were impressed with McClellan, they weren't alone. As Washington Irving wrote, "M'Lellan was a remarkable man. He had been a partisan under General Wayne, in his Indian wars, where he had distinguished himself by his fiery spirit and reckless daring, and marvelous stories were told of his exploits. His appearance answered to his character. His frame was meagre, but muscular; showing strength, activity, and iron firmness. His eyes were dark, deep-set, and piercing. He was restless, fearless, but of impetuous and sometimes ungovernable temper."[3]

The stories told about the athletic McClellan were marvelous indeed, growing more fantastic with each retelling. Some said he routinely jumped over tall horses with ease, others that he had outrun a horse somewhere between Mercersburg and Fort Loudon, Pennsylvania. Just as impressive was the account of McClellan jumping over a team of oxen simply because they were blocking his way.[4] But the best-known legend easily topped the list.

In June 1795, hundreds of soldiers gathered at Fort Greene Ville, Mad Anthony Wayne's fortress and the largest American fort west of the Appalachians (near present Fort Greenville, Ohio). A palisade ten feet high enclosed the fifty-acre camp, complete with officers' quarters, barracks for enlisted men, a huge council house, shops, gardens, stables, and a slaughterhouse. Wayne had summoned the Miami, Shawnee, Delaware, Ojibwa, Ottawa, and Kickapoo Nations to treaty negotiations, and a multitude of Indians were now camped outside the fort. One soldier present, twenty-five-year-old Lieutenant William Clark, wrote his sister that "the eye is constantly entertained with the splendor of dress and equipage, and the [ear] with the sounds of drums, fifes, bugles, trumpets, and other instrumentals. We have daily parades & maneuvers, when we are amused by the roaring of the cannon, and the yells of the guards that perform those maneuvers daily." In the midst of this revelry, McClellan had competed with other soldiers in a contest of strength and skill, relegating any feats of the others to distant memory when he charged down an incline and leaped over a covered wagon eight and a half feet tall. Or so the story went.[5]

"Mr. McClellin receved us very politely," Clark wrote, "and gave us all the news and occurrences which had taken place in the Illinois within his knowledge." McClellan also told of his plans to proceed up the river and trade with the Omaha and Yankton Sioux Indians in present Nebraska and South Dakota. Given the good conversation—and the good wine—Lewis and Clark were hardly inclined to push on down the river. "The evening proveing to be wet and Cloudy we Concluded to continue all night," Clark added.[6]

Two of McClellan's passengers were well known to Lewis and Clark— Pierre Dorion Sr. and Joseph Gravelines, a French-Canadian interpreter who had lived among the Arikara Indians for many years. The captains had employed Gravelines during the winter of 1804–1805, and at their request he had accompanied an Arikara chief named Arketarnarshar, "Eagles Feather," east to meet Thomas Jefferson and other officials. The chief had been well received, but in April of 1806, while still in the East, he had died of an illness. Now Gravelines and Dorion had the unenviable task of going upriver to the Arikara villages (in northern South Dakota) to announce Arketarnarshar's death. The two interpreters carried gifts and a letter from Jefferson. "Every thing we could do to help [Arketarnarshar] was done," the president wrote, "but it pleased the great Spirit to take him from among us."[7]

"Mr. Durion was enstructed to accompany Gravelin," noted Clark, "and through his influence pass him with his presents & by the tetons [Lakota] bands of Sieux."[8] Dorion and Gravelines were the best men to handle such Indian diplomacy, but even they would be helpless to forestall the brewing trouble that would reach its apex late in the summer of 1807.

On the morning of September 13, a Saturday, McClellan and his crew headed up the river. Hospitable to the last, McClellan gave the captains three bottles of wine and each of the men a dram of whiskey. Whether McClellan knew that his future partner Ramsay Crooks was a week behind him—or whether the two had even met—is unknown. But Crooks was on his way, and on the afternoon of September 20, his group had docked their fleet of flat-bottomed, thirty-foot Canadian *bateaux* on the shore opposite the hamlet of La Charette, Missouri, when they spotted several canoes and pirogues hastening downstream. Inside those dugouts, two and a half dozen adventurers, accompanied by a Mandan chief, an interpreter, and their families, "sprung upon their oars" with surprising enthusiasm, firing off three rounds and shouting out a huzzah as they pulled up to the shore. A handful of traders seized their flintlocks and discharged a welcome.[9]

The affable Crooks stepped forward to befriend the boatmen, introducing himself to their commanders only to discover he had just met Lewis and Clark. Crooks and his fellows were both delighted and "much astonished" at the captains' safe return. "They informed us that we were supposed to have been lost long since and were entirely given out by every person," wrote Clark.[10]

Clark added that he and Lewis "were very politely received" by Crooks and his companion, a trader by the name of Reed, quite possibly John Reed, who went west with the Dorions and Crooks and McClellan in 1811. "Those two young Scotch gentlemen furnished us with Beef [,] [flour] [,] and Some pork for our men, and gave us a very agreeable supper," wrote Clark. Sitting around a campfire with Crooks and Reed, Lewis and Clark no doubt related a few selected episodes from their fascinating voyage of discovery. The autumn chill in the night air made the fire particularly inviting, with Lewis and Clark—who had delighted in the sight of cattle earlier that day—savoring fresh milk offered by friendly French boatmen. Newly acquired Kentucky whiskey—the perfect complement to the cold, creamy milk—made the conversation that much more pleasant, and the captains likely "pointed out . . . places where the beaver most abounded," "making enquires and exchanging answers &c. until near midnight," as they had lately done with other traders. Then, with rain looking likely, Crooks and Reed invited the weary explorers to lodge in one of their tents for the evening.[11]

Born in Greencok, Scotland, in 1787, Crooks had sailed for Canada with his widowed mother and three siblings in 1803. Within a year, the young man was clerking for a Montreal mercantile house, earning a reputation for his "judgment, enterprise, and integrity." Crooks was a hard-working, gentle soul with a talent for gaining the trust of others—his hopes of becoming a prominent trader were hardly misplaced. At the time of his meeting with Lewis and Clark, however, neither he nor they could have imagined that he would cross the continent at a younger age than either of them had done.[12]

Two days after bidding farewell to Crooks and Reed, on September 23, 1806, Lewis and Clark returned to a rousing St. Louis welcome. Two weeks after that, the Frankfort, Kentucky, *Palladium* printed a Clark letter depicting the great waterways of the West, the "tremendous mountains . . . covered with eternal snows," and the "generally friendly" Indians, adding that not a single man had been lost after leaving Fort Mandan. Scores of newspapers reprinted the letter, and when Clark's description was combined with Lewis's bold declaration that "the Missouri and all its branches from the Cheyenne upwards abound more in beaver and common otter than any other streams on earth," it was not surprising that a throng of aspiring mountain men made the pilgrimage to St. Louis.[13]

From their homes in Kentucky, John Hoback, Jacob Reznor, and Edward Robinson could thus have known of the captains' triumphant return by October; they could have also heard rumblings that the prominent St. Louis entrepreneur Manuel Lisa was planning to ascend the river in the spring. Exactly when they arrived in St. Louis is not known, but there is no indication they knew each other when they signed three-year contracts with Lisa and his partners Pierre Menard and William Morrison around April of 1807.[14]

Hoback and Reznor hailed from central Kentucky (Mercer County and Nelson County, respectively); Robinson was from western Kentucky's Livingston County. All three owned plantations and had wives and children—presumably grandchildren in Robinson's case. The tenderfoots hoping to go upriver must have snickered at the sight of these graybeards—especially sixty-two-year-old Robinson—but Lisa always looked first for seasoned hands. The three hardly presumed to make history, but as Robert M. Utley has written, "[T]hey deserve to be remembered as the first white men to traverse a vast country soon to became the heartland of the Rocky Mountain fur trade."[15]

The "doomed trio" of Hoback, Reznor, and Robinson had not yet met Crooks and McClellan or Pierre Dorion Jr., and the six of them would not go west together for another four years, but all of them journeyed up the Missouri during the historic and turbulent summer of 1807 and found themselves right in the thick of things.[16]

In April of 1807, seven months after meeting Lewis and Clark on his way up the river, Ramsay Crooks found his role reversed. This time he was the one riding with the current and heading for St. Louis when he encountered an expedition going upstream near La Charette, Missouri. The impressive outfit of fifty or sixty men and two keelboats was valued at $16,000 and was commanded by Lisa on the first of three historic missions to the upper Missouri.[17]

No one who ever met him seemed to lack an opinion of the shrewd, hard-driving Lisa. Henry Marie Brackenridge called him an enterprising gentleman; Meriwether Lewis dubbed him a scoundrel. Whether Crooks had met Lisa or not, he certainly knew of him. Lisa got the most from his men, even though many despised him and some vowed to kill him. If Crooks met them on the river, they were all pushing, pulling, or rowing the boats upstream or out hunting. If he met them in the evening, they were securing the boats, digging latrines, gathering and chopping wood, unpacking gear, putting up tents, dressing freshly killed deer or elk, building fires, cooking, cleaning their guns, standing guard, or handling other chores ordered by Lisa. As the fur hunter's contract made clear, each man was "obliged to do, to obey, to execute with promptness, & diligence all reasonable orders . . . given by those in command of the expedition."[18]

The six Lewis and Clark veterans in the group—Pierre Cruzatte, George Drouillard, Baptiste Lepage, John Potts, Peter Weiser, and Richard Windsor—probably recognized Crooks from the previous autumn. Hoback, Reznor, and Robinson were meeting Crooks for the first time. Like Lisa's other hands, the three were chomping at the bit to get up the river and start making money. An average beaver skin, or *plew*, weighed a pound and a half and could be sold in St. Louis for five dollars or more. Even after returning half their plews to the company (in exchange for a horse, five traps, ten pounds of powder, twenty pounds of lead, a kettle, and a few knives, hatchets, and awls), four trappers could *theoretically* expect to conclude a season with twenty-five packs of beaver in hand, with sixty plews per pack, for a total of close to $2,000 per man. Toussaint Charbonneau, by contrast, had earned a respectable $400 for two and a half years of service to Lewis and Clark. Expert interpreters and hunters had lately signed government contracts for $1 a day, but the prospect of garnering a thousand dollars or more in a single season was unheard of. What had been said a few months earlier about John Colter and two companions also applied to Hoback and his two friends: "They tells us that they are determined to stay . . . and trap and hunt until they make a fortune before they return."[19]

What everyone conveniently ignored was that the licenses issued to Lisa and his competitors authorized them to *trade*, not to *hunt*. The whole point was to protect Indian lands but still encourage commerce by allowing traders to obtain furs and skins from the Indians in exchange for "goods, wares, and

merchandize"—but not "spiritous liquors." Furthermore, traders were permitted to reside at Indian "towns and not at their hunting camps." The Indians were to do the trapping and exchange the furs at official trading posts,
or "factories," while the traders stayed clear of Indian hunting grounds and
transported the furs down the river to sell them. So, when Lisa or one of the
other business owners contractually bound their men to "hunt, and trap the
beaver of the Missouri the best that [they] can," they were violating the
agreement they had signed with the government. [20]

But for men like Reznor and Robinson—presumably unaware of such
technicalities—there was something else, something that ultimately proved
more alluring than the prospect of wealth. Jedediah Smith said it best: "I
must confess that I had at that time a full share of that ambition (and perhaps
foolish ambition) which is common in a greater or less degree to all the
active world. I wanted to be the first to view a country on which the eyes of a
white man had never gazed and to follow the course of rivers that run
through a new land." [21]

On May 1, 1807, Crooks appeared at the office of territorial secretary Frede-
rick Bates and obtained a two-year license to trade with the Indians on the
Missouri River. Crooks brought with him an oath and bond signed by
McClellan. The two men had apparently met and formed their partnership the
previous winter at McClellan's camp in northeastern Nebraska. The high-
strung McClellan had wisely chosen a partner in many ways his opposite. As
Hiram Martin Chittenden, the great historian of the fur trade, later wrote,
Crooks "was always open and above board in his dealings," a man of "extraordinary energy" despite chronic illness. [22] While McClellan was a hero of
the Indian wars of the 1790s, Crooks made his name as a competitive but fair
entrepreneur almost half a century later.

The same day he obtained the license from Bates, Crooks delivered a
letter from his new partner. Composed at a camp in the Omaha, or "Mahaw,"
Indian country and written in a businesslike hand, the letter was addressed to
Governor Meriwether Lewis but delivered in his absence to William Clark,
now a militia general and a U.S. Indian agent. More than any other document, the two-page epistle sets up the context and introduces the main
players in the intricate drama that unfolded during the historic summer of
1807.

First, McClellan stated his intent to "visit the upper parts of the Missouri
as soon as I possibly can after my arrival at St. Louis." [23] This is exactly what
he and Crooks did, going upriver with eighty men sometime in July.

Second, he offered to escort the Mandan chief Sheheke "to his respective
home." Often remembered for his kindness to Lewis and Clark, Sheheke had
accepted their invitation to go downriver in 1806, bringing his wife, Yellow
Corn, and two-year-old son, White Painted House. They had visited Thomas

Jefferson and were now back in St. Louis. "I will with pleasure take him under my charge," McClellan wrote, "as there will be but little danger to fear. I shall have two boats well manned and armed." Crooks soon discovered, however, that William Clark had already made arrangements "to send the Mandan Chief" and "several bands of the Sioux Nation . . . to their country in safety." A few weeks after Crooks' arrival in St. Louis, "70 men, exclusive of the 18 Indian men, 8 women, and 6 children," started up the river in keelboats, pirogues, and canoes. Commanding Sheheke's military escort was Nathaniel Pryor, a veteran of the Lewis and Clark Expedition. "Ensign Pryor's party will consist of 48 men," Clark wrote, "which will be fully sufficient to pass any hostile band which he may probably meet with."[24]

Crooks' future traveling companion, Pierre Dorion Jr., was also among those accompanying the Indians back to their homelands, as was his father, Pierre Sr. The elder—who for some unknown reason had returned to St. Louis rather than continuing on to the Arikara Nation with Gravelines—had signed on as one of Pryor's interpreters, and "Young Dorion" was on his way with "a boat and 10 men" to trade with the Sioux.[25]

Third, McClellan told of "a Canadian who obtained licenses to trade with the Sioux & Ponca for the year 1806. [He] proceeds on a voyage this spring up the Missouri." Lewis and Clark had met this French trader, Charles Courtin, on September 14, 1806, two days after meeting McClellan. Because he had accepted Joseph Gravelines—on his way to deliver news of Arketarnarshar's death to the Arikara Nation—as a passenger, Courtin's voyage had evolved into a delicate diplomatic mission. Although Secretary of War Henry Dearborn had promised to send Gravelines "in a light boat, with a sober, discreet Sergeant & four faithful sober soldiers, up to the Ricara Nation," that had not developed. Then the plan to go with the savvy Dorion Sr. had also fallen through, and Gravelines and the innocent bystander Courtin were left to themselves.[26]

Fourth, McClellan's letter was full of oblique references to the major presence on the river. His offer to escort Sheheke or take on other government assignments and an urgency to get back up the river all reflected McClellan's ambition to outdo his chief competitor: Lisa.

Although McClellan did not mention a former army officer by the name of John McClallen, he had met him on the river in 1806, just as Lewis and Clark had done. "This gentleman [McClallen] an acquaintance of my friend Capt. Lewis," wrote Clark. "[He] informed us that he was on rather a speculative expedition to the confines of New Spain, with the view to introduce a trade with those people." McClallen's purported plan was to stop at the Platte River, establish a trading post, and later proceed southwest to Sante Fe. What McClallen did not tell Lewis and Clark was that he had purchased trade goods in Baltimore and that Governor James Wilkinson (discovered after his death to have spied for the Spanish) had used government funds to ship the goods to St. Louis. Nor did he reveal his true destination. Rather than stopping at the Platte River, he intended to proceed right up the Missouri and reach the prime trapping territory of Montana well ahead of Lisa.[27]

The stage was now set: a host of traders, officers, infantrymen, riflemen, *engagés*, hunters, trappers, fishermen, blacksmiths, gunsmiths, interpreters, cooks, clerks, vagabonds, and imposters had fixed their gaze on the upper Missouri. By midsummer they would be strung out from its mouth near St. Louis to the springs marking its beginnings in western Montana and all along its meandering 2,700-mile course. The mysterious McClallen was leading the pack, commanding a large keelboat with fifteen hands, an interpreter, and a clerk onboard. He would reach Montana sometime in June. Next came Courtin, who trailed McClallen by several weeks and 500 miles, commanding his own keelboat and ferrying the bearer of bad news, Joseph Gravelines. Lisa, with his two keelboats, his fifty men—including Hoback, Reznor, and Robinson—and his uncanny negotiation skills, lagged almost two months and a thousand miles behind Courtin. Pryor and his seventy-odd men, Dorion Sr. and Jr. among them, were charged with both military and trading missions and left a month and a few hundred miles behind Lisa. Last of all came Crooks and McClellan, with eighty men and two keelboats, departing late in the season, six weeks after Pryor and five or six hundred miles behind him.

Two years earlier, Lewis and Clark had followed the Missouri to its source, crossed the Continental Divide into Idaho, and navigated the Columbia River system all the way to the western coast. None of these groups had any intention of doing that—they were bound for North Dakota and Montana. Indeed, by the summer of 1807, even the visionary John Jacob Astor had not yet announced plans for a fur-trading venture headquartered near the Pacific Ocean. As James Ronda has written, "Astoria flickered into life sometime late in 1807. It was then that Astor first mentioned his western idea to De Witt Clinton."[28] Still, events set in motion earlier in 1807 would eventually unite Hoback, Reznor, and Robinson, the Dorions, and Crooks and McClellan, place them in Astor's employ, and drive them into the electrifying but harrowing West. By pure happenstance, they would take a more southerly course than Lewis and Clark and become the first pioneers to travel what decades later would be called the Oregon Trail.

May of 1807 found Lisa pursuing his course up the Missouri, keeping the keelboats near the bank to avoid the overpowering current at midriver. His boats were about seventy feet long and ten feet wide with a cabin and a square-rigged sail in the middle and seats for ten rowers at the bow. Cleats nailed to the running boards enabled seven hands on each side "to have a foot-hold in forcing the boat up stream by long pike poles about twelve feet long with sharp iron sockets at one end and a flat button on the other." Putting their "shoulders to the wheel," the men leaned into their poles and "walked" the boat forward, with each man hurrying back to his original position after reaching the stern. When deep water or a soft bottom rendered the poles useless, a crewman threw a length of rope ashore and a host of hearty men followed, fighting their way through mud, rocks, brambles, and mosquitoes as they hauled the boat upstream. As a contemporary observer noted, "The men employed as hands upon these boats were none other than the hardiest race of men, of romantic nature, and athletes, for none other could perform such service, and withstand the exposure."[29]

The voyagers were burned by sun and pelted by hail; rain "violent with hard claps of thunder and sharp lightning" kept them awake at night and soaked their bedding; high winds halted them for hours at a time; blowing sand blinded them; collapsing river banks startled or injured them; sawyers—trees swept into the river somewhere upstream—snagged the boats, ripped them open, or capsized them; an *embarrass*—a reeking mass of driftwood, dead buffalo, and whatever else congealed in the sludge—often grew larger and larger until it broke free of an island or a sawyer and slouched downstream with an irresistible force that made the river unnavigable. All of this fluctuated from minute to minute, shifting course like the river itself, but the never-failing constants from spring through fall were "mosquitoes excessively tormenting."[30]

Lisa's chief lieutenant, and undoubtedly his most valuable crew member, was George Drouillard, the skilled hunter, scout, and interpreter who had proved himself time and again during Lewis and Clark's journey. No one could question that Lisa and Drouillard were the perfect team to find and lay claim to the best trapping territory. So it was particularly ironic that three weeks into the hopeful journey, Lisa and Drouillard did something that would cast a pall over the entire excursion, foreshadowing Drouillard's death three years later.

On May 14, as Lisa's men passed several small islands and fought an "exceedingly rapid" current, they saw a large river flowing in from the south—the Osage, an impressive four hundred yards wide but still not half as wide as the Missouri. Perhaps hearing from the Lewis and Clark veterans that there were "fine springs and streams" and salt licks nearby and that deer were plentiful, Lisa stopped his boats. A few white hunters were camped nearby, and one of them offered to enlist. Lisa agreed, and the young man gathered his few supplies to stow on the keelboat.[31]

Whether they introduced themselves then or in the coming days, Hoback, Reznor, and Robinson soon became the first of the future Astorians to meet the new recruit, an individual destined to become a legendary and controversial mountain man, whose career in the West spanned a quarter century of intrigue and close calls before he fell at the hands of Arikara warriors in present Montana—the formidable Edward Rose. Said to be part European, part African-American, and part Cherokee, Rose was a sort of everyman by birth, although like other "half-breeds," his heritage was disparaged in the nineteenth century. Born and raised near Louisville, Kentucky, he left home at seventeen or eighteen and worked his way down the Ohio and Mississippi Rivers to New Orleans, where, according to his friend and biographer, Reuben Holmes, "[H]e became celebrated for the eagerness with which he espoused the quarrels of his comrades, and particularly so as a true supporter of the dignity of 'Old Kentuck.' He could lay claim to a large share of consideration on that subject, for, to the moment of his death, his visage most conspicuously displayed the marks of turmoil and strife." The most conspicuous of these marks, an unsightly scar at the tip of Rose's nose "made by the meeting of the upper and lower jaws of a 'big' Chillicothean," had given Rose the nickname *Nez Coupé* or Cut Nose.[32]

No record remains of Rose's activities that day, but it would have been typical of him to boisterously join Lisa's hunters, brag about his shooting skills, and then back up the boast by returning with fresh venison. But Rose had barely joined the trapping expedition when another man abandoned it. Just as the boats pulled away, someone yelled out that a trapper named Bissonnet (also called Bazine) was missing. Lisa promptly ordered the boats back to shore. Thinking that Bissonnet had been accidentally left behind, several men called out for him, but there was no reply. Concluding the man had deserted, Lisa summoned Drouillard. "George, go and find this Bazine," he demanded, "and bring him *dead* or *alive*." Drouillard got his rifle and ammunition. Then, accompanied by Benito Vasquez, another of Lisa's lieutenants, Drouillard "started into the woods." Meanwhile, Lisa and two others were checking their own firearms and preparing to leave in a canoe. "If I meet him I will shoot him on first sight," Lisa announced as he and the others paddled for a small river about two leagues distant.[33]

A gloom fell over Hoback, Reznor, Robinson, and the other forty-odd men as they waited. This kind of idle time was not what they had wanted. "Some time after [Lisa] left I heard a rifle shot," said Antoine Dubreuil. A half-hour after that, Drouillard and Vasquez came out of the woods and walked toward the keelboats. Drouillard announced that he had shot Bissonnet "and was sorry for it." He asked for help bringing the wounded man back, and four men stepped forward. Drouillard led them into the woods, and when they returned some time later they were carrying Bissonnet, who was still alive. Drouillard, one of Lewis and Clark's best marksmen, had shot him in the back, near one of his shoulders.[34]

Dubreuil reported what happened next: "As soon as [Lisa] landed, George Drouillard announced to him that he had wounded the man. [Lisa] said, 'It is well done. He's a rascal who got what he deserved.' He went up to [Bissonnet] and spoke to him in an angry tone, blaming him for the condition in which he had put himself and which was purely his fault."[35]

An unnamed witness took up the account, saying that Bissonnet "was then asked why he had deserted. He replied he could give no reason—it was a misfortune for him. He was also asked if anyone treated him ill. He answered, no, it was an unlucky fate that awaited him."[36]

Dusk was falling by this time. Lisa had no physician aboard, so some of the men did what they could, probably sitting up with Bissonnet all night. The next morning Lisa assigned a man to take Bissonnet in a canoe back to St. Charles—a day and a half away—"to receive surgical aid." But no one was surprised when Bissonnet died in the canoe a few hours later.[37]

The somber mood prevailing among Lisa's men aptly portended the rest of the trip: they would see one crisis after another. As for Lisa and Drouillard, on their arrival in St. Louis fifteen months later, both would be charged with murder.

About the same time that Bissonnet succumbed to his wounds, Robert McClellan left his camp in Nebraska and started down the river, bringing with him an unwilling companion by the name of Francis Hortiz. Commissioned by Governor Wilkinson to "seize the person and property of all unlicensed traders," McClellan had detained Hortiz—and his keelboat—because the latter had no license. "[Hortiz] solemnly declares he has obtained licenses and lodged them in the hands of his father at St. Louis," McClellan had written to Lewis. That was not good enough for McClellan, and he had ordered Hortiz back to St. Louis.[38]

On June 3, near present Kansas City, Kansas, McClellan and Hortiz met Lisa's contingent coming up the river. The meeting between McClellan and Lisa could not have been cordial. The two had disputed a debt in 1805, and the next year Lisa sued McClellan for $2,000. McClellan countersued for $5,000, but the court had awarded Lisa $810.50 while rejecting McClellan's claim. Lisa and a partner then brought another suit against McClellan and won that one as well, for $1,185.33 1/2, plus court costs. When the two met on the river, it's hard to imagine that Lisa did not remind McClellan how much he owed—down to the half cent.[39]

The three men somehow set aside their various disputes long enough to take care of a matter of business. McClellan and Hortiz acted as witnesses while an engagé by the name of Francois Lecompt, who had apparently been traveling with one of them, reversed his course on the river—as so many others would do—and signed a three-year contract with Lisa.[40]

McClellan knew several of Lisa's men, but he was likely delighted to be introduced—or reintroduced—to John Hoback, who, like McClellan, had served in one of the elite military companies of the era: Mad Anthony Wayne's Kentucky Scouts and Spies. Though not a member of that select group himself, William Clark had known men who were and perhaps had them in mind a decade later when describing what he sought in recruiting

men for the expedition: "The young men that I have engaged . . . are . . . the
best woodsmen and hunters, of young men in this part of the country." Clark
added—and this was true for Wayne as well—that "a judicious choice of our
party is of the greatest importance to the success of this vast enterprise."[41]

It was hardly a coincidence that Clark had found his exceptional frontiers-
men and marksmen in Kentucky, "the dark and bloody ground," where the
Daniel Boone legacy of living off the land and forever pushing westward—
and displacing Indians—was thriving. To a man, Clark's enlistees—and
Wayne's—felt more at home in the wilderness than in the city, preferring—
as Lewis did on the last night of his life—to sleep on a buffalo robe rather
than a bed. These were men who naturally picked up Indian languages, who
relished the feel of buckskin, who could start a fire and get comfortable in the
wettest and coldest of conditions.

Among Wayne's recruits were William May, Dodson Tharp, Joseph
Young, and a number of other skilled men, but McClellan and Hoback were
the only scouts and spies known to have gone up the Missouri that summer.
They had served under different captains—McClellan under the celebrated
William Wells and Hoback under James Flinn—but they would forever be
brothers in arms. Hoback had no doubt heard the story of the Miami squaw
McClellan had taken captive only to discover she was a white woman kidnapped years earlier. Grateful to be rescued—even though McClellan had
initially intended to kill her—she astounded the band of scouts with her
pluck. When her former people launched an attack, she handled a flintlock
effortlessly, fighting alongside McClellan and his men. Next she guided them
safely through the woods in the midst of a violent squall. Some had expected
the bachelor McClellan to court this amazing woman proper and marry her.
He hadn't.[42]

About a week after meeting Lisa, McClellan and Hortiz had reached
present Saline County, Missouri, when they saw two keelboats making their
way up the river, surrounded by a hodgepodge of pirogues and canoes. This
was Pryor's group of soldiers and traders, with young Auguste Pierre Chouteau commanding a keelboat stocked with trade goods and with Pierre Dorion Sr. and Jr. both present. McClellan soon learned there would be no hefty
government contract in the offing because Pryor's passengers included Sheheke and his family.

Hearing that Lisa was several days ahead hardly pleased Pryor, who had
hoped to combine their parties to yield a formidable force of four keelboats,
multiple cannons, and one hundred men, virtually ensuring safe passage all
the way to North Dakota. Although Lisa had told Frederick Bates in St.
Charles that he would wait for Pryor, he did no such thing. If anything, he
seems to have rushed ahead to gain a trading advantage among the nations of
the upper Missouri. Pryor had little chance of catching him.[43]

Pryor focused his attention upstream, McClellan downstream, hoping that Crooks was now arranging financing so that he could get busy buying keelboats, canoes, boat hooks, and chains; rifles, pipe tomahawks, knives, lead, powder, and flints; portable soup, rock salt, spices, and whiskey; kettles, spades, axes, rope, and needles and thread; blankets, coats, overalls, and flannel; powdered bark, calomel, opium, lancets, and syringes; white wampum, spun tobacco, medals, red silk handkerchiefs, and ear trinkets. The dependable Crooks did not disappoint.[44]

On June 3, the same day that McClellan and Hortiz witnessed Lisa and Lecompt's contract, Courtin and Gravelines reached the Arikara villages, set amongst so many sandbars that the main channel was difficult to discern. This nation, called "Ricaras" or "Rees," had lost much of its population to smallpox in the last decade, with a dozen villages now reduced to three. They were governed by so many chiefs that one trader described them as "captains without companies." Farmers who raised "squashes of three different kinds," as well as corn and pumpkins, they dwelled in "neat lodges covered with earth and picketed about."[45]

Moments after unloading Gravelines's gifts, Courtin discovered that the Indians had plundered most of his goods. As if that weren't disheartening enough, Courtin was asked to read Thomas Jefferson's letter announcing Arketarnarshar's death, with trader Joseph Garreau translating. Not only was the chief dead, white men had interred the body in some unknown land, depriving the family of healing burial rituals. The elders were not pleased. Gravelines attempted to ease the tension by presenting nine muskets to Arketarnarshar's sons; three hundred dollars' worth of goods—probably including white and red glass beads, calico shirts, blankets, copper kettles, silk handkerchiefs, and thimbles, needles, and thread—to Arketarnarshar's wives and children; and one hundred pounds of powder and a corresponding quantity of lead, to the chiefs.[46]

Arketarnarshar's family and fellows accepted the gifts but were not impressed. They announced "that there was no other liar but their Father [Jefferson], and that . . . they had resolved to do the same as the Sioux in stopping and plundering all and every boats that would ascend as far as their villages and that they would also kill all those who would oppose their designs because the Americans were uncapable of revenging themselves."[47]

Courtin was an innocent bystander in this course of events and Gravelines was the man who had urged Arketarnarshar to go east, so it was more than a little ironic that Courtin was held against his will while Gravelines was freed. When Courtin wrote his letter on June 22, he didn't know if and when the people he called "brute but coward" would release him.[48] Gravelines, however, was soon on his way back to St. Louis with Courtin's letter in hand. He met Lisa, then Pryor, and finally Crooks and McClellan as he followed the

Missouri, but we have no record of what he told them about the Arikara. We just know that none of the three groups turned back.

Toward the end of June, Manuel Lisa and his crew came upon a mammoth river rolling in from the west. More than six hundred yards wide at its mouth, it flowed with "great velocity," dumping huge amounts of sand into the tamer Missouri. This was "the Great River Platte," flowing into the Missouri just south of present Omaha, Nebraska. The Lewis and Clark veterans may have directed Lisa north to a "point convenient for observations," with clumps of oak, walnut, and elm trees, where three years earlier they had "cleared away the willows and pitched [their] tents and built boweries." The deer hunting here was good, which no doubt accounted for the packs of wolves stalking the prairie.[49]

The next morning the men spotted something on the river, a speck on the horizon that gradually came into focus. Then they made out a solitary boatman paddling downstream. A welcoming shot brought him toward the shore. Which of his former companions first recognized the lone traveler is not known, but his name was likely buzzed among the trappers and engagés, bringing smiles and nods of appreciation from several. John Colter was back.

Ten months earlier, at the Mandan villages in North Dakota, Colter and his two new partners, Joseph Dickson and Forrest Hancock, had climbed in a small canoe and paddled up the Missouri to make a fortune trapping beaver. They had not been heard from since, and it was somehow fitting that of all people, Charles Courtin was the first to chronicle what had become of two-thirds of the triad, managing in his unlucky way to witness one key event after another. Ten days after his arrival at the Arikara villages, Courtin had watched as Dickson landed in his canoe, barely escaping when Indians shot at him and tried to steal his furs. A week later, Courtin reported in his letter, Hancock had received a more friendly reception. Courtin's epistle had not mentioned Dickson and Hancock's erstwhile partner, but Colter had likely passed the Arikara villages himself a few days before Dickson. Thomas James, who met Colter two years later, left this memorable description: "[Colter's] veracity was never questioned among us and his character was that of a true American backwoodsman. He was about thirty-five years of age, five feet ten inches in height and wore an open, ingenious, and pleasing countenance of the Daniel Boone stamp. Nature had formed him, like Boone, for hardy endurance of fatigue, privations and perils."[50]

Knowing that Colter's "knowledge of the country and nations rendered him an acquisition," Lisa offered him a job, perhaps sweetening the offer by making him a "free trapper," meaning that once the party stopped he could trap and trade without any obligation to Lisa. A free trapper might even have one or two engagés bound to him. Although Colter had apparently lost his first wife through divorce or death, his son Hiram was at least three years old.

So Colter was two weeks from home and had a son waiting for him, as well as 320 acres of land and $300 in cash. But if he deliberated or hesitated, no mention of that was recorded, only that he "was persuaded to return."[51]

Within days, Lisa's men met Dickson canoeing down the river; Hancock, a few days after that. Dickson, who declined any invitation to join Lisa, reached St. Louis with his cargo intact and made a good profit on his plews, but Hancock, like Colter, signed on with Lisa and reversed his course to face the dangers north- and westward. But the immediate danger came not from Indians but from a discontent crewmember by the name of Bouché. He had been trouble from the start and was now refusing to work, trashing supplies—including meat—and even conspiring to kill Lisa. In addition, the hunters had hit a streak of bad luck, bringing in so little game that rations were reduced to a fourth of a pound of meat per man per day.[52]

Things hardly got better when Lisa reached the Arikara villages (arriving not long after Courtin's release). "Two or three hundred warriors were drawn up and on [Lisa's] approach, . . . discharged a volley before his boat, to indicate the place where he should land. He accordingly put to shore, but made it known, that no one of them was to enter his boat; while the chiefs appointed warriors to stand guard and keep off the crowd." Lisa's cocksureness, often ridiculed by his enemies, served him well (and continued to serve him well, for he never found himself in a battle with Indians). When an Indian rushed forward and slit open bags of corn being offered for trade by Arikara women, Lisa "instantly called his men to arms, pointed a couple of swivels which were fixed on his boats, and made every preparation for defense." Colter, Rose, Hoback, and the others were now bonded the way Lewis and Clark's men had been when they faced off with the Lakota in 1804. Lisa's action was perfectly timed, and the Arikara "dispersed in confusion" even though they considerably outnumbered the trappers. When the chiefs reappeared, they came with peace pipes, seeking friendship. "They came to him, and according to their custom, stroked him on the shoulders, begging him not to be displeased, declaring that the Indian who had offended him was considered a bad man."[53]

At least this was the report of Henry Brackenridge, who got his information from Lisa himself, but another source describing Lisa's encounter with the Arikara painted quite a different picture.

By the time Lisa made his way into North Dakota in mid-August, John McClallen had crossed the Rocky Mountains—and the Continental Divide—in western Montana and adopted a new persona, creating a historical riddle that would not be solved for a century and a half. The unlucky Courtin, who had now been robbed at least twice, was in eastern Montana, approaching Blackfoot country. Downstream from Lisa, Pryor's contingent was somewhere near the Nebraska/South Dakota border.

The latecomers, Crooks and McClellan, were about halfway across the state of Missouri, getting away from St. Louis none too soon for McClellan, who had barely arrived in that city when he had been arrested for trespass, with the warrant claiming he had "committed an assault upon Francis Hortiz," that he "did take and detained one barge manned and loaded with goods, the property of Francis valued [at] $7000." In his suit, Hortiz claimed that McClellan had illegally impounded 902½ pounds of deerskin, 167½ pounds of beaver pelts, and 230 raccoon skins.[54]

It seems that Hortiz had been telling the truth about his license. McClellan argued, however—and William Clark agreed—that Hortiz had violated the law by not having the license with him. Clark even convinced the attorney general to take the case against Hortiz to a grand jury, but they had refused to prosecute. Instead, McClellan had been "bound in $8,000 to appear before the court in September term." As Clark put it, "Mr. McClellan's attorney has some faint hopes of bringing forward his business in another shape; if he does not succeed, McClellan will pay most probably, severely for his solicitude to do a service to his country."[55]

Already facing financial ruin because of Lisa's successful lawsuits against him, McClellan had done the only logical thing: he had gone up the Missouri with Crooks as planned, confident he could manage grizzly bears, flash floods, buffalo stampedes, famine, pestilence, mutinous crew members, and warring Indians—as long as he was free of constables and lawyers, warrants and subpoenas. When the September term came around, McClellan was six hundred miles away, with nary a judge or jury in sight. The record is silent on how the officials reacted to his failure to show, but they hardly forgot about him. They waited patiently for his return.[56]

By mid-September Crooks and McClellan had passed the Platte River and were near Council Bluffs when they saw a flotilla coming downstream—Pryor's group. McClellan had last seen this party in western Missouri, where he learned of their plans to escort Sheheke home and trade among the Indians. Knowing how long such a trip would take, McClellan had not expected to see them returning for weeks, but now the confidence so evident among Pryor's men in June had been supplanted by anguish. With all the boats docked, Pryor had a chance to explain that when he arrived at the Arikara villages, a Mandan woman held captive for several years boarded his boat and informed him that Lisa "had passed up some time before" and had found himself threatened by the Arikara, a circumstance that "probably obliged [Lisa] to divert the storm which threatened *his own boat*, by directing the attentions of the Ricaras to *ours*." Lisa had reportedly told the Arikara chiefs "that two boats might be very soon expected; that we had the Mandan chief on board; and that we were to remain for the purposes of trade. . . . On this, they pillaged [Lisa] of about the half of his goods, and suffered him to pass on, determining in their councils at the same time, to murder the Mandan and his escort as soon as we should arrive."[57]

If Lisa had acted in bad faith when he reneged on his pledge to wait for Pryor, he was now guilty of the ultimate betrayal—jeopardizing Pryor's men to get himself out of a jam. Crooks had apparently given Lisa the benefit of the doubt in the past, but his future contempt of Lisa may well have taken root on hearing this report from Pryor. McClellan had needed no convincing.

Although Pryor had attempted to negotiate, the Arikara were "determined on plunder and blood." Several of them seized the cable of Chouteau's barge—"as his contained merchandise and had no soldiers to defend it." Moments later "the Indians now raised a general whoop, and as they retired to the willows, fired on the men on the beach as well as on both boats in the same instant."[58]

Pryor's men responded with a "well-directed volley" of fire from swivel-mounted cannons, blunderbusses, and rifles, but the Indians were also well armed, and a full-fledged battle erupted. One man reported firing more than forty shots himself, even though he was wounded. Amid the booms of the cannons and the retorts of the rifles came the moans of the wounded and the distinct smell of gunpowder, a smoky haze obscuring the view on both sides. Pryor ordered a retreat and launched his boat cleanly, but Chouteau's men "were obliged to drag the barge while exposed to the continual fire of the enemy."[59]

The irony was that between them Gravelines and Lisa had supplied a good deal of the lead and powder and several of the rifles now being used against Pryor's men. Chouteau finally got free, and both boats took their flight down the river, the engagés paddling or poling furiously while gunmen covered them. When they were out of range of Arikara guns, they lashed their boats together and attended to their wounded.[60]

As with most expeditions that went up the river in those years, a host of specialists were onboard–from interpreters to gunsmiths to marksmen and boatmen–but not a single physician, so men with little medical know-how did what they could for the nine seriously wounded victims. Crooks and McClellan could offer sympathy and a few medical supplies but little else.

Although he could have easily been killed, Dorion made it back to a keelboat unscathed. He accompanied Pryor back to St. Louis, so it is safe to assume that the first ones to hear of the conflict were Pierre Jr. and Marie, who lived among the Yankton Sioux almost two hundred miles upstream from Crooks and McClellan's position. Pierre Jr. would have been particularly interested not only because his father had been present but also because he himself had traveled with Pryor's group as far as Sioux country. The attack could not have surprised him. Violent encounters with Indians were a fact of life among those who ventured west. Four of Chouteau's men had been lost—three during the melee and another who died nine days later. One of the killed was apparently Lewis and Clark veteran Joseph Field, who had served with his brother Reuben. Lewis had noted that the Field brothers were "engaged in all the most dangerous and difficult scenes of the voyage, in which they uniformly acquitted themselves with much honor."[61]

Three of the wounded were also Lewis and Clark men—René Jusseaume, temporarily with the party in 1804, and permanent members George Gibson and George Shannon. Gibson's wound did not appear fatal, but Jusseaume had been "badly wounded in the thigh and shoulder," and Shannon had taken a ball that mangled his leg below the knee. Jusseaume and Shannon had suffered constantly in the two weeks since the fight, and medical help at St. Charles was another two or three weeks away. Could either man survive that long? [62]

Questions also swirled around Crooks and McClellan's partnership. Pryor's description of the "most unhappy affair" had convinced them to abandon their hopes of reaching Mandan and Hidatsa country that season; they pushed back to the mouth of the Nodaway River, north of present St. Joseph, Missouri, not far from where McClellan had met Lewis and Clark in 1806. At the edge of a grassy plain, "a series of the most rugged cliffs" lined the river, some of them exhibiting "perpendicular faces at least a hundred feet in height," and it was here, at the foot of these forested bluffs, that Crooks and McClellan built their "wintering house." Taking advantage of the abundant red and white oaks, they "constructed comfortable quarters, the house having three rooms."[63]

No list of the eighty-odd men who accompanied Crooks and McClellan has been found, but we can identify two of them—"an American named Ayers" and John Day, "a hunter from the backwoods of Virginia," who was "six feet two inches high, straight as an Indian; with an elastic step as if he trod on springs, and a handsome, open, manly countenance."[64] Both of them found their way into the history books—but not for happy reasons.

As David Lavender noted, "The Indians of the vicinity were used to normal trade customs, and it is not likely that Crooks and McClellan risked offending them by using to any great extent the traps they had brought along." So, with their plans in limbo, they tasked their men with hunting the plentiful deer, smoking meat, guarding the trade goods, erecting shelters, and stocking firewood, but they unavoidably "found themselves paying wages to and providing food for several unnecessary hands."[65] What they would do in the spring was uncertain, but a hard plains winter was coming on—that was one of the few things not in doubt.

Chapter Two

"A Powerful Company Is Forming"

Pryor's beleaguered band reached St. Charles in mid-October 1807, with George Shannon teetering between life and death; the doctor who treated him "found one of his legs in a state of gangrene caused by a ball having passed through it" and to save his life was "under the necessity of amputating the limb above the knee." René Jusseaume had also survived but reported to Thomas Jefferson that "I am now crippled and to all appearances for the rest of my days."[1]

Nathaniel Pryor detailed the battle and the loss of Auguste Pierre Chouteau's men in a letter written to William Clark on October 16. By that time, John McClallen and Charles Courtin had both established their winter camps in present Montana—McClallen along the Flathead River, north of the future site of Missoula, and Courtin at Three Forks, where the Jefferson, Madison, and Gallatin Rivers converge to form the Missouri. Courtin was still in U.S. territory, although right in the heart of Blackfoot country. McClallen had crossed the Rocky Mountains, going so far west that he was no longer within the huge parcel of land deeded to the United States by the Louisiana Purchase—richly ironic because on August 13 two Kutenai Indians had arrived at the camp of the famed Canadian explorer David Thompson, 350 miles north of McClallen's huts, and handed him a letter from an American army office named *Zachary Perch*—apparently McClallen's alias—warning Thompson about "carrying on a Traffic with the Indians within *our* Territories."[2]

So, of the five companies that had left St. Louis that spring and summer, only one was still fighting the Missouri in late October: Manuel Lisa's. He had reached the Mandan and Hidatsa villages in present North Dakota in mid-September, but the normally friendly Indians had given him a hostile reception—"his presents were rejected, and the chief demanded some powder, which was refused. . . . [Lisa] told them that they might kill him, but that his property would be safe. They were finally compelled to accept of such presents as he offered."[3]

Just days later, Lisa caught sight of a powerful Assiniboine war party approaching, "some on horseback, others on foot, and all painted for war." Not hesitating, Lisa "charged his swivels and made directly across to the savages, and when he had come within an hundred yards, the match was put, while there was at the same time, a general discharge of small arms." The strategy worked perfectly—at least according to the nonwitness Henry Marie Brackenridge—and the startled warriors "fell back, tumbled over each other, and fled to the hills," leaving Lisa to smoke the peace pipe with a few chiefs.[4]

Whatever the exact details, Lisa escaped again, reaching the confluence of the Missouri and Yellowstone Rivers (just east of the North Dakota/ Montana border) about the same time that Pryor arrived at St. Charles. Up to this point, Lisa had followed the same westward route as Lewis and Clark, but he now abandoned the captains' course along the Missouri for one along the Yellowstone, the first in a series of cutoffs that would transform the original Oregon Trail across North Dakota and Montana into a southerly path that bypassed those states entirely. Lisa likely chose the Yellowstone because Clark had experienced a nonviolent homeward journey along that river in 1806, but Lewis and three companions had skirmished with Blackfoot warriors and killed two of them while traveling the Missouri.[5]

Richard Edward Oglesby, Lisa's biographer, represented a host of historians when he wrote that Lisa's "hardy band" that "set out for the mountains in the spring of 1807 [was] the first organized trading and trapping expedition to ascend the Missouri to the Rocky Mountains," but as already noted, Lisa and his men were not the first and not even runners-up because they trailed both McClallen and Courtin. Lisa was recognized as the first simply because he returned to the "States" to tell his story, while neither McClallen nor Courtin ever did. Until the late twentieth century, they were relegated to the category of "other groups of traders on the river" whose "activities, successes, or failures have yet to come to light."[6]

Lisa's movements, by contrast, were well documented. Continually delayed by Bouché's antics, the group did not reach its planned destination until mid-November, more than a month behind schedule and too late to take advantage of the valuable fall trapping season. With a northern winter crashing down on them, Edward Rose, John Colter, John Hoback, Jacob Reznor, Edward Robinson, and the others scrambled to raise temporary shelters and a trading house with two rooms and a loft in a wooded patch between the confluence of the Yellowstone and Bighorn Rivers. The encampment was christened Fort Remon, after Lisa's son, but soon anglicized to Fort Raymond (also called Manuel's Fort, Fort Lisa, and Fort Manuel Lisa). This was the perfect site for a trading post—with a good supply of both water and wood, good country for both beaver and game. More importantly, the neighboring Crow Indians were friendly and they were interested in commerce. And the key to Crow commerce—indeed a key to Crow culture itself—was a creature technically known as *equus ferus caballus*.

Sometime around 1730, the Crow acquired the horse, which had arrived in the New World with Hernán Cortés in 1519 and had transformed Indian life as it made its way either through trade or larceny from Mexico northward into the entire American and Canadian West, initially by way of Mississippi to the northeast, New Mexico to the north, and California to the northwest. Arguably more than any other Indian nation, the Crow had mastered the art of capturing, riding, and trading horses. As Colin G. Calloway has written, "They built up a lucrative trade and guarded it jealously," obtaining horses from their Salish, Nez Pearce, and Shoshone allies in the west and "driving the herds east to the villages of their Hidatsa relatives, where they exchanged them for corn, tobacco, and European goods."[7]

Charles McKenzie, a North West Company clerk present in 1805 when a Crow caravan arrived in Hidatsa country, wrote that "they consisted of more than three hundred Tents, and presented the handsomest sight that one could imagine—all on horseback. Children of small size were lashed to the Saddles, and those above the age of six could manage a horse." The Crow had driven two thousand head of horses across the high plains, and the sight reminded McKenzie of a great army. Gathering on a rise behind the Hidatsa village, the Crow horsemen were addressed by a chief—"they then descended full speed—rode through the Village, exhibiting their dexterity in horsemanship in a thousand shapes—I was astonished to see their agility and address:—and I could believe they were the best riders in the world." Dressed in leather, they looked "clean and neat—Some wore beads and rings as ornaments. Their arms were Bows and arrows, Lances, and round stones enclosed in leather and slung to a shank in the form of a whip."[8]

Lisa had no doubt heard such stories, and he wasted no time befriending the Crow. Brackenridge wrote that Lisa "dispatched Coulter . . . to bring some of the Indian nations to trade. This man, with a pack of thirty pounds weight, his gun and some ammunition, went upwards of five hundred miles to the Crow nation; gave them information, and proceeded from thence to several other tribes." Making a journey that would be the stuff of legend—and controversy—Colter traveled to the southwest, into Wyoming's Bighorn Basin, to the present site Cody. From there he veered to the south and slightly to the east, eventually picking up the Wind River and ascending it to its source at Brooks Lake. Then he went northwest, into present Yellowstone Park, seeing Yellowstone Lake but missing Old Faithful and other wonders to the west. His northeast route then took him to Clark's Fork of the Yellowstone, which he followed to the Yellowstone and from there back to the fort.

Colter likely encountered a number of Crow villages, including one at the mouth of Pryor Creek and another on Clark's Fork.[9]

Showing his confidence in Lewis and Clark's men, Lisa also selected two others as emissaries to the surrounding Indian nations—George Drouillard and Peter Weiser. Drouillard made two trips, one to the Bighorn Basin and another to the Little Bighorn River, and visited a number of Crow camps, such as one near the headwaters of Rosebud Creek and another on the Bighorn River. Weiser apparently went west to the Three Forks area, ascended the Madison River, and crossed the Continental Divide into present Idaho, possibly meeting both Blackfoot and Shoshone Indians in the process.[10]

Of course, Colter, Drouillard, and Weiser had extensive experience as explorers, woodsmen, and Indian diplomats, but Lisa's fourth choice was a surprise—the greenhorn Edward Rose. According to Reuben Holmes, proofs of Rose's "reckless bravery," "strong and vigorous constitution," and "his tact and facility in overcoming sudden difficulties and dangers . . . had not escaped the scrutiny of Mr. Lisa." Rose was thus "selected to spend the winter with the Crow Indians," where he learned their language "with considerable facility," "engaged in their pursuits with them," and "found that he could run a buffalo or a Black-foot as well as they could."[11] Exactly where Rose went is unknown, but he may well have gone east, since none of the others ventured in that direction. He took to Indian life like few other trappers had ever done.

Leaving in the dead of winter, the four nomads probably made their own snowshoes, just as earlier explorers in the region had done, and disappeared into the cold one-by-one, loaded down with their buffalo robes, their trade goods, their pemmican, their flint and steel, their tomahawks and scalping knives, and their rifles and ammunition.[12] The others watched them leave and then returned to building shelters, guarding the fort, hunting deer and elk, smoking meat, and digging coal from a nearby deposit. Given their later history, we have every reason to believe that Hoback, Reznor, and Robinson were among those wishing to trade places with the four pathfinders. If so, they would get their wish soon enough—and one too many times.

Pierre Dorion had voyaged up the Missouri with Pryor's group in the spring of 1807, going as far as the southeast corner of present South Dakota, where he stopped with the Yankton Sioux he was escorting. He apparently remained there with Marie, and sometime that year their son Baptiste was born. As far as is known, the little family lived a peaceful life among the friendly Yankton during 1807 and 1808, dwelling in a typical Sioux tepee—described by Clark as "snug" and "handsum" and "made of Buffalow Skins Painted different Colour"—with Pierre interpreting for any white men who came by or hunting buffalo with his Yankton comrades.[13] Each day was filled with labor, but they had good shelter, sufficient food, and the fellowship of friends.

Four or five hundred miles upstream, another French-Canadian interpreter and his Indian wife—Toussaint Charbonneau and Sacagawea—were living quite a similar life, only in a Mandan village. They also had a young son named Baptiste. Both boys would become interpreters and guides in their own right, and in a development no one in 1807 could have predicted, both would die in a fertile coastal land coveted by Spain, Britain, Russia, and America—a land dreamed of and longed for by countless immigrants who journeyed there along treacherous trails in covered wagons: Oregon.

Reliving his experience from a year earlier, Ramsay Crooks canoed down the Missouri in the spring of 1808 and applied to go back up the river later in the summer. He strode into the governor's office on May 2, one year and one day after making his 1807 application, but this time the new governor was present. Appointed in March of 1807, Meriwether Lewis had lingered in the East for a year before making his way to St. Louis. He and Crooks had plenty to talk about, but the details of any conversation they had have been lost. We simply know that Crooks was granted permission to "ascend the Missouri with provisions for [the] trading house" he and Robert McClellan were operating. He may have learned from Lewis himself that obtaining provisions would not be easy because in the midst of a simmering conflict with Britain the United States had cut off imports from that country and had passed an embargo act prohibiting U.S. vessels from sailing to foreign ports, bad news for entrepreneurs like Crooks and McClellan who needed such English goods as "manufactured cloth, tools, guns, and so forth" to trade with the Indians. Nevertheless, the determined Crooks eventually made arrangements to travel to Michilimackinac, a key trading center situated on present Mackinac Island between Lake Michigan and Lake Huron, to see if he could buy the needed supplies there. He arrived in mid-August, made the purchase, and then visited a U.S. official named George Hoffman to apply for a license to transport the supplies back to St. Louis. Suspicious that Crooks was British-Canadian—which he was—Hoffman requested that Crooks take an oath to demonstrate his loyalty to the United States, but Crooks "refused taking it— alledging that he conceived himself an American Citizen, that he was concerned with one Mc.Cleland, an American born," and that he had no allegiance to the British trading firm in the area. The reluctant Hoffman reported to Frederick Bates that he therefore granted Crooks a "*Common* Clearance."[14]

With a boatload of valuable goods, Crooks and his hands voyaged to Green Bay by way of Lake Michigan, ascended the Fox River to the southwest, and then made a portage to the Wisconsin River, which they followed to the Mississippi. Crooks reached St. Louis about the middle of September and found the city buzzing about a trial scheduled to start on Monday, September 19. The defendant was Drouillard; he and Lisa had returned from Fort Raymond on August 5 only to be arrested three days later, with the prosecutor arguing that the killing of Bissonnet sixteen months earlier "was perpetrated thro' express malice and that it was murder in the fullest and most strict sense of the term."[15] The plan was to prosecute Drouillard first and then Lisa in a separate trial.

Crooks met up with McClellan, who had arrived a few weeks earlier. Coming downstream, McClellan had happened upon six boats transporting eighty-one soldiers going in the opposite direction. They were under the command of William Clark, who was coming overland with another eighty men on horseback. Their destination was an area along the river known as Fire Prairie, in present western Missouri. The combined force would construct a trading and military post, soon called Fort Osage, on a grand bluff overlooking the winding river.

As historian Jay H. Buckley has noted, "the site could easily control the Missouri River trade since all passing craft would fall within the gun range of the fort on the bluffs."[16]

McClellan had apparently kept his presence quiet, avoiding legal action related to the Hortiz suit, and was therefore not likely to show up at Drouillard's trial. But if Crooks attended all or part of the proceeding, he quickly learned Shannon's fate when he saw the young man, newly fitted with a peg leg, sitting in the jury box with Pierre Didiere, Patrick Lee, and nine others. The trial occupied the entire week and was possibly attended by Meriwether Lewis and Frederick Bates, both of whom had taken a special interest in Shannon, visiting and assisting him during his convalescence. If so, they would have been unavailable to deal with Crooks and McClellan, who were eager to renew their trading license and get back up the river. Any attempt to secure the license was further complicated when William Clark arrived from Fire Prairie on Thursday, September 22, and presumably reported to Lewis.

As for Drouillard, Lewis and Clark both viewed him with great admiration, particularly Lewis, who called him "a man of much merit" and added that he deserved "the highest commendation" for his service on the expedition. So the two friends were no doubt tremendously relieved when Shannon and his fellow jurors returned with a verdict of not guilty—after deliberating for only fifteen minutes—convinced by the defense that "the killing was perfectly justifiable, both by the laws of God and man."[17]

The trial ended on Friday, September 23, and the next day Crooks and McClellan, likely accompanied by John Day, who had come down the river with Clark's party, officially filed their application with the governor's office. The license was granted but with the curious stipulation that they could "trade at the Fire Prairie, with authority to the Agent or Sub Agent of that place, so to extend the licence, as to embrace such portion of the upper country as he (said Agent) may judge proper."

Crooks and McClellan were not pleased, however, because they wanted to trade on the upper Missouri, and when they got to Fort Osage, the sub-agent, either Reuben Lewis (Meriwether's brother) or Pierre Chouteau Sr., told them they could make their winter camp at the Black Snake Hills, at the present site of St. Joseph, Missouri, not far to the south of where they had spent the previous winter. As David Lavender so aptly put it, "[I]t is within possibility that in being exiled to the Black Snake Hills the partners were feeling the claws of a new monopoly that hoped to absorb every bit of the trade from the mouth of the Platte to the head of the Missouri." The "reluctant initiator" of this new monopoly was none other than Manuel Lisa, who had made another remarkable escape when the prosecutor had declined to pursue murder charges against him because of Drouillard's acquittal, even though many observers had likely been convinced, as the defense argued, "that if any one was to blame [for Bissonnet's death], it was Mr. Lisa who ordered [Drouillard] to bring the deceased '*dead or alive.*'"[18]

Although each man was about to spend a fourth consecutive winter on the Missouri, their business had been largely frustrated and neither Crooks nor McClellan had reached the prime trading territory among the Mandan and Hidadtsa Indians in present North Dakota. Now, with the U.S. embargo, powerful competitors, or hostile Indians hindering their every move, they were about to give up, a decision they would formalize during the coming winter. But the partners were unaware of a development that would convince them to try anew, a development that would alter the course of their lives, mentioned in surprisingly specific terms in a letter that Governor Lewis had received in August of 1808 from Thomas Jefferson. "A powerful company is at length forming for taking up the Indian commerce on a large scale," Jefferson wrote. "They will employ a capital the first year of 300,000 [dollars] and raise it afterwards to a million." The President added that the company would "be under the direction of a most excellent man, a Mr. Astor."[19]

Chapter Three

"Dissolved by Mutual Consent"

By the summer of 1808, John Hoback, Jacob Reznor, and Edward Robinson had been at Fort Raymond for more than six months and had received no news from "the States" since their departure from St. Louis in the spring of 1807. Nor would they hear of any happenings in the East for another thirteen months, but this was a fact of life among those who ventured to the Rocky Mountains as hunters and trappers. Still, they had seen their share of fascinating events, and like those in St. Louis, they had watched as Manuel Lisa dodged another scrape with danger.

George Drouillard, Peter Weiser, and John Colter, the three Lewis and Clark veterans sent out the previous fall to the Crow and other Indian nations, had all returned safely by spring, and while the first two provided valuable information about present Wyoming and Idaho, Colter had the most amazing story to tell. As Washington Irving wrote in 1837, Colter had discovered "natural curiosities, which are held in superstitious awe" by the Crow. "A volcanic tract . . . on Stinking River . . . was first discovered by Colter, a hunter belonging to Lewis and Clarke's exploring party, who came upon it in the course of his lonely wanderings, and gave such an account of its gloomy terrors, its hidden fires, smoking pits, noxious streams, and the all-pervading 'smell of brimstone,' that it received, and has ever since retained among trappers, the name of 'Colter's Hell!'"[1]

The men had hardly had time to trade opinions about these claims before Lisa dispatched the ever-active Colter once again, this time "to the forks of the Missouri, to endeavor to find the Blackfeet nation, and bring them to his establishment [at Fort Raymond] to trade." Lisa was apparently hoping that the Blackfoot Indians near Three Forks would not know of (or not care about) Meriwether Lewis's violent encounter with Blackfoot warriors a few hundred miles to the north in 1806. Unknown to Lisa, of course, Charles

Courtin and his men had founded a post at Three Forks late in the summer of 1807 and were still there.[2]

Colter, however, had neither the chance to meet Courtin nor to appeal peacefully to any Blackfoot Indians because he "fell in with a party of the Crow nation, with whom he staid several days." The Crow were accompanied by a large number of friends from the Salish tribe—often called Flatheads—and the combined party was "attacked by their enemies the Blackfeet. Coulter, in self-defence, took part with the Crows." A friend of Colter's (who got the story from Colter) reported that eight hundred Crow and Salish were pitted against fifteen hundred Blackfoot. "The battle was desperately fought on both sides," with the Blackfoot first engaging the Salish, "whom they attacked in great fury. The noise, shouts and firing brought a reinforcement of Crows to the Flat-Heads, who were fighting with great spirit and defending the ground manfully." Colter "distinguished himself very much in the combat," and although he was "wounded in the leg, and thus disabled standing," he "crawled to a small thicket and there loaded and fired while sitting on the ground." When his allies took the upper hand, the Blackfoot band retreated, although they "retired in perfect order and could hardly be said to have been defeated." But they would not forget that they had "plainly observed a white man fighting in the ranks of their enemy."[3]

Colter made it back to the fort, probably assisted by Crow friends, and was recovering from his wound when a fabled dispute broke out between Lisa and one of his trappers—and it wasn't Bouché. After a long sojourn among the Crow, where he made fast friends and adapted surprisingly well to Indian life, Edward Rose had returned to Fort Raymond, arriving sometime in June, "about the time Mr. Lisa was completing his arrangements for descending the river to St. Louis. Rose was, of course, called upon to show his 'returns,' or account for the goods," but flattered by the Crow villagers he had lived with, he had freely given away all of his trade supplies, down to the last bead. "Whether he reported his goods as lost in crossing a creek, or whether he reported them stolen by the Indians," is not known, but Lisa was not happy. He and Rose were alone in the counting room when Rose decided he had heard enough of Lisa's haranguing and "sprang, like a tiger" upon Lisa, overpowering him, and "would probably have killed him, had not the noise of the scuffle brought a man, by the name of Potts . . . to the relief of Mr. Lisa. His coming saved Mr. L., but he suffered severely by the interference."[4]

Taking no thought for Potts, another of Lewis and Clark's men in the group, Lisa hightailed it out to his boat "with the intention of embarking immediately," but as the boat "swung around into the current" of the Yellowstone River, the enraged Rose "ran to a swivel . . . and quickly directing its line of fire, 'touched it off' with his pipe." A barrage of buckshot volleyed through the cargo box of the keelboat, but miraculously injured none of the

crew, which included Drouillard. "Rose immediately commenced re-charg-
ing the swivel, but was prevented from completing his object by the intervention of about fifteen men"—likely including Hoback, Reznor, and Robinson—"who could barely restrain the effects of his ungovernable passion."[5]

Lisa made his escape, probably viewing his arrest several weeks later in
St. Louis as tame by comparison, and within days Rose packed up "whatever
goods he could wheedle or frighten out of those remaining in the fort, and
started for the Crow nation," where he immediately gave the goods as gifts,
adopted Crow "dress and costume, head-gear and all, exchanged a favorite
rifle and accoutrements for a wife, and slung a bow and quiver to his back."
He "seemed born" for Crow life, "almost always recklessly and desperately
[seeking] death where it was most likely to be found. No Indian ever preceded him in the attack or pursuit of an enemy."[6]

As summer turned to autumn, autumn to winter, and winter to spring, the
men at Fort Raymond saw nothing of Rose, perhaps concluding he was gone
forever, but Hoback, Reznor, and Robinson had not see the last of the "celebrated outlaw."

Any discouragement Ramsay Crooks and Robert McClellan had felt as they
canoed back up the Missouri in late September of 1808 only deepened during
the long winter. The trader Joseph Robidoux III and his six sons (one of
whom founded St. Joseph, Missouri) had established a virtual monopoly in
the local Indian trade, so business was bad. On top of that, the value of fur
had plummeted and was likely to continue dropping as long as the embargo
was in place. Then one of Crooks and McClellan's men was killed by unknown Indians. Given all of this, it was hardly a surprise that the partners
prepared an announcement:

> Take Notice
> The partnership formerly subsisting between us under the firm of McClellan
> and Crooks, is this day disolved by mutual consent.
> All persons indebted to said firm are requested to make immediate payment
> and those who have claims on the same, will present them to Ramsay Crooks;
> who is fully authorized to settle all the affairs of said partnership.
> Robert McClellan
> Ramsay Crooks
> Black Snake Hills, River Missouri, 17th Feb. 1809[7]

As soon as weather permitted, Crooks launched his canoe southward, making
what had essentially become his annual spring pilgrimage to St. Louis (this
was the fourth year in a row he had made the trip). The first matter of
business was delivering his and McClellan's announcement to Joseph Charless, editor of the *Missouri Gazette*, who printed it on April 12, leaving
Crooks to an uncertain future. His partnership with McClellan had seemed so

promising—he must have felt a pang of regret at the dissolution of the company and how circumstance had conspired against him and McClellan. The amazing thing was, this young man Crooks, now a veteran Missouri River trader, was barely twenty-two years old. Given the good reputation he had established, his prospects were good, regardless of his exact plans. But whatever intentions he had remain a mystery because circumstance suddenly turned in his favor. Within weeks he probably regretted delivering the notice to Charless so promptly. Indeed, he soon acted as if he and McClellan had not composed and published the announcement at all—although McClellan wouldn't know for months, Crooks and McClellan were back in business.

The exact sequence of events is not known, but about the same time the notice ran in the *Gazette*, a surprising but welcome report came from Washington: on March 1, three days before leaving office, Thomas Jefferson had signed legislation repealing much of the embargo act. The *National Intelligencer* had flooded the capital with extra copies of its newspaper, proclaiming the news bound to thrill farmers, trappers, shop owners, entrepreneurs, businessmen, and laborers of all stripes, for although the embargo had ostensibly been aimed at foreign countries, especially Britain, the Americans were the ones who had felt the brunt of it. Fur prices would certainly jump, and trade goods would be much more accessible.

The other piece of good news came from a young St. Louis businessman by the name of Wilson Price Hunt. Only four years older than Crooks, Hunt had arrived in St. Louis from New Jersey in 1804 and formed a partnership with John Hankinson. As James P. Ronda has written, "The two were general-merchandise agents, selling everything from soap and grain to whiskey and boats. They even dabbled in the fur market, trading with the Chouteaus and Astor's St. Louis agent, Charles Gratiot."[8]

Crooks, of course, had had frequent dealings with St. Louis merchants and almost certainly knew Hunt. It does not seem unreasonable to conclude, with David Lavender, that Hunt approached Crooks with the "electrifying news" that Crooks and McClellan were being invited "to join an expedition being formed by John Jacob Astor to follow Lewis and Clark's route to the Pacific." According to Lavender's scenario, Hunt suggested that an advance party headed by Crooks and McClellan could "press up the Missouri ahead of the main overland group and prepare a winter base for the overlanders to use the following winter, 1810-1811."[9]

Not only did this development resurrect Crooks and McClellan's trading hopes, it offered an incredible opportunity for them to compete with or even surpass their chief enemy: Lisa. The monopoly that Lisa had reluctantly initiated during the fall of 1808 and the subsequent winter was the St. Louis Missouri Fur Company. Although Lisa, Pierre Menard, and William Morrison had each claimed furs worth an impressive $2,667.50 from Lisa's 1807 expedition up the Missouri and Yellowstone Rivers (with Lisa receiving an additional $985.00 for leading the group), they worried that other well-connected traders in St. Louis—and there were several—could dart in front of them. They were apparently therefore "constrained to take part with others in order to avoid a ruinous competition."[10]

As William E. Foley has noted, this venture "attracted a host of notable investors who joined together to forge a powerful alliance linking business and government. The firm's list of subscribers read like a who's who of Upper Louisiana's commercial and political power brokers." On March 7, 1809, Lisa, Menard, and Morrison were joined by William Clark, Pierre Chouteau and his son Auguste Pierre, Benjamin Wilkinson, Sylvestre Labbadie, Andrew Henry, and Reuben Lewis in signing the articles of incorporation of the new company. Governor Meriwether Lewis, who "in all likelihood, was a secret partner in the new firm," was determined to break the British stranglehold on upper Missouri trade and "agreed to give [the company] free rein in the region by suspending all trading restrictions there."[11]

Of course, two names conspicuously missing were Crooks and McClellan, and there is no indication that they were invited to join the new company. Not only that, but the subagent who had assigned them to the Black Snake Hills, either Reuben Lewis or Auguste Pierre Chouteau, was now a partner in the St. Louis Missouri Fur Company and had likely seen hints or intimations of future developments before making the assignment. Such a one could not be expected to be impartial. All of this would have thrown Crooks and McClellan into an unwinnable situation, but the offer from Hunt tipped everything topsy-turvy. Although they had not yet signed an official contract, Crooks and McClellan had the prospect of going up the river backed by a tycoon with considerably more capital and connections than anyone in St. Louis.

Presumably carrying a letter of credit from Hunt, Crooks hurried north, leaving in May. He had to get to Michilimackinac and purchase trade goods as soon as possible. He had no time to waste because the St. Louis Missouri Fur Company had garnered a hefty contract to travel up the Missouri, and Crooks wanted to be right behind them.

This contract was hardly a run-of-the-mill agreement between private parties. In a move that would simply be unthinkable in the twenty-first century (and was even objectionable in the nineteenth), "His Excellency Meriwether Lewis, Governor of the . . . Territory of Lousiana, and Superintendent of Indian affairs" had agreed to pay a company that included his brother and his best friend $7,000 to escort Sheheke and his family back to their North Dakota home (the same assignment McClellan had sought in the spring of 1807). Not only had Lewis leveraged his position to give the St. Louis Missouri Fur Company an unfair advantage over their competitors—particularly Crooks and McClellan—he had drawn up and executed the contract on February 24, 1809, two weeks before the company partners had even signed their own articles of agreement (and, by mere coincidence, one week after Crooks and McClellan had signed the announcement of their dissolution). And although the contract listed its ostensible objective as the "safe convey-ance and delivery of the Mandan Chief, his Wife, and child, to the Mandan Nation," there was no doubt that this well-financed journey up the Missouri would give Pierre Chouteau, the commander of the detachment, and his associates an unparalleled opportunity to make crucial trade agreements on the way. Making this trade advantage explicit, the contract specifically prom-ised that Lewis would not "authorize any other person or persons to ascend the Missouri any higher . . . than the Mouth of the River La Platte, for the purpose of Trading with the Indians," nor "permit any party accompanying the said detachment or any other party, to ascend the River, go before or in advance of the said detachment commanded by said Choteau from the mouth of the said River La Platte, to the Mandan village."[12]

Not only would the company be well compensated for its efforts, it was virtually guaranteed first trading rights with the Omaha, Yankton Sioux, Lakota Sioux, Mandan, and Hidatsa Nations.[13] We have no record of how Hunt and Crooks responded to this amazing course of events, but perhaps they were content in the hope that their well-financed expedition would give them ample opportunity to establish their own monopoly in the Rocky Mountains and along the Pacific coast. Crooks simply made plans to pur-chase goods and supplies and ascend the Missouri right after Chouteau's group. To run matters as smoothly as possible, Crooks apparently brought in a new man to assist with the operation. His name was Joseph Miller, and according to Washington Irving, he was "well educated and well informed, and of a respectable family of Baltimore. He had been an officer in the army of the United States, but had resigned in disgust, on being refused a furlough, and had taken to trapping beaver and trading among the Indians."[14] In a few years, Miller would achieve a rather unique status among the founders of the Oregon Trail: he would be the only man who set out with the westbound Astorians and returned with the eastbounders but never made it to Oregon or the Pacific Ocean, even though he saw his share of present South Dakota, Wyoming, and Idaho.

Miller likely recruited men and arranged for a keelboat as Crooks went north for goods. Meanwhile, Chouteau and the partners who would go upriv-er with him—Lisa, Menard, Henry, Labbadie, and Reuben Lewis—tried to get their massive mission off the ground. The contract required them to enlist 120 men, 40 of whom had to be Americans and expert riflemen. They also had to "furnish the said detachment . . . with good and suitable Fire Arms, of which at least fifty shall be Rifles, and a sufficient quantity of good Ammuni-tion." Then came an endless list of supplies that included everything from knives, gun slings, coats, axes, spades, rope, awls, iron spoons, portable soup, and lamps and wicks to glass beads, needles and thread, spun tobacco, red silk handkerchiefs, and fishing hooks (all gifts for the Indians), to canoes, paddles, chains, boat hooks, calomel, lancets, and ointment. Lewis and Clark had gone to great lengths to equip and feed around 50 men traveling in one keelboat and two pirogues, and yet the St. Louis Missouri Fur Company had to provide for approximately 350 men going upriver in thirteen keelboats and barges, accompanied by canoes of all shapes and sizes. It was little wonder that a list of partial expenses showed $6,171.14¼ worth of goods purchased from F. Regnier and Company and another £6,861/98/6 worth provided by Pierre Chouteau. But it was not quite as understandable how the company could miss a crucial deadline. The contract plainly demanded a departure date of April 20, which could be postponed to May 10 in the event of "any unforseen accident." And even though the penalty for not leaving by May 10 was a fine of "three thousand dollars, lawful money of the United States"—almost half the scheduled payment—and even though no unforeseen circumstances interfered, Chouteau and his group of about 160 men did not depart until May 17. Smaller groups followed over the next few weeks, and Lisa finally got away exactly one month later, on June 17. Luckily, Governor Lewis did not impose a fine.[15]

Among the men who signed on with Lisa was Thomas James. Born in Maryland in 1782, he was an experienced frontiersman who was hired as steersman or "captain" of one of the barges. He had twenty-four men, all Americans, under his command. James said the expedition was "raised for trading with the Indians and trapping for beaver on the head waters of the Missouri and Columbia rivers." He enlisted for three years with the expectation of receiving traps and ammunition when the men arrived at the hunting grounds, as well as the assistance of four hirelings, or *engagés*. ("The 'company' made us the fairest promises in St. Louis, only to break them in Indian country," wrote James.) The outspoken and observant James kept a journal of the trip, and although he lost the journal, he later described the voyage in fascinating detail in his book, *Three Years among the Indians and Mexicans*, which he published in 1846, one year before his death. The volume not only makes for compelling reading but also offers the only full-length account of the first—and most historic—mission of the St. Louis Missouri Fur Company.[16]

In the course of his travels, James met up with Hoback, Reznor, and Robinson at Fort Raymond in 1810 and with them survived a Blackfoot attack. By that time, he was well acquainted with another man who would also survive the hostilities, "a Yankee, named Pelton, . . . a jovial, popular fellow" who was a crewmember on the barge captained by James. Archibald Pelton "greatly amused the company in coming up the river, by his songs and sermons. At every stopping place he held a meeting for the mock trial of offenders and exhorted us in the New England style to mend our courses and eschew sin."[17] Like John Day and Miller, Pelton would go west with Hoback, Reznor, and Robinson—and Crooks and McClellan—making his name as a founder of the Oregon Trail. His story would be entertaining, exciting, astonishing, and ultimately heartbreaking.

Another member of the crew would become a well-known and well-respected mountain man, with a "fabulous career spanning the period from Lewis and Clark to the Civil War." He was "most evidently calm, cool, competent, highly efficient and effective, not prone to homicide, drunken celebration or other colorful habits." His name was John Dougherty, and he was only eighteen when he signed on with the company in 1809. Over the course of his long career in the West, Dougherty was never employed by Astor's American Fur Company—"he was, in fact, a noted adversary of that company"—but he shared trials, adventures, and narrow escapes with Hoback, Reznor, Robinson, and Pelton.[18]

James and his crew viewed Lisa with contempt. "He . . . bore a very bad reputation in the country and among the Americans," wrote James. Lisa and some of his colleagues "required all the boats to stop in company for the night," but James's barge was "large and heavily loaded, [and] the crew frequently had great difficulty in overtaking [the other boats] in the evening." Rather than sympathizing, Lisa "lorded it over the poor fellows most arrogantly, and made them work as if their lives depended on their getting forward, with the greatest possible speed."[19]

James's contingent was hardly the only unhappy crew. On reaching the mouth of the Osage River, Menard wrote that he and the other partners found "about eighty men, of which one half are American hunters and almost all revolted. It was necessary to make new arrangements with them, but I hope all will be better in the future." But things did not improve, and Lisa sent Clark regular reports about men who had deserted. By June 24, approximately eighteen men had defected. A week later, Lisa wrote to Clark that two more men, John Davis and John Bly, had deserted and taken company rifles with them. "We are going very slow," Lisa continued. "We left a large Barge"—because they didn't have a crew to man it. "Reuben Lewis commands the Boat in which the americans are together"—the same boat James was steering—"two men for each oar and still they complain. I am fearful that more will desert and that we shall be obliged to leave another Boat." Lisa ended the gloomy letter by informing Clark that four or five men were sick.[20]

On July 8, the exasperated Lisa reached Fort Osage, where a few small comforts of home might have been enjoyed, but he had nothing but worries. He urged Clark to "make all possible diligence to arrest our deserters" if they arrived in St. Louis. "I wish you to see Mr Chouteaus Son and enquire where, those deserters have left their plunder, I wish you to have them punished, for they have made us suffer." Lisa also included the amounts these men owed the company—down to the half cent. He wrote of more sickness, of having to leave a boat and a quantity of corn behind "for want of men," of five barrels of pork "found to be rotten, not fit for use."[21] It was one thing after another.

But Lisa was also fretting about something else: Crooks had arrived at Fort Osage, and Lisa was worried that Crooks and McClellan might try to get to the upper Missouri before the St. Louis Missouri Fur Company men. "Mr Crouks left this [place] yesterday to join Mr McClellan," wrote Lisa. "He said and promised that he would wait for us [at the mouth of the Platte River]. If we do not find him there I will be obliged to take an assortment [of men] and go after him with my boat which is the fastest going boat we have."[22]

His streak of good luck continuing, Crooks had made a quick trip southward on Lake Michigan by boarding the sailing ship *Selina* and having his barges towed behind. Leaving a crew behind to transport the goods, he likely "hurried ahead in a conoe or light bateau to St. Louis. There he gave the bills of lading for the barges to Joseph Miller, so that Miller could transfer the material to a keelboat and start it up the Missouri."[23]

As Lisa mentioned to Clark, Crooks had left Fort Osage on July 9, on his way to meet McClellan (and no doubt bring him up to date on all the surprising news). But when Lisa suspected that Crooks might break his pledge and rush up the river, he was simply revealing that he did not know Ramsay Crooks very well. Governor Lewis had legally restricted travel on the Missouri, and, as Hiram Martin Chittenden wrote, Crooks was a "vigorous and relentless enemy when he took up a contest," but "he opposed clandestine, quite as much as open, violations of the law." Although Crooks spent most of his life "connected with a business where the temptation to use lawless methods was so great, there is no record of any attempt on his part to do anything that he had not a legal right to do."[24]

James wrote that a few weeks after leaving Fort Osage "our allotted provisions gave out and we were compelled to live on boiled corn, without salt. At the same time all the other boats were well supplied and the gentlemen proprietors in the leading barge were faring in the most sumptuous and luxurious manner. The French hands were much better treated on all occasions than the Americans." The irony was, the boat that James and his comrades were rowing and pulling up the meandering Missouri was loaded down with thirty barrels of pork that the Americans were not allowed to touch. Their resentment turned to anger and their anger to fury. "Their boiled corn without salt or meat, did not sustain them under the fatigue of navigating the barge," wrote James, "and the contrast between their treatment and that of the French enraged them." In a scene reminiscent of Rose's assault on Lisa a year earlier, some of the crew threatened a mutiny. A Tennessean "about six feet high and well proportioned," who "figured as ring-leader on this occasion," was a man by the name of Cheek; one day when the flotilla stopped at noon he rolled a barrel of pork onto the deck, raised a tomahawk, and cried out to James, "Give the word Captain."[25]

James forbade opening the barrel and "went ashore to find Lewis, who had left the boat at the beginning of trouble." When James confronted Lewis, the latter hurried to a nearby boat where Lisa had gathered with several other partners. "I could see them in their cabin, from the shore where I stood," James remembered, "playing cards and drinking." When Lewis announced that "James' crew were taking the provisions," Lisa "seized his pistols and ran out" to confront James. "What the devil is the matter with you and your men?" he asked. "We are starving," James answered, "and we must have something better than boiled corn." Meanwhile, "Cheek was brandishing his tomahawk over the pork barrel and clamoring for the 'word' . . . while the rest of my crew were drawn up in line on the boat, with rifles, ready for action." Lisa and the others relented and gave the crew a large supply of pork. A few days later, the pork was removed and replaced with a supply of lead.[26]

Things had changed considerably in the two years since Lisa had ordered a man shot for deserting. Now he sought no retribution for James's men but left well enough alone. "We continued our ascent of the river without any occurrence of importance," reported James. "Below Council Bluffs we met Capt. Crooks, agent for John J. Astor, and who was trading with the Mohaws [Omaha Indians]."[27]

True to his word, Crooks had waited for the Missouri Fur Company men. And although James did not mention McClellan, Dr. William Thomas, the company surgeon, who was riding on James's boat, recorded further details: "August 1st arrived at the river Platte on the south side. Met with Mr. M'Clelland, waiting for the Ottos, whom he expected in great numbers to trade with."[28]

Although Thomas had encountered a long line of influential and note-worthy men during the trip up the river, he had offered no commentary on any of them, but Crooks's partner was an exception. Showing an admiration for McClellan that was not untypical, Thomas wrote: "Mr. M'C[l]elland has weathered many storms in his life, and it appears that each day seems to throw something bitter in his cup; brave, generous and kind, he meets the untutored Indian with the smile of complacency," adding that, if in peril, McClellan "discovers exalted courage, surrounded with Indians, with his rifle, pistols, and sword, he bids defiance to whole nations; threatening or executing extermination to all who attempt to plunder him."[29]

Crooks and McClellan continued their trade with the local Indians—they could not proceed north until Miller arrived with the keelboat. The company partners and their men, of course, pushed on up the river, enjoying good weather and relative calm among the hands. They were about thirty miles south of present Sioux City, Iowa, when they reached the Omaha Indian village. Dr. Thomas noted that it was situated "on a prairie on the south side [Nebraska side], four miles from the river, resembling at a distance, the stack yard of an extensive farmer, having their huts in the form of a cone, about 15 feet high. Their council house is built in the centre, large enough to contain 300 men; the materials consists of split sticks and pieces of timber; covered with earth."[30]

A few days earlier, the Omaha had lost several warriors in a skirmish with the Sioux, but this did not prevent them from greeting the American traders, and with a festive meal. "Here we were served with the first dish of dog meat," wrote Thomas. "[I]t is esteemed delicate, and none partake of it but those they wish to honour." Sheheke was the guest of honor—he had donned "an elegant full dress suit of regimentals, with his horse covered with the most showey ornaments, he set out accompanied by thirty Maha chiefs on horse back, in their best dress."[31]

Whether the group met Pierre Dorion Sr. during or before this feast is unknown, but Meriwether Lewis had told Chouteau that Dorion had "been ordered to join you at the mahas Village and Place himself under your direction." Chouteau had been contractually obligated to hire at least two interpreters in St. Louis, and Lewis had recommended Noel Mongrain, Joseph Gravelines, and Baptiste Dorion (son of Pierre Sr. and brother of Pierre Jr.). Which of them actually accompanied Chouteau is unclear, but Dorion Sr.'s services would be invaluable regardless. No man was better qualified to act as interpreter and negotiator as the armada made its way into Yankton, Lakota, and Arikara territory.[32]

The ubiquitous Pierre Dorion Jr. was also hired as an interpreter for the St. Louis Missouri Fur Company in 1809; Washington Irving wrote that Pierre Jr. "conducted their traders in safety through the different tribes of the Sioux," proving himself "faithful and serviceable."[33] Since he is not known to have joined the company in St. Louis (and was not mentioned by Lewis) it is quite likely that he and his father enlisted together at the Maha village in August. Since the company seemed financially solid and planned on making regular trips up and down the Missouri, Pierre Jr. had every reason to seek long-term employment with them. That arrangement would have worked out fine for both parties because his skills were highly desired. During his stay at Fort Mandan, however, Pierre Jr. got himself in a predicament that would directly impact his decision to go west with the Astorians.

So, with two and possibly three Dorions aboard, the motley collection of keelboats, barges, canoes, businessmen, clerks, steersmen, boatmen, hunters, trappers, engagès, and even a physician continued up the river, leaving their Omaha friends on August 13. The Dorions did not disappoint, and conflicts with both the Yankton and Lakota (who understandably wanted to trade for the valuable goods being delivered to Sheheke's people) were avoided. Meeting the Arikara Nation, of course, was a different matter because of how the Arikara had attacked the party of Pryor and Chouteau and killed several men two years earlier. There had been no contact between the Arikara and the U.S. government since then, and Governor Lewis had ordered harsh measures, telling Chouteau to have the Indians most responsible for the attack (or others substituted in their place if necessary) "shot in the presence of the [Arikara] nation," and to incite the Mandan and Hidatsa Nations to attack the Arikara if needed. Fortunately, Chouteau took a much more judicious approach. His team arrived in the area on September 12. "On approaching their village," wrote James, "we took precautions against an attack. A guard marched along the shore, opposite to the boats, well armed. My crew composed a part of this force. When within half a mile of the village we drew up the cannon and prepared to encamp." Chouteau reported that "the Ricaras expecting their Village was to be attacked, sent away their Old men, women and children." Nor would the Arikara chiefs agree to sit in council with Chouteau. When he finally convinced them to do so, he announced: "The first time you Permitted Yourselves to fire upon the colours of your father, and to attack his men. I have orders to destroy your nation, but the chiefs of the sioux and mandan nations have United together and interceded for your pardon. . . . You may call Back your old men, your wives and children."[34]

The Arikara "expressed extreme sorrow at the recollection of their own differences with Lieut. Prior; and their profuse hospitality in given [giving] corn and meat, evinced their satisfaction at the return of friendly intercouse." Chouteau thus negotiated a new peace, and the Arikara chiefs took Sheheke by the hand, begged his forgiveness, and guaranteed his secure passage this time. Indeed, a week later, Sheheke arrived safely at his home—after a three-year absence. Not only had Chouteau accomplished his key mission of "the safe conveyance of the Mandan Chief, his Wife, and child, to the Mandan Nation," he had averted any further violence, even though "five or six hundred of the ricaras believing they would be attacked had Provided themselves with Guns, Amunition and Horses."[35]

Two independent accounts of this crucial meeting with the Arikara noted that when Chouteau's men first approached the Indian villages, a mysterious horseman appeared. "An old chief rode out at full speed," wrote James, "and with violent gestures and exclamations, warned and motioned back his countrymen from before our cannon. . . . He supposed we were about to inflict a proper and deserved punishment . . . [and] drove back all who were coming out to meet us." Reuben Holmes picked up a similar narrative, merging his story seamlessly with that of James and describing the rider's "dress and comparisons [as] those of an Indian dandy: . . . On his head was a dress of eagle and raven's feathers, worked in porcupine; his war club, adorned with plumes and ribbons, was in his hand, and his bow, ready strung, was brought around in front of his body, apparently for immediate use, if necessary." He rode a white stallion, a gift from an Arikara chief, which was marked with the red impressions of a man's hand, one of which was placed in the middle of the horse's forehead. The horseman's face "was painted, one half red, and the other half black. Such was the appearance of the man who came to the shore where the boats lay." But this reinsman was not an old man at all—he wasn't even an Indian—and some of the experienced engagès making their second or third trip up the Missouri discovered his identity "by the gleam of his eye (the only natural thing about him)." Much to their "surprise and amusement," they realized the man who had approached the shore at a full gallop was their old confidant Edward Rose.[36]

Although he had left Fort Raymond to dwell among the Crow, Rose had soon moved farther east, into Arikara country, "and was received by them in the most friendly manner. Here he was a perfect Indian. There was not an article of dress, or of any other description about him, that was not purely Indian." Earning the respect of the Arikara by learning their language and by acting with his usual reckless courage, Rose had gained enough trust to act as their emissary. But now, as he approached the keelboats and barges lining the shore, "surprise awaited Rose also, for, contrary to his expectations, he found Mr. Lisa in charge of the boats. He knew that he had cause to be remembered, and he knew that Mr. Lisa was not the man to forget the scene which had passed between them at the mouth of the Yellow Stone." Rose was right—he certainly had cause to be remembered—he likely would have killed Lisa a year earlier if John Potts had not interfered. What Lisa was thinking he never said, but he soon approached with a rifle in his hand. The unpredictable Rose engaged Lisa in conversation and "pretended to explain his former conduct. He laid the blame upon those who were with him among the Crows, and after telling a long story about things that never occurred, Mr. Lisa became, to all appearance, reconciled."[37]

Although he may have vowed never to rehire Rose and likely even plotted revenge, Lisa was first and foremost a businessman, a pragmatist who "saw that Rose might be useful to the company—first by refraining "from instigating the Indians, which it was in his power to do," and second by "furnishing information, interpreting, &c.—and [Lisa] accordingly again employed him."[38]

On September 22, the Dorions witnessed the joyous homecoming of Sheheke, his wife, Yellow Corn, and their five-year-old son, White Painted House. Minutes after landing, Chouteau's barges were "soon crowded with natives, and mutual congratulations took place" as the wanderers were "received with the greatest demonstration of joy." Sheheke, outfitted in "his full dress of uniform suit," was presented with a majestic horse, which the newly arrived chief "displayed considerable taste in dressing . . . in scarlet and gold laced housings, with a highly mounted bridle and saddle." Sheheke had returned with a bundle of impressive presents, including "[g]oods, wares,

Merchandizes[,] articles, and utensils," which his friends the Hidatsa chiefs eagerly awaited. "However," observed Dr. Thomas, "their hopes were vain: Sheheken was as anxious to retain his property, as they were to receive it." Although Chouteau had demanded that Sheheke distribute the gifts, the chief declined. "This seemed to occasion Jealousies and diffculties among all the tribes," wrote Chouteau, "and the more so as 'One Eye' the Great Chief of the minnetaries (Hidatsa) had in a quarrel a few days before murdered one of the principal men of the mandans." But Sheheke insisted on keeping the goods to himself, oblivious to the implications. "To Prevent Any further misunderstandings," said Chouteau, "and to appease the Jealousies which had been Created by the refusal of the mandan Chief to have the presents distributed, I distributed among them Sixty Pounds of Powder, and one hundred & Twenty Pounds [of balls] . . . and ten pounds of Vermillion, and one hundred and fifty Pounds of tobacco, which seemed to restore harmony amongst them." Sheheke's reputation, however, was hardly restored, and Dr. Thomas noted that "murmurs took the place of mirth, and on our departure from the village, [Sheheke's] popularity was on the decline."[39]

This was not the outcome Chouteau had hoped for, but he and his partners had nevertheless fulfilled their part of the agreement by delivering Sheheke safely to his home. Now they got down to other matters of business. First of all, they were concerned by reports that the North West Company "had erected a fort at the three forks of the Missoury. This information is believed to be true from the Circumstance of about thirty american hunters, who had used to visit the mandan Village, not being seen nor heard of since about Eighteen months." Had Chouteau been able to investigate this alarming news, he would have found that neither the North West Company nor Hudson's Bay had built a fort at Three Forks. The post in question had been built by Courtin and his men in 1807. By 1808, however, Courtin had crossed the Rocky Mountains and entered Salish country, where he built a fort on the Jocko River (which flows into the Flathead River) near present Ravalli, Montana. As Harry Majors speculated, Courtin "was most likely driven across the Continental Divide to the Flathead country by a war party of [Piegan Blackfoot] during the fall of 1808." If a Blackfoot war party had driven Courtin west, it could have been the same group that fought a battle against Crow and Salish enemies earlier that summer along the Gallatin River—the battle in which Colter was wounded.[40]

John McClallen—or Zachary Perch—and his men were less than ten miles northwest of Courtin's new post, near present Dixon, at the confluence of the Jocko and Flathead Rivers. He and Courtin must have met, but any record of their interaction has been lost. McClallen and his men were presumably continuing to trap beaver and cache the valuable pelts, but getting those pelts back to St. Louis presented serious challenges. First because the hostile Blackfoot Indians stood in the way and second because McClallen's group was on the wrong side of the watershed. They could not load their merchandise into a boat and float downstream—like the trappers at Fort Raymond could do (assuming Indians along the way would let them pass). Using water transportation, at least initially, was therefore out of the question because the Flathead, as well as other rivers in northwestern Montana, flowed north, right into areas dominated by the likes of David Thompson, Finan McDonald, and other Canadian trappers. What McClallen had in mind is not clear—perhaps he hoped to build friendships with the Blackfoot, or find ways to avoid them. Regardless, there is no indication that he had attempted to send beaver packs back to St. Louis since arriving in the Rockies in 1807.

Although Chouteau and his partners knew nothing of Courtin or McClallen, they soon got a report from Benito Vasquez, who had been in charge of Fort Raymond for the last year. The news wasn't good. More than one group of hunters had tried to trap the beaver-rich Three Forks area, but Blackfoot warriors had driven them all out—probably about the same time Courtin had fled west. A group of four men led by Casè Fortin had sent word of hiding twenty packs near Three Forks before presumably crossing the Divide to winter with the Salish Nation. They were never heard from again. Another group had gone south to trap the "River of the Spaniards," apparently Wyoming's Green River, and still another, led by a promising young trapper by the name of Baptiste Champlain, had headed into Crow country. Vasquez and those remaining—Hoback, Reznor, and Robinson quite likely among them—had closed up the fort and returned to the Mandan villages to await the next expedition coming up the Missouri.[41]

If Vasquez had offered a preview of Colter's amazing adventure, the partners got the full story when they traveled ten or twelve miles above the Hidatsa villages to construct the company's main trading post. "Information was received here," wrote Dr. Thomas, "that the Blackfoot Indians, who reside at the foot of the mountains, were hostile. . . . One of the survivors, of the name of Coulter, who had accompanied Lewis and Clark, says, that he in company with another was fired on by these Indians." Colter's companion was John Potts, the man who had saved Lisa from Rose's wrath, and the two of them left Fort Raymond for Three Forks as soon as Potts recovered from the beating administered by Rose. Surprised by a large Blackfoot war party as they were trapping the Jefferson River, Colter and Potts knew they had no chance of escaping. Convinced he was already a dead man, Potts raised his rife and shot one of the warriors. He was immediately "made a riddle of," as Colter later said. In the first published account of what would become one of the most celebrated legends in Western lore, long since known as "Colter's Run," Dr. Thomas wrote that Colter's "canoe, cloathing, furs, traps and arms were taken from him, and when expecting to receive the same fate as his comrade, he was ordered to run off as fast as possible; which he coldly complied with. Observing one of the young men following at full speed, armed with a spear, he pushed on to some distance, endeavouring to save his life. In a few minutes the savage was near enough to pitch his spear, which he [had] poisoned, and threw with such violence as to break the handle and miss the object." Colter now "became the assailant, turned on the Indian and put him to death with the broken spear. Naked and tired he crept to the river, where he hid in a beaver dam from the band who had followed to revenge the death of their companion. Having observed the departure of the enemy, he left the river and came to the Gros Ventres, a tribe of the Mandans, a journey of nine days, without even mowkasons to protect him from the prickly pear, which covered the country, subsisting on such berries as providence threw in his way."[42]

Dr. Thomas never saw the area of Colter's escape himself and likely had only a vague notion of Colter's route, but his account was largely confirmed by subsequent, more detailed versions, including one by the best-selling author Washington Irving that memorialized Colter's Run.

Thomas James heard the story along with Dr. Thomas, and then took care of more practical matters: his own supplies had been confiscated by the company, contrary to his signed contract, according to James, so he bought from Colter "a set of beaver traps for $120, a pound and a half of powder for $6, and a gun for $40. Seeing me thus equipped, Liza, the most active, the meanest and most rascally of the whole, offered me new and good traps, a gun and ammunition. I told him he appeared willing enough to help when help was not needed, and after I was provided at my own expense . . . I prepared to begin business." James and two partners then felled a tree, built their own canoe, and paddled up the Missouri to trap on their own.[43]

Pierre Dorion Jr. took up residence at the new trading post, hunting, trapping, negotiating with Indians, and taking on any other tasks requested by the company. With Toussaint Charbonneau and Sacagawea living in the area, Dorion may have met them, especially since he and Charbonneau had so much in common—they were both French-speaking interpreters born to Canadian heritage. Both had lived along the upper Missouri for years; both were married to Indian women; both had assisted Lewis and Clark, but this was their first opportunity to meet because Charbonneau had joined the captains after Dorion had completed his service. Of the two, Dorion had a better reputation—because of both his language skills and his work ethic. As Washington Irving observed, Dorion was reliable when sober, but "the love of liquor, in which he had been nurtured and brought up, would occasionally break out, and with it the savage side of his character." It was this weakness that "embroiled him with the Missouri Company. While in their service at Fort Mandan, on the frontier, he had been seized with a whiskey mania; and, as the beverage was only to be procured at the company's store, it had been charged in his account at the rate of ten dollars a quart."[44] How many quarts

Dorion consumed is not known, but the clerks at the store allowed him to run up a considerable bill, something that would eventually push Dorion and his young family into the West, with all its allures and dangers.

Disappointed that Vasquez's report had not been more favorable, the company partners were still optimistic that a large force could successfully harvest the plentiful beaver at the source of the Missouri River. Reaffirming that Chouteau and Lisa would return to St. Louis (as originally planned), the partners also decided that Henry would take forty men on horseback and go overland to Fort Raymond while Menard and his men traveled to the same location by boat. In the spring (of 1810) the combined party would proceed to Three Forks. Menard confessed in a letter to a friend that "the manner of some of my associated displeases me. I love to see things done frankly, which is not at all the case here and often causes small difficulties." Giving weight to James's accusations, Menard added that he was "obliged and forced to say that we are wrong at least three times out of four with the engagès and the hunters. Thank God this is about to end." As for trapping at the convergence of the Jefferson, Madison, and Gallatin Rivers, Menard acknowledged, "It is said that one cannot imagine the quantity of beaver that there is [at Three Forks], but there is the difficulty of the savage Black Feet who plunder often." Despite all this, Menard found reason to be hopeful. "I have a lot of confidence in the party of Mr. Henery. He admits everything perfectly with his humor as well as his honesty and his frank manner and without beating around the bush. I will also say to you . . . nobody sees clearer than I the advantages and resources of the Missouri. There is no doubt that if one finds the means to exploit it, it will make him a great fortune."[45]

Indeed, company partners and trappers alike set their sights on 1810 as the dawn of a new era, when the tremendous potential of the Missouri would begin to be realized. "Expectations were high: the company hoped to obtain three hundred packs of beaver in the first year—a small fortune worth as much as $150,000."[46] Within months, however, Henry, Menard, and all the others would be sorely disappointed.

In August of 1806, as Lewis and Clark descended the Missouri, Clark composed a letter to Charbonneau, who had remained at the Hidatsa villages with Sacagawea and their son Baptiste. Clark expressed his affection for Baptiste, whom he called "my boy Pomp," and offered to "educate him and treat him as my child." Clark added this promise: "Charbono, if you wish to live with the white people, and will come to me I will give you a piece of land and furnish you with horses cows & hogs." Charbonneau had declined this offer in 1806, but by 1809 he had changed his mind. When Chouteau and Lisa and their men left the Mandan and Hidatsa villages in early October, Charbonneau's little family was aboard one of the keelboats, hoping to take advantage of Clark's kind offers.[47]

Of the trip down the river, Chouteau wrote: "On my return I saw at the river Platte Messrs. McClellan, Crooks and Miller who were licensed to trade & Hunt in the Upper Parts of the Missoury. In passing the Prairie Sioux [Lakota] they with a party of chosen men had been stopped, and Fortunately saved themselves by stratagem, taking advantage of the Night and returned to pass the winter where I saw them."[48]

For the second time in three years, Crooks and McClellan had been thwarted in their attempts to reach the key trading center at the Mandan and Hidatsa villages in present North Dakota. Thomas Biddle fleshed out the incident in an 1819 letter: "Encouraged . . . by the attempt of the Missouri Fur Company, they followed their boats in the spring of 1809. They were met, however, by the Sconi band of the Sioux [Lakota], who refused to permit them to pass, and compelled them to remain among them. By affecting to submit, and commencing to erect houses, the Indians were thrown off their guard; and the party, taking advantage of their absence on a hunting excursion, embarked with their goods, and descended the river to the Ottoe village, where they passed the winter of 1809-'10." Biddle added that Crooks and McClellan "have always attributed their detention by the Sioux to the Missouri Fur Company, or some of its members, who to procure themselves a passage, informed the Sioux that the boat coming up was intended to trade, and that they must not permit her to pass. Considering the character of Indian traders, when in competition, the fact is very far from being improbable."[49]

According to Hiram M. Chittenden, a band of Lakota, "some six hundred strong, appeared upon a high bank in a concave bend of the river and ordered the boats to turn about and land farther down the stream." Crooks and McClellan had no choice but to obey, so they "set about making a post with every appearance of good faith." Seeing this, most of the Indians traveled to their village some twenty miles distant to obtain articles to trade, leaving only a handful of warriors behind to guard the Americans. Crooks and McClellan leveraged the situation to "carry out in part the purpose of their expedition and also to revenge themselves upon the Indians. They clandestinely sent a party of hunters and trappers up the river in a canoe with directions to collect such furs as they could and to await favorable opportunities to return." As soon as the hunting party was thought to be well beyond Lakota country, the others packed up their goods and supplies, "left a message for the Indians not calculated to mollify their feelings," and raced down the river.[50]

Biddle's assertion that Crooks and McClellan "attributed their detention" to "some" members of the Missouri Fur Company was a classic understatement. The two partners blamed *one* member of the company for the betrayal—Lisa—and they were enraged. Neither ever said why they suspected Lisa, but they could have heard it directly from the Lakota. If so, they would have been reminded of Pryor's claim two years earlier that Lisa had betrayed him in a similar way. That accusation had come from a Mandan woman who had no reason to lie. Whatever the source of their information, Crooks and McClellan were convinced that Lisa was the culprit—they had to be particularly incensed that they had honored their pledge to wait for the Missouri Fur Company boats only to find themselves cut off from the upper river. Chittenden is correct in his assessment that "of direct evidence [of Lisa's involvement] there is none."[51] But there is also no doubt that Lisa worried about Crooks and McClellan going upriver surreptitiously and no doubt that he was fully capable of deceiving the Lakota into holding the duo as virtual hostages.

Chittenden states that Crooks and McClellan spent the winter near Council Bluffs, "on the west bank of the river a little above the mouth of Papillon Creek and therefore near the latter site of Bellevue [Nebraska]." They did their best to carry on trade, but things did not turn out well. On June 10, 1810, Charles Gratiot wrote John Jacob Astor that "Mr. Crooks who had been equipped from [Hunt] last fall, is returned [to St. Louis] yesterday from his Winter ground, which has been very indifferent on account of the Indians being at War with each other during the Season."[52]

Chouteau, Lisa, their crew, and their passengers—Charbonneau, Sacagawea, and Pomp—arrived in St. Louis on November 20, 1809. There was no chance to exchange pleasantries with whoever greeted them because they instantly heard the news—the *only* news being talked about in St. Louis: Meriwether Lewis was dead. "But what has been my surprise since I arrived here three days ago," Chouteau wrote in a letter. "I learned of the tragic and untimely death of Gov. Lewis."[53]

Less than two months after his thirty-fifth birthday, as he traveled to the nation's capital, Lewis had died a lonely death in the backwoods of Tennessee in the early morning hours of October 11. The only details available had come from newspaper articles, with a touching tribute running in the *Missouri Gazette* on November 2:

> By last mail we received the melancholy account of the premature death of his Ex'y. Governor Lewis; he landed at the Chickasaw Bluffs much indisposed, and shortly after set out on his way to the Federal City via Nashville; about 40 miles east of the river Tennessee, the party stopped for the night and became much alarmed at the governor's behavior, he appeared in a state of extreme mental debility; and before he could be prevented, discharged the contents of a brace of pistols in his head and breast, calling to his servant to give him a bason of water; he lived about two hours and died without much apparent pain. The governor has been of late very much afflicted with fever, which never failed of depriving him of his reason; to this we may ascribe the fatal catastrophe! Alas Lewis is no more—his bodily conflicts are over—his days have been numbered—the scene is closed for ever—He was no less conspicuous for

his native affability, suavity of manners, and gentleness of disposition, than
those domestic virtures which adorn the human character—a dutiful son, an
effectionate brother, a kind and feeling friend.—Reader, picture to thyself, the
poignant feelings of a fond and doting parent on being informed of the death of
a son, whose general worth was highly appreciated by those who knew him.
Adieu! kind friend, thy own harmonious ways,
Have sculpur'd out thy monument of praise;
Yes: they'll survive till times remotest day,
Till drops the bust, and boastful tombs decay. [54]

To make matters worse, Lewis's best friend, the one man who could have
brought a sense of calm to the distraught city, William Clark, was nowhere to
be seen. He had left on an extended trip to the East on September 21, the day
before Chouteau's party had safely delivered Sheheke and his family to their
home. Clark would not return to St. Louis for ten months.

In a prescient insight into how Lewis's death portended a gloomy future
for the Missouri Fur Company, Robert Lucas, son of the prominent St. Louis
judge John B. C. Lucas (who had presided over Drouillard's murder trial)
wrote to a friend: "The hopes of the Fur Company which ascended this River
have died with their patron and benefactor Gov. Lewis[.]" From the reports
of Chouteau and Lisa, continued Lucas, "the situation of the Compy is critical and the prospects of advantage commerce but slender except the Mandan
and ricara Nations, all the Missouri Indians were unfriendly & inclined to
Commit depradations in the Property of the Company."

Chapter Four

"We All Now Became Blind from the Reflection of the Sun's Rays"

In the autumn of 1809, after buying a gun, ammunition, and traps from John Colter, Thomas James had teamed with one partner named Miller (not the Joseph Miller who had signed on with Crooks and McClellan) and another named McDaniel, both of whom were also well supplied with weapons, powder, lead, traps, and naive aspirations. "We were young, and sanguine of success," James remembered. "No fears of the future clouded our prospects and the adventures that lay before us excited our hopes and fancies to the highest pitch."[1]

The three were promptly disabused of their fancies. They intended to "ascend to the 'Forks' and head waters of the Missouri and the mountains," but they soon hit violent November winds then freezing rain. Negotiating waves that had nearly drowned a Mandan woman, they "pushed or rather paddled on in a shower of rain, till late that night and encamped." The next morning, wrote James, "we went on in snowstorm and in four days the ice floating in the river, prevented further navigation of the stream with a canoe. We stopped on the south side of the river, built a small cabin, banked it round with earth and soon made ourselves quite comfortable."[2]

But not comfortable for long. On Christmas day James "froze" his feet and "became so disabled as to be confined to the house and unable to walk. Miller and McDaniel soon after started back to the Fort, with [a] stock of beaver skins to exchange them for ammunition." The days dragged on, and the two men failed to return. When they had been gone twice as long as they predicted, James began to consume the last of his rations "and should have suffered for food, had not a company of friendly Indians called at the cabin and bartered provisions for trinkets and tobacco." Next he met two Canadians and an American, employees of the Missouri Fur Company who were delivering dispatches for the groups commanded by Pierre Menard and Andrew Henry that had gone on to Fort Raymond. James identified the Canadians as Marie and St. John and the American as Ayers, the same man who had gone up the Missouri earlier with Ramsay Crooks and Robert McClellan.[3] His first name is not known, nor the names of his parents, the place or year of his birth, or his background before taking up the trapping life in 1807.

The three men informed James "that Miller and McDaniel had changed their minds; that they did not intend to continue further up the river and seemed to be in no haste to return to me." Then, invited to join Ayers and his companions, James accepted. He buried Miller and McDaniel's traps and supplies in a corner of the lodge and left them a note on a piece of bark. "I learned on my return in the Spring," he added, "that both of them had been killed as was supposed by the Rickarees. Their guns, traps, &c., were seen in the hands of some of that tribe; but they were never heard of afterwards."[4]

James, Ayers, Marie, and St. John started overland on horseback for Fort Raymond on February 3, 1810. Following the Missouri and Yellowstone Rivers, while eventually taking them to the fort, would also have taken them northwest—and hundreds of miles out of their way. So they rode west, through the snow and wind and cold, along the south bank of the Missouri for approximately fifty miles until they "struck the Little Missouri a branch from the south."[5] James and the others clearly had some knowledge of the Little Missouri, a winding, five-hundred-mile river that rises in northeastern Wyoming and flows through part of Montana and South Dakota before reaching North Dakota. The river had an intriguing history both before and after the four horsemen followed it south. In 1803, the French-Canadian trapper Jean Baptiste Lepage (who went west with Lewis and Clark the next year) became one of the first white men to explore the river, finding through his solitary, harrowing trip by canoe that certain sections were simply not navigable.[6] If he reached the river's source he saw a spectacular stone monolith (*igneous intrusion* or *laccolith* in technical language) to the east, a landmark now known as Devils Tower, that dominated the landscape and was held sacred by a host of Indian nations, including the Arapaho, Cheyenne, Crow, Kiowa, Lakota, and Shoshone.

Three-quarters of a century after James and the others were advised by Indians "to keep up the banks of [the Little Missouri] for two days [before] turning northwardly," an easterner still in his twenties, who had been sickly as a child and was labeled a "pale, slim young man with a thin piping voice . . . the typical New York dude" by a newspaper reporter, made a name for himself in the badlands along the Little Missouri. When a band of outlaws stole a boat from one of his ranches, this dude followed them down the Little Missouri, captured them, then "navigated an ice-ridden stream, battled his way through Sioux country with his captives aboard, and eventually hired a prairie schooner to transport the thieves 15 miles overland to the nearest town. When he arrived with the thieves in tow, an eyewitness called him 'the most bedraggled figure I'd ever seen.'" The young New Yorker won respect, with an old-timer concluding that Theodore Roosevelt "was a Westerner at heart and had the makings of a real man."[7]

James and his companions left the Little Missouri and traveled northward, as instructed, but did not find the Powder River (called the "Gunpowder river" by James) as expected and soon found themselves lost on the high plains of eastern Montana. "No game was to be seen and we were destitute of provisions," wrote James. "For five days we tasted not a morsel of food, and not even the means of making a fire . . . alone in that vast desolate and to us limitless expanse, of drifting snow, which the winds drove into our faces and heaped around our steps. Snow was our only food and drink, and snow made our covering at night. We suffered greatly from hunger."[8]

They trudged on, "about to ward off starvation by killing a horse and eating the raw flesh and blood," when they ascended a mound and saw a herd of buffalo. They killed "several of these noblest animals of game," then made a fire and cut up the meat, but were "so voracious in [their] appetites, as not to wait for the cooking, but ate great quantities raw." They "ate and ate and ate," wrote James, as if there was no limit to their capacity, as if no quantity could satisfy them. Predictably, when the four men finally concluded their gluttonous feast, they were too sick to sleep. "In the morning we arose, without having rested, feverish and more fatigued that when we supped and retired the night before. Our feet, limbs, and bodies were swollen and bloated, and we all found ourselves laid up on the sick list, by our debauch on buffaloe meat."[9]

They were immobile for more than a day then slowly resumed their northwestward march. Luckily, they soon found the Yellowstone, "the river which [they] had suffered so much in seeking, and bent [their] course up the stream, crossing its bends on the ice." Following the river, they gradually recovered from their "unnatural surfeit and gross gormandizng of buffalo meat," partaking now in moderation of the vast buffalo herds but still enduring bitter cold and "much suffering." They rode southwest for several days along the south bank of the Yellowstone, eventually reaching a river bottom thick with cottonwood trees. Through the trees they saw a wide river flowing in from the south, knowing it had to be the Bighorn. Then, as they rode out of the trees and onto the ice of the Bighorn they saw the welcome sight of the fort, straight ahead, on a bluff rising above the river bottom.[10]

We don't know what the fort looked like, but it may have been similar to Manuel Lisa's Fort Mandan, constructed in the fall of 1809, which "consisted of a square blockhouse, the lower part of which was a room for furs," the upper part offering living quarters for a partner and some hunters, with a number of "small outhouses, and the whole . . . surrounded by a pallisade, or piquet, about fifteen feet high."[11]

James and his new friends got a warm welcome. "Here I found Cheek, Brown, Dougherty and the rest of my crew rejoicing to see me," he wrote. Archibald Pelton was also there, as well as John Hoback, Jacob Reznor, and Edward Robinson, now old hands at Fort Raymond. Two of the top hunters and scouts from the Lewis and Clark Expedition were also present—George Drouillard and Colter. Drouillard had returned to St. Louis with Lisa in 1808 and had planned on visiting his family in the coming months, but the plan was scuttled when he exhausted his funds paying his defense attorneys. He had come back up the river with Pierre Chouteau's group in the summer of 1809, glad to be back in the territories, away from courthouses. Colter, of course, had not been back to St. Louis since leaving in 1804 with Lewis and Clark. He had just spent the winter at Fort Raymond—his sixth consecutive winter in the wilderness. Leaving a trace of himself for posterity, Colter had carved an inscription into a sandstone rock: *Colter 1810*. The only other inscription on the rock was one left in the early weeks of the founding of the fort: *M Lisa 1807*. As for Lisa, James was overjoyed to find that he had returned to St. Louis. The partners present were Menard, Henry, and Reuben Lewis, and James had particularly kind thoughts for Menard: "Col. M. was an honorable, high minded gentleman and enjoyed our esteem in a higher degree than any other at the company."[12]

Considering what James, Ayers, Marie, and St. John had endured over the last several weeks, Fort Raymond offered amazing comforts—ointment, powdered bark, and Epsom salts to treat cuts and bruises, aches and pains; heated water for makeshift bathing; a chance to mend or replace tattered clothes and moccasins; warm bunks at night; fellowship around an indoor fire, with singing and fiddle playing; and, best of all, something to eat besides frozen jerked buffalo meat—portable soup transported from Missouri the previous summer; squash or corn obtained from Indians; dried grapes, berries, or currants; cutthroat or rainbow trout fresh from the river; and a wonderful variety of meat—including venison, elk, beaver, grizzly bear, bighorn sheep, and pronghorn antelope—all cooked in bear grease and flavored with salt and other delectable spices.

Had James and the others arrived two years earlier, they could have enjoyed the comforts of the fort while trapping the surrounding rivers and streams, but steady "hunting" had blunted the seemingly endless supply of beaver pelts to be taken near the mouth of the Bighorn. Now, even men working out of Fort Raymond were making long trips to find beaver. Young John Dougherty, one of James's crew, had arrived at the fort in the autumn of 1809, and "during the course of the winter had extended his hunting excursions a considerable distance up the Bighorn & Little Bighorn Rivers." As Mark W. Kelly has noted, "With beaver likely trapped out within an easily accessible radius of [Fort Raymond] by the earlier inhabitants of the post,

Dougherty made his way up the Big Horn," probably going as far as the mouth of the Shoshone River in present Wyoming.[13]

But there was no question where the St. Louis Missouri Fur Company should center its first major trapping effort: everyone knew that a prime and untapped beaver ground lay to the west, almost but not quite due west, 170 miles away—as the crow flies, that is. James was not surprised that "after remaining at this Fort or camp a few days we started westward for the 'Forks' and mountains." Menard and Henry were capable leaders—more than capable—but they had never seen this country before, so they called on someone who had, a man well acquainted with the Three Forks area. "Our guide on this route was Colter, who thoroughly knew the road," said James, "having twice escaped over it from capture and death at the hands of the Indians." The first escape had come around August of 1808, when he made his legendary run—after Blackfoot warriors had stripped him of his weapons, clothes, and moccasins. The second escape came several months later, in the dead of the winter of 1808–1809, when the courageous—or foolhardy— Colter had "recovered from the fatigues of his long race and journey [and] wished to recover the traps which he had dropped into the Jefferson Fork" when John Potts was killed. Supposing "the Indians were all quiet in winter quarters," Colter returned to the Gallatin River and "had just passed the mountain gap, and encamped on the bank of the river for the night and kindled a fire to cook his supper of buffalo meat when he heard the crackling of leaves and branches behind him in the direction of the river." He could see nothing in the darkness but instantly smothered his fire when he heard the cocking of guns. "Several shots followed and bullets whistled around him, knocking the coals off his fire over the ground. Again he fled for life, and the second time, ascended the perpendicular mountain which he had gone up his former flight fearing now as then, that the pass might be guarded by In- dians."[14]

Colter "promised God Almighty that he would never return to [the Three Forks area] again if he were only permitted to escape once more with his life." His prayer was answered, and he "made his way with all possible speed, to [Fort Raymond]." Colter had kept his promise—at least temporari- ly—and by September of 1809 he was back at the Hidatsa villages near the confluence of the Knife and Missouri Rivers, where he met James and Dr. Thomas. At that time, Colter was clearly preparing to go home to St. Louis. He sold his traps and gun to James—a sure sign of his intentions. Perhaps he had already arranged to make the return trip with Chouteau and Lisa. If so, Menard or Henry had gotten word of that plan and stepped in to convince Colter to go back to Fort Raymond and guide the party west to Three Forks in the spring. No one left a record of the negotiations, but something con- vinced Colter to tempt God and return to the Forks. James explained it by saying that men like Colter, "and there are thousands of such, can only live in a state of excitement and constant action. Perils and danger are their natural element and their familiarity with them and indifference to their fate, are well illustrated in these adventures of Colter."[15]

Colter was so drawn by perils and dangers that he found the lure of the West almost irresistible. This was the third time he had been homeward bound only to change his mind, reverse his direction, and head back to the wild (a pattern that would be echoed in the false starts of Hoback, Reznor, and Robinson). The first time had come in August of 1806, at the Mandan and Hidatsa villages, when he bade farewell to Lewis and Clark, climbed in a small canoe with his new partners Dickson and Hancock, and paddled up the Missouri. Not quite a year later, in the summer of 1807, Lisa's northbound group, which included Hoback, Reznor, and Robinson, had been camped near the mouth of the Platte when they spotted Colter coming down the river, this time alone in a canoe. He was only two weeks from home, but Lisa had no trouble persuading him to turn back. Even the eventful and dangerous year of 1808—which included the two escapes and the pledge to God already mentioned, as well as the earlier battle between the Crow and Salish Indians on one side and the Blackfoot on the other, in which Colter had been wounded—had not cured Colter of his wanderlust. He had changed his mind a third time and returned to Fort Raymond with either Menard or Henry in the autumn of 1809. But he had to replace the gun, powder, and traps he had already sold to James, and he apparently obtained at least some new supplies among the effects of Jean-Baptiste Lepage, a fellow trapper—and fellow Lewis and Clark veteran—who had died a nonviolent death at the fort. A clerk was handling Lepage's affairs, and Colter signed a promissory note for $36.50 to Lepage's estate on December 31, 1809.[16] (Most of the men were unlikely to have either currency or coin—they bartered by trading goods or signing notes, and a promissory note was exactly what James had given Colter.)

Colter's experience with Lewis and Clark hardly qualified him to lead a group of trappers from Fort Raymond to Three Forks. True, he and other members of the Corps of Discovery had traversed the Three Forks area when they arrived from the northeast in July of 1805 and from the northwest a year later, but during the expedition, Colter never saw the regions directly west or south of Three Forks—nor did he ever travel along the Yellowstone River or even see the Bighorn. On both the trip west and the trip east through Montana, Colter had taken the northern route along the Missouri River, the route that at least briefly appeared to be laying the foundation for a national path of westward migration.[17] More than anyone, however, Colter had nudged that path to the south, first by leading Lisa's group along the Yellowstone River (rather than the Missouri) in 1807 (probably because he, Dickson, and Hancock had found good and safe trapping along the Yellowstone during the winter of 1806-1807), and second by leading Menard and Henry and their men even farther south in 1810.

Rather than following the Yellowstone River (as many historians have assumed), Colter cut to the southwest. Two people with him left sketchy but valuable accounts of the route: James and John Dougherty. James left no map and few geographical details, but the information he did provide supplements and confirms what are called the Dougherty Map and Dougherty Narrative. Sometime around 1818, a correspondent whose name has been lost carefully interviewed Dougherty, then about twenty-eight and about to begin a long and notable career in government service as an interpreter, guide, Indian agent, and army officer. The unnamed interviewer produced a map—now in the National Archives—with a narrative describing Dougherty's experiences on the other side. Mark W. Kelly, who has combined an exhaustive study of the map, the narrative, and other contemporaneous documents with firsthand field research throughout the entire region, has noted that the available evidence "renders any attempt to delineate [the] route with specificity an exercise in futility." What is known, however, is that the journey began at the mouth of the Bighorn and ended at Three Forks; "the Yellowstone River proper was not followed upstream; [and] the trek encompassed no fewer than three hundred miles in length, taking ten to twelve days to effect."[18]

As Kelly notes, "the route, as recorded in the Dougherty Narrative, indicates the extent of John Colter's respect for the Blackfoot Confederacy. Colter . . . was keenly aware of the likelihood of encountering the Blackfoot should he lead Henry's brigade directly up the Yellowstone, certainly the most expeditious route. Colter thus contrived to lead them southward into Crow lands, thence northward, in an attempt to surreptitiously circumvent the Blackfeet domain," arrive at Three Forks, and build a fort before being discovered.[19]

Kelly's analysis, when combined with James's statement that Colter "thoroughly knew the road, having twice escaped over it from capture and death," casts new light on Colter's Run. After finding himself naked and unarmed at the Madison River, he could have run——limped—a westerly course over Bozeman Pass to the Yellowstone River, taking the shortest possible route back to Fort Raymond, but that route would have also kept him in the heart of Blackfoot country. So he went southeast, getting out of Blackfoot territory as fast as possible, even though the trip would be eighty, ninety, maybe one hundred miles longer. But the extra distance was offset by Colter's knowing at least a good portion of the area ahead of him: during that memorable winter of 1807–1808, on assignment from Lisa, he had trekked southwest from Fort Raymond into the Bighorn Basin and as far south as the Wind River before circling back to the fort. Henry and Menard and their men were thus tracing Colter's Run in the reverse direction, as well as part of what William Clark called "Colter's Route," as they made their way to Three Forks.

They left in mid-March of 1810—sixty mounted men well armed and well supplied eager to take full advantage of the spring trapping season—with Colter in the lead. The veterans who had built the fort in 1807 knew well how harsh the Montana winters could be—and how long those winters could last—but they were nevertheless likely surprised when they hit a blizzard their first day out. They were soon drenched through and through, chilled to the core, but when the longed-for sun finally appeared it was too bright, overpowering, making them wish for another storm. "My friend Brown became blind from the reflection of the sun on the snow," James wrote. "His eyes pained him so much that he implored us to end to his torment by shooting him. I watched him during that night for fear he would commit the act himself."[20]

"Our second day's journey brought us to an Indian lodge," wrote James. "Stripped, and near by, we saw a woman and boy lying on the ground, with their heads split open, evidently by a tomahawk." These were the wife and son of a friendly Shoshone Indian, "he having saved himself and his younger wife by flight on horseback." Two trappers had also escaped the violence. "They told us that a party of Gros Ventres had come upon them, committed these murders, and passed on as if engaged in a lawful and praiseworthy business."[21]

"Evidently by a tomahawk." The murdered woman and boy lay perfectly still. We don't know how Hoback, Reznor, and Robinson responded to the bloody scene—to the stench and the flies buzzing—but they likely felt the same stoical revulsion experienced by James. In the three years since they had left St. Louis, they had grown accustomed to the brutal world of the West. They knew the danger of arriving uninvited in Arikara, Lakota, Crow, or Blackfoot country. Their friend John Potts had been killed and then dismembered by Blackfoot fighting men. Their friend Casè Fortin and three others had disappeared, possibly suffering a similar fate. But Hoback, Reznor, and Robinson had lived on the advancing frontier for decades and also knew the risk of invading Miami, Cherokee, Delaware, or Shawnee territory.

Reznor had likely roamed into the Illinois country and heard stories of what happened fifteen years earlier, when Indians massacred 630 of General Arthur St. Clair's troops. "The bodies of the dead and dying were around us," wrote one survivor, "and the freshly scalped heads were reeking with smoke, and in the heavy morning frost looked like so many pumpkins through a cornfield in December."[22]

Serving under Mad Anthony Wayne, Hoback may have fought (along with a young lieutenant named William Clark) in the Battle of Fallen Timbers in 1794, where Wayne's troops won a decisive victory against an Indian confederacy that included members of the Kickapoo, Iroquois, Wyandot,

Shawnee, and Miami Nations. After the battle, Wayne's men did their best to starve the surviving Indians by "cutting down and destroying hundreds of Acres of corn & Burning several large Towns besides small ones." As the Miami chief Little Turtle said, "We raised corn like the whites, but now we are poor hunted deer."[23]

Robinson knew the realities of frontier life better than anyone. As early as 1777 he had served with the militia in present West Virginia. In a letter written on August 2 of that year, a fellow soldier described a scene that was all too typical: "Charles Grigsby's wife and child killed and scalped on July 31; pursuing party out."[24] Robinson had next continued west, to the alluring bluegrass of Cain-tuck-ee, where he fought in several battles with Indians, probably alongside his contemporaries Daniel Boone and George Rogers Clark.

As if endeavoring to outdo each other, the Indians and Europeans traded atrocities during the 1780s and 90s. "Whole families are destroyed without regard to Age or Sex," one man wrote to Thomas Jefferson. "Infants are torn from their Mothers Arms and their Brains dashed out against Trees . . . Not a week Passes some weeks scarcely a day with out some of our distressed Inhabitants feeling the fatal effects of the infernal rage and fury of those Excreable Hellhounds."[25]

The soldiers burned Indian villages by the score and acres of Indian corn by the hundreds, sometimes digging up Indian graves to take scalps. When a group of militiamen captured close to one hundred Christian Delaware Indians, they concluded the Indians could have obtained their European kettles and dishes only by killing whites. After taking a vote, the soldiers methodically butchered the forty-two men, twenty women, and thirty-four children with clubs and hatchets. One man reportedly killed fourteen Indians with a mallet before proclaiming, "My arms faile me. Go on with the work. I have done pretty well."[26]

This was the Kentucky legacy, the price paid for elbow room. The countryside was striking, with one settler saying it "beggars description. Poetry cannot paint grooves more beautiful, or fields more luxuriant."[27] But it was also the "dark and bloody ground," something that Hoback, Reznor, and Robinson knew perfectly well. So, when the three of them headed west with Lisa in 1807 to make a fortune, they understood the risks.

Menard, Henry, and their men rode on, "bearing west-southwest toward the Pryor Mountains," according to Kelly's proposed route, "keeping the Big Horn River and its guardian Big Horn Mountains on [their] left." They followed Pryor Creek upstream and through the Pryor Gap. Next they crossed into the Bighorn Basin of present Wyoming. They continued southwest until they approached Heart Mountain (north-northwest of Cody).[28]

"Our course now lay to the north-west for the Forks of the Missouri," wrote James. Colter had likely been in this area at least three different times.

He led them northwest to Clark's Fork of the Yellowstone River, which they ascended "to a low pass (today's Colter Pass) over which he crossed to the headwaters of Soda Butte Creek. Angling southwest now, downstream, the Colter-led brigade traveled the easily-defined Bannock Trail leading to the Lamar River [whereupon they entered present-day Yellowstone Park]." They next headed northwest, following the Lamar to its confluence with the Yellowstone. They followed the Yellowstone northwest, back into present Montana, to "a breach in the Gallatin Range between the Yellowstone and Gallatin rivers, the location being identified on the Dougherty Map with the inscription '18 miles across.'"[29]

James wrote that the party had been traveling for ten or twelve days when they reached this gap in the mountains, "where it commenced snowing most violently and so continued all night. The morning showed us the heads and backs of our horses just visible about the snow which had crushed down all our tents. We proceeded on with the greatest difficulty." The men pushed on to a ravine, where they fought their way through the tremendous snow drifts surrounding them. "The strongest horses took the front to make a road for us, but soon gave out and the ablest bodied men took their places as pioneers. A horse occasionally stepped out of the beaten track and sunk entirely out of sight in the snow."[30]

That night they reached the Gallatin River, the east fork of the Missouri. Colter led most of the group through an opening in the mountain to the north, but James and three others forded the river and "encamped and supped (four of us) on a piece of buffalo meat about the size of the two hands." Adding misery to misery, the four were already suffering "from indistinct vision, similar to Brown's affliction . . . . We all now became blind as he had been, from the reflection of the sun's rays on the snow. The hot tears trickled from the swollen eyes nearly blistering the cheeks, and the eye-balls seemed bursting from our heads."[31]

At first their sight had been obscured, but now they could not see well enough to move at all, and they had nothing to eat. "In this dreadful situation we remained two days and nights." When they partially recovered their vision, they were ready to kill one of the packhorses for food, but one of them was able to shoot a goose. "We made a soup and stayed the gnawings of hunger. The next day our eyes were much better, and we fortunately killed an elk, of which we ate without excess, being taught by experience, the dangers of gluttony after a fast."[32]

Following the Gallatin downstream, James and the others spotted the main group on the opposite shore. The larger party had suffered an even more severe case of snow blindness. Unable to hunt, they had slaughtered and devoured two horses and three dogs, and James found to his dismay that his pet dog, a present to him from an Indian, was one of those killed. These men had been so helpless that thirty Shoshone Indians "came among them, and left without committing any depredation. Brown and another, who suffered less than the others, saw and counted these Indians, who might have killed them all and escaped with their effects with perfect impunity. Their preservation was wonderful."[33]

The irony was that four years and five hundred miles away, Hoback, Reznor, and Robinson—three of the men debilitated by snow blindness—would receive quite a different reception from another group of Shoshone Indians.

The next day they reached the spot where two years earlier Colter had fought with the Salish and Crow against the Blackfoot. James and the others saw the human remains scattered in great numbers over the battlefield as Colter told of the fight. The day after that, April 3, 1810, they at last reached Three Forks. Although Lewis and Clark had noted any number of places in present Montana where beaver were plentiful, the founders of the Missouri Fur Company had concluded that this was the best spot of all. "The resources of this country in beaver fur are immense," Menard wrote.[34] The Gallatin, Madison, and Jefferson Rivers were each fed by lesser rivers, streams, and creeks, in a broad, flat, fertile plain offering a supreme natural habitat for beavers. So Menard and his men came, despite hearing firsthand accounts of hostile Blackfoot warriors from Colter.

Still, Colter's tales had a chilling effect on Menard's trappers. "As we passed over the ground where Colter ran his race," wrote James, "and listened to his story an undefinable fear crept over all. We felt awe-struck by the nameless and numerous dangers that evidently beset us on every side. Even Cheek's courage sunk and his hitherto buoyant and cheerful spirit was depressed at hearing of the perils of the place." The change in Cheek was dramatic, undoubtedly inspiring fear in several of the men. "He spoke despondingly and his mind was uneasy, restless and fearful. 'I am afraid,' said he, 'and I acknowledge it. I never felt fear before but now I feel it.'"[35]

The next day, April 3, 1810, wrote James, "we reached the long sought 'Forks of the Missouri,' or the place of confluence of the Gallatin, Madison and Jefferson rivers. Here at last, after ten months of travel [from St. Louis], we encamped, commenced a Fort in the point made by the Madison and Jefferson forks, and prepared to begin business."[36]

James, his former crewmates Dougherty and Brown (whose first name is unknown) and another man by the name of Weir agreed to trap together "on the Missouri between the Forks and the Falls [near the future site of Great Falls], which lie several hundred miles down the river to the north." The four men "made two canoes by hollowing out the trunks of two trees," and three or four days after arriving at the Forks prepared to set off down the river. Cheek was remaining with the main company, and he and James each tried to convince the other to join his party, but neither prevailed. As James and the others left in two freshly built dugout canoes, Cheek "said in a melancholy tone, 'James you are going down the Missouri, and it is the general opinion that you will be killed. The Blackfeet are at the falls, encamped I hear, and we fear you will never come back. But I am afraid for myself as well. . . . I may be dead when you return.'"[37]

"His words made little impression on me at the time," wrote James, "but his tragical end a few days afterwards recalled them to my mind and stamped them on my memory forever."[38]

About the same time that James and his companions departed, a group of eighteen men, including Cheek and Colter, "determined to go up the Jefferson river for trapping, and the rest of the company under Col. Menard remained to complete the Fort and trading house." James's group paddled down the Missouri without incident and on the third day encountered "a scene of beauty and magnificence combined, unequalled by any other view of nature" that James had ever beheld, which he compared to the Garden of Eden, with "the peaks and pinnacles of the Rocky Mountains" shining in the sun and with "Buffalo, Elk, Deer, Moose, wild Goats and wild Sheep; some grazing, some lying down under the trees and all enjoying a perfect millenium of peace and quiet." It was little wonder that Dougherty, "as if inspired by the scene with the spirit of poetry and song, broke forth in one of Burns' noblest lyrics, which found a deep echo in our hearts." They stopped to prepare supper and set their traps; when they checked the traps before retiring, they "found a beaver in every one, being twenty-three in all." All four men were "cheered with thoughts of making a speedy fortune."[39]

They were jolted back to reality the next morning. Brown and Dougherty's canoe overturned when they stuck a submerged rock—they lost their guns and most of party's ammunition and beaver pelts. It was decided that Brown and Dougherty would return to the fort to obtain additional guns and ammunition. They took one musket with them and left the other one for James and Weir. "They reached the Fort the first night, having saved a great distance by crossing the country and cutting off the bend of the river which here makes a large sweep to the east." They arrived at the fort long after dark and may have had a chance to snatch a little sleep when "early the next morning the whole garrison was aroused by an alarm" made by a trapper named Francois Vallé. The previous evening, as Brown and Dougherty made their way south to the fort, Vallé and several French-Canadian trappers had been fleeing north, riding all night to make the forty-mile trip from their camp on the Jefferson River. Someone opened the gate, and Vallé and the others, distressed, "as if pursued by enemies," led their exhausted horses into the cramped, half-finished fort, and Vallé announced that his trapping party had been attacked, men had been killed, and an attack on the fort could be imminent. "The whole garrison"—including Hoback, Reznor, and Robinson—"prepared for resistance."[40]

Vallé gave the sad report to his friend Henry and also to Menard, who offered details in a letter to Chouteau: "A party of our hunters was defeated by the Blackfeet on the 12ᵗʰ [of April]. There were two men killed, all their beaver stolen, many traps lost, and the ammunition of several of them, and also seven of our horses. . . . The party which was defeated consisted of eleven persons, and eight or nine of them were absent tending their traps when the savages pounced upon the camp." The two men killed, explained Menard, were "James Cheeks, and one Ayres, an engage of Messrs. Crooks and McLellan."⁴¹

Colter and a few others soon arrived, unhurt, and reported that they had not seen any Indians near the fort. Menard now dispatched Dougherty and Brown—who had had little, if any, rest since their strenuous trek the previous day—back to their Missouri River camp to warn James and Weir and escort them back to assist in the defense of the fort. Luckily, they were "well mounted" this time and also took horses for James and Weir, whom they met early in the evening. The four loaded gear and beaver pelts onto their horses and rode south, seeing eight Blackfoot warriors but escaping unnoticed. They approached the fort at 2:00 in the morning, probably about twenty-four hours after Dougherty and Brown had arrived the first time. "We forded the [Jefferson] river with great difficulty," wrote James, "and went towards the Fort," when several dogs began barking furiously. "I spoke to the dogs, and a voice hailed us from the Fort, with 'who's there'? I answered promptly, and thus saved ourselves from a volley, for . . . the whole garrison was drawn up with fingers upon triggers . . . expecting an attack every moment . . . all in the greatest consternation."⁴²

James, of course, already knew that his friend Cheek had been killed, as well as Ayers, who had befriended him and invited him to join with Marie and St. John in making the journey to Fort Raymond. Now James heard details from men who had been on the scene. On their third day of trapping, the company of eighteen men had pitched their tents on the bank of the Jefferson. Colter and most of the others went out hunting while Cheek, Ayers, and a man named Hull prepared the camp. Suddenly thirty or forty Indians appeared on the prairie south of them, some on horses and some on foot, running toward the camp. Vallé and two others rushed into the camp and warned Cheek and his trapping partners to mount their horses and escape.

"This Cheek refused to do, but, seizing his rifle and pistols, said he would stay and abide his fate. 'My time has come, but I will kill at least two of them, and then I don't care.' His gloomy forebodings were about to be fulfilled through his own recklessness and obstinacy." Meanwhile, "Ayers ran frantically about, paralysed by fear and crying, 'O God, O God, what can I do.'" His horse was within reach, he had the chance to save himself, but he could not. The polar opposite was Hull, who "stood coolly examining his rifle, as it for battle." As James so aptly put it, "Courage and cowardice met the same fate, though in very different manners."[43]

With the Blackfoot rapidly approaching, Vallé and his two companions gave up and prodded their horses away from the river. As soon as they got out on the open prairie, they urged their horses to a gallop, probably gripping the reins in one hand and the mane in the other, hanging on for precious life, riding north, glancing over their shoulders at the mounted Indians pursuing them. "The sharp reports of Cheek's rifle and pistols were soon heard, doing the work of death upon the savages, and then a volley of musketry sent the poor fellow to his long home."[44]

Referring to Cheek and Ayers, Menard wrote, "In the camp where the first two men were killed we found a Blackfoot who had also been killed, and upon following their trail we saw that another had been dangerously wounded. Both of them, if the wounded man dies, came to their death at the hand of Cheeks, for he alone defended himself." Including harsh details even in a letter to his wife, Menard added: "I have always before my eyes the barbarity of the Blackfeet—they mutilated with their knives the two they had killed. We reciprocated on one of theirs who had been killed by James Cheaque before he himself."[45]

James wrote that the dead Indian was found "with two bullets in his body, supposed to be from Cheek's pistol. The body was carefully concealed under leaves and earth, and surrounded by logs." He added that he and the others "found and buried the corpses of our murdered comrades, Cheek and Ayers; the latter being found in the river near the bank."[46]

Besides the two men killed, wrote Menard, "three others are missing and from their possessions we have found we believe that they are either dead or prisoners. It would be much better for them if they were dead rather than prisoners." At least one man had been taken alive, however. On the day of the attack, a trapper by the name of Michael Immell, later to become re-nowned, had returned from hunting with others about dusk, "ignorant of the fate of their fellows, and seeing the tent gone they supposed the place of the camp had been changed." Then Immell heard a noise near the river and walked down to the bank to investigate. "He saw through the willows, on the opposite side, a camp of thirty Indian lodges, a woman coming down to the river with a brass kettle which he would have sworn was his own, and also a white man bound by both arms to a tree. He could not recognize the prisoner, but supposed he was an American." Immell and those with him then hastened to the fort, arriving the next morning.[47]

Hull, who had been in the same camp with Cheek and Ayers, and who had faced death—or worse—with such eerie calmness, was one of those who had gone missing, along with Freehearty and Rucker, who had been trapping a stream about two miles farther south. (None of their first names are known.) To rescue anyone still alive, and also to seek revenge, the men pursued the Indians but could not overtake them. "We followed the trail of the savages for two days," said James, "when we missed it and gave up the chase. Many of the men wished to pursue them into the mountains, but Col. Menard judged it imprudent to go further in search of them, as we should, probably, come upon an army of which this party was but a detachment. . . . We accordingly retraced our steps to the Fort, and remained in it, with our whole force, for several days, expecting an attack. No attack was made, however." Menard said the men's "greatest sorrow" was that they "did not encounter the party in order to revenge the outrages of the Blackfeet monsters."[48]

"Hull was never heard of [again]," wrote James, who could have said the same for Freehearty and Rucker. But, as Menard had written to his wife, it would be better for the three missing men to have been killed than have been taken prisoner. So, apparently concluding that the details would be too much for the families to bear, the thoughtful Menard softened his report when he was interviewed by a newspaper editor on his arrival in St. Louis in July. The resulting article reported, in part: "A hunting party which had been detached from the Fort to the Forks of Jefferson River were attacked in the neighborhood of their encampment on the 12th of April by a strong party of the Blackfeet, whom they kept at bay for some time, but we are sorry to say unavailingly, as the Indians were too numerous; the party consisted of 14 or 15, of whom 5 were killed . . . Hull, Cheeks, Ayres, Rucker and Freehearty." There was no mention that three men had almost certainly been taken alive and tortured to death, no mention of cowardice or scalping, no mention of a man being tied to a tree. The news was delivered as gently as possible—if it were delivered at all, for no one ever left any record of if or when the families were notified. Those living in the St. Louis area—or their friends— may have discovered the life-altering announcement in the course of browsing the third page of the July 26, 1810, issue of the *Louisiana Gazette*. One notice on that same page urged readers who had not yet paid for their subscriptions to "settle with the respective Post Masters from whom they receive their papers"; another informed the public that Heslep & Taylor, "Windsor & Fancy Chair-makers," had just received "an extensive assortment of materials necessary for elegant and plain chairs" from Pennsylvania; another expressed the need to "hire by the year, a negro boy of from 10 to 15 years of age, to work in a tobacco manufactory." Not only that, but four marriages were also announced, including that of Lieutenant Benito of the U.S. Army to Miss Emilie Vincent. One could almost have missed the article stating, "A few days ago, Mr. Menard, with some of the gentlemen attached to the Missouri Fur Company, arrived here from their Fort at the head waters of the Missouri."[49]

But just as dying at the hands of the Indians was preferable to being taken prisoner, finding notice in the newspaper of a son's, brother's, or husband's death was preferable to waiting day after day and year after year without knowing what had become of him. There is little doubt, however, that the family of Cheek, Ayers, Hull, Rucker, or Freehearty—or maybe even all five families—found themselves in that endless state of dread.

The attack left the men in a state of despair. Reuben Lewis was convinced that "the Blackfeets are urged on by the British Traders" and that "it will be impossible to trap on this River Unless we could have [two or three hundred] men in this Country."[50] But nothing reflected the melancholy running through the camp like Colter's reaction to narrowly escaping the Indians who had killed Cheek and Ayers.

"He came into the Fort," wrote James, "and said he had promised his Maker to leave the country, and 'now,' said he, throwing down his hat on the ground, 'If God will only forgive me this time and let me off I *will* leave the country day after tomorrow and be d—d if I ever come into it again.'"[51]

Colter made arrangements to leave with William Bryan, a young man from Philadelphia, and another trapper whose name is unknown. Knowing that Colter was leaving, Menard and Lewis wrote letters for Colter to deliver. Menard wrote one to his business partner and brother-in-law, Pierre Chouteau, and another to his wife, Angelique. "I hope," he wrote to Chouteau, ". . . to see the Snake and Flathead Indians. My plan is to induce them to stay here, if possible, and make war upon the Blackfeet so that we may take some prisoners and send back one with propositions of peace—which I think can easily be secured by leaving traders among them below the Falls of the Missouri. Unless we can have peace . . . or unless they can be destroyed, it is idle to think of maintaining an establishment at this point." Encouraging war among the Indian nations seemed out of character for Menard—perhaps he had a change of heart because there is no evidence he pursued the plan. He revealed a much more gentle side in his letter to his wife, whom he called "Doll." "Kiss our dear child for me and tell him to expect me in July," he wrote.[52]

"Dr Brother," Reuben Lewis wrote to his brother Meriwether, "The return of your oald acquaintance Coalter, gives me an opportunity of addressing you a few lines." He went on to discuss the disheartening situation at Three Forks, his future with the Missouri Fur Company, and claims that "Martens abound" near the Spanish River and that "the upper branches of the Columbia are full of beavers." He concluded with a report of his good health and signed the letter thus: "with high esteem your affectionate brother Reuben Lewis."[53] What he did not know, of course—and what he would not learn for another fifteen months—was that Meriwether Lewis had died six months earlier of self-inflicted gunshots.

Menard and Lewis wrote their letters on April 21, probably sitting near an evening campfire inside the fort. If others gathered around the fire felt pangs of homesickness and wrote or dictated letters to loved ones, those letters have been lost. One indication that at least one letter disappeared was Reuben Lewis's mention that he wished to write to his mother "by this opportunity," apparently meaning that he intended to include a letter for his and Meriwether's mother in the same packet of mail that Colter was carrying east.[54] But no such letter to Lucy Meriwether Lewis Marks has ever been discovered.

Colter and his two companions left the next day, as promised. James, who apparently met Colter the next year after his own return to St. Louis, reported that Colter and the others "were attacked by the Blackfeet just beyond the mountains, but escaped by hiding in a thicket, where the Indians were afraid to follow them, and at night they proceeded toward the Big Horn, lying concealed in the daytime. They reached St. Louis safely."[55]

"We kept the flag flying a month," continued James, "frequently seeing Indians without getting an interview with them; they always fleeing at our approach. We then pulled down the flag and hoisted the scalp of the Indian whom Cheek had killed. By this time the Fort was completed and put in a good state of defense." The men subsisted by hunting in small groups—leaving the fort before dawn, riding twenty or thirty miles if necessary, killing a buffalo or elk, and returning with their horses laden with meat.[56]

"The Grizzly Bears frequently made their appearance and we killed great numbers of them," wrote James. One day James, Pelton, and a few others went out to check their traps. Pelton was alone, a short distance from the others, "when he heard a rustling in the bushes at his right, and before turning around he was attacked by a large bear, which grasped him by the breast, bore him to the earth and stood over him." The quick-thinking Pelton "screamed and yelled in a most unearthly manner, and his new acquaintance, as if frightened by his appearance and voice, leaped from over his body, stood and looked at him a moment, over his shoulder, growled, and then walked off." James and the others had come running in the direction of Pelton's cries and met him, "grumbling and cursing, with his head down, as if he had been disturbed in a comfortable sleep, and altogether wearing an air of great dissatisfaction." Pelton told them what happened, adding with his typical wit that he owed his escape to his own "bearish eyes which disconcerted his friendly relation in the act of making a dinner of him."[57] This was the last humorous story recorded about Archibald Pelton.

The men stayed near the fort, always careful, always expecting an attack, but no attack came. "Thus we passed the time till the month of May," wrote James, "when a party of twenty-one, of whom I was one, determined to go up the Jefferson river to trap." At first they stayed together but, finding the trapping unprofitable, they changed their plan and began separating into groups of four—with two men trapping while the other two stood guard. "In this manner we were engaged, until the fear of Indians began to wear off, and we all became more venturous." The man among them who feared Indians the least was Drouillard, whom James called "Druyer, the principal hunter of Lewis & Clark's party." Son of a French-Canadian father and Shawnee mother, Drouillard boasted that he was "too much of an Indian to be caught by Indians." He went up the Jefferson alone one day and returned the next day with six beavers. Despite a warning from James, "the next day he repeated the adventure and returned with the product of his traps, saying, 'this is the way to catch beavers.'"[58]

Perhaps Drouillard was reliving his glory days from the Lewis and Clark Expedition, when he had seemed invincible, accompanying Lewis on every dangerous mission but never suffering harm, not even when he and Lewis and the Field brothers had a scrape in which they killed two young Blackfoot warriors. Perhaps he was wishing he could be free of the shadow cast over him when he shot Bissonnet that day in May of 1807. Perhaps he was inviting danger, wishing for a chance to live—and die—like the brave and honorable man of the expedition and not like Lisa's underling who had shot a fellow trapper in the back. If so, his wish was granted. He went up the river again on the third day, alone, brushing off pleas to stay with the others, and found the chance to face death like the person Meriwether Lewis had called "a man of much merit," who encountered "all the most dangerous and trying scenes of the voyage [and] uniformly acquited himself with honor."[59]

At the same time that Drouillard departed to check his traps, wrote James, "two Shawnees left us against our advice, to kill deer. We started forward in company, and soon found the dead bodies of the last mentioned hunters, pierced with lances, arrows and bullets and lying near each other." Checking their weapons, James and the others proceeded up the Jefferson. "Further on, about one hundred and fifty yards, Druyer and his horse lay dead, the former mangled in a horrible manner; his head was cut off, his entrails torn out and his body hacked to pieces. We saw from the marks on the ground that he must have fought in a circle on horseback, and probably killed some of his enemies, being a brave man, and well armed with a rifle, pistol, knife and tomahawk."[60]

A report of Drouillard's death apparently made its way north, to the Canadian trapper Alexander Henry. "While on a war excursion last summer [1810]," wrote Henry, "these people (the Falls Indians or Gros Ventres of the Prairies) fell upon a party of Americans whom they confess that they murdered, and robbed of considerable booty in utensils, beaver skins, etc. . . . From the description the Bloods gave of the dress and behavior of one whom they murdered, he must have been an officer or trader; they said he killed two Bloods before he fell. This exasperated them and I have reason to suppose they butchered him in a horrible manner."[61]

The newspaper article announcing Menard's return to St. Louis offered further details: "It appears from circumstances that Drouillard made a most obstinate resistance as he made a kind of breastwork of his horse, whom he made to turn in order to receive the enemy's fire, his bulwark, of course, soon failed and he became the next victim of their fury. It is lamentable that although this happened within a short distance of relief, the [gun]fire was not heard so as to afford it, in consequence of a high wind which prevailed at the time." James added: "We pursued the trail of the Indians till night," remembered James, "without overtaking them, and then returned, having buried our dead, with saddened hearts to Fort,"[62]

Less than four years earlier, in July of 1806, also in present western Montana, Meriwether Lewis, Drouillard, and Joseph and Reubin Field—all strong, healthy, and fearless men in their mid-twenties or early thirties—had survived a sudden an unexpected fight with a group of young Blackfoot men in which they killed one of the Indians and fatally wounded another (the sole violent encounter during the expedition). As Stephen E. Ambrose has written, they were "four whites in the middle of a land with hundreds of Blackfoot warriors who would seek revenge the instant they heard the news. It was imperative that Lewis get himself and his men out of there. Immediately." The four horsemen rode toward the mouth of the Marias River, hoping to meet Sergeant Ordway's group, which was descending the Missouri in canoes. "The party retreated at a trot, covering about eight miles an hour. . . . They rode through the morning and midday not stopping until 3:00 p.m.," when they stopped to rest their horses. "They had covered sixty-three miles." After a ninety-minute break, "they mounted up and rode off, to cover seventeen more miles by dark. Then they killed a buffalo and ate, mounted up again and set off, this time at a walk." With frequent lightning showing the way, they rode on until 2:00 a.m., when they rested again, having covered close to one hundred miles in the last twenty-two hours. At dawn they resumed their march, meeting Ordway and his men after riding another twenty miles. "The men quickly took the baggage from the horses and put it in the canoes, turned the horses loose, and set off."[63] Now, less than four years later, three of the men who had shared that incredible adventure were dead.

Drouillard's death was soon followed by another violent and disheartening incident, but this time nature had seemingly joined in league with the Blackfoot. James's former traveling companions St. John and Marie arrived at Three Forks from Fort Raymond. "Marie's right eye was out and he carried the yet fresh marks of a horrible wound on his head and under his jaw," wrote James. One morning after setting his traps on a branch of the Yellowstone River, Marie had come upon a grizzly, which didn't notice him until he fired at the bear and missed. Marie wounded the animal with his next shot, then "plunged into the water above [a beaver] dam." The grizzly followed him right into the river, watched as he dived several times, then "seized him by the head, the tushes piercing the scalp and neck under the right jaw and crushing the ball of his right eye." St. John came running to the rescue, felling the bear with a shot to the head, "then dragged out Marie from the water more dead than alive. I saw him six days afterwards, with a swelling on his head an inch thick, and his food and drink gushed through the opening under his jaw, made by the teeth of his terrible enemy."[64]

When the men weren't making narrow escapes from Indians, James wrote that they were making "still narrower" escapes from bears. "Game became very scarce and our enemies seemed bent upon starving us out. We all became tired of this kind of life, cooped up in a small enclosure and in perpetual danger of assassination when outside the pickets. The Blackfeet manifested so determined a hatred and jealousy of our presence, that we could entertain no hope of successfully prosecuting our business, even if we could save our lives in their country." Most of the American trappers, like James, found their enthusiasm for the trapping life completely sapped—they just wanted to go "back to the settlements," back home. They made preparations to go east with Menard. "Col. Henry and the greater part of the company," however, "were getting ready to cross the mountains and go onto the Columbia beyond the vicinity of [their] enemies." Most of those going with Henry were French-Canadian, but there were "a few Americans" in the party, including Hoback, Reznor, and Robinson, who had apparently made no compact with God. After everything—after seeing what happened to Potts, to Cheek, to Drouillard, to poor Marie and the others—they had turned down a chance to return to their wives and children and brothers and sisters and friends and neighbors in Kentucky and were not only staying in the wild but were crossing the Rocky Mountains and going farther toward the only point on the compass that interested them: West.[65]

Chapter Five

"Whiskey Flowed Like Milk and Honey in the Land of Canaan"

About the same time that George Drouillard went down fighting in the Three Forks country, Ramsay Crooks left his winter camp near Council Bluffs and came down the Missouri, arriving in St. Louis on June 9, 1810. He apparently talked with Charles Gratiot shortly after his arrival and learned that Wilson Price Hunt, who had gone to New York the previous November to meet with John Jacob Astor, was not back yet. From all indications, however, Astor's plan to establish a trading post on the Pacific coast was still in force.[1]

As David Lavender notes, Crooks, Robert McClellan, and Joseph Miller had probably "long since decided that Crooks should go as usual to Michilimackinac and try to make arrangements for another outfit they could use for their own trade if Hunt did not appear." But if Crooks did meet Hunt, he would be prepared to join with him on the journey west, reuniting with Miller and McClellan along the way. So Crooks headed north, up the Mississippi and then the Illinois, now just as familiar to him as the Missouri. At Chicago he was once again lucky enough to hitch a ride on the *Selina*. Reminiscing more than half a century later, a woman by the name of Lydia Pomeroy remembered that in Chicago "we met Mr. Crooks, who Embark^d. with us on our return [to Mackinac] to join his friends for the Rocky Mountains."[2]

Mrs. Pomeroy had a good memory, for Crooks did indeed meet Hunt at Mackinac, probably in early August, and Hunt brought him up to date on recent happenings. On June 23, 1810, in New York, the final papers had been signed to organize the Pacific Fur Company and formalize plans for a trading post on the Pacific coast. Astor, who would manage the company and invest up to $400,000, had received fifty of the one hundred shares of stock. Alexander McKay, Donald McKenzie, Duncan McDougall, and David Stuart, all veterans of the North West Company, and Hunt, the lone American partner present at the formal organization, all received five shares each. Two of Stuart's shares went to his nephew, Robert Stuart, on September 10. Hunt signed for Crooks, who received five shares, and for McClellan and Miller, who received two and a half shares each. The other fifteen shares were reserved for the company to use as it saw fit. Astor agreed to cover all losses during the first five years.[3]

Alexander Ross, who became one of the first employees of the new company when he signed on as a clerk, wrote that Hunt, "a person every way qualified for the arduous undertaking," proceeded to Montreal to recruit men, accompanied by McKenzie, a man who "had already acquired great experience in the Indian countries, . . . bold, robust, and peculiarly qualified to lead Canadian voyageurs through thick and thin. Mr. Astor placed great confidence in his abilities, perseverance, and prudence."[4]

Although "crowds of blustering voyageurs, of all grades and qualities, flocked thither to enroll themselves under the banner of this grand undertaking," and McKenzie wanted to sign all the men they needed, Hunt "gave a decided preference to Americans, and . . . this was the plan ultimately adopted: so that no more Canadian voyageurs were taken than were barely sufficient to man one large canoe." One man who enlisted in Montreal as a clerk was Jean Baptiste Perrault, who "contracted for Five years at the rate of 80 [pounds] per year." Perrault wrote that his wife had just given birth to a son and was "very much grieved" when he announced his plans to be gone for five years. Giving her what little money he had, he "arranged with a friend to provide for the small Needs she would have in my absence." That evening, wrote Perrault, "I left my wife in her bed." Soon he departed with McKenzie, Hunt, and the others for Mackinac, where they arrived on July 17.[5] They had been there for perhaps two weeks when Crooks arrived.

At Mackinac, wrote Ross, Hunt and McKenzie "in vain sought recruits, at least such as would suit their purpose; for in the morning they were found drinking, at noon drunk, in the evening dead drunk, and in the night seldom sober. . . . Every nook and corner in the whole island swarmed, at all hours of the day and night, with motley groups of uproarious tipplers and whiskey-hunters." He added that "Mackinac at this time resembled a great bedlam, the frantic inmates running to and fro in wild forgetfulness; so that Mr. Hunt, after spending several weeks, could only pick up a few disorderly Canadians, already ruined in mind and body . . . [and] now saw and confessed his error in not taking M'Kenzie's salutary advice to engage more voyageurs at Montreal."[6]

Meanwhile, Perrault was a deeply worried man. "We reached mackinac," he wrote, "and I had been there Ten days, thinking and imagining all sorts of things constantly about my family. This kept me in such a state of anxiety that I could no longer render Account of myself." What happened next revealed a good deal about Hunt and McKenzie (and possibly Crooks, who arrived about this time). "The gentleman perceiving it, said to me at noon, while dining, 'perrault, you seem . . . sorrowful. You are doubtless worrying about your family. Necessity has compelled you to separate from them, but At your discretion we will give you your Release.'" The grateful Perrault accepted the offer. A few days later, Hunt told Perrault that he had recommended him to Otis Denum, who planned to take an outfit to Lake Superior. That afternoon, McKenzie and Hunt introduced him to Denum, who offered a contract. Perrault signed the next day and was thus able to see his family much sooner than if he had gone west with the Astorians. The man hired to replace Perrault was a "rough, warm-hearted, brave old Irishman," John Reed, perhaps the same Reed who had met Lewis and Clark with Crooks in 1806, certainly the same Reed whose fate was wrapped up with those of John Hoback, Jacob Reznor, and Edward Robinson, though he had not yet met them.[7]

According to Ross, "the cross breeds and Yankees [at Mackinac] kept aloof, viewing [Hunt and McKenzie's] expedition, as an army views a forlorn hope, as destined to destruction. Mr. Hunt . . . regretted most of all the precious time they had lost to no purpose at Mackina, and therefore set about leaving it as soon as possible." They made their final preparations and left Mackinac on August 12, 1810, crossing over Lake Michigan to Green Bay, where they ascended the Fox River into present central Wisconsin, made a short portage to the Wisconsin River, and followed that waterway to the Mississippi, which took them to St. Louis. They arrived on September 3. Miller was there to greet them, but McClellan was somewhere on the upper Missouri.[8]

During this same period, things were happening fast in the East. On August 23, Astor had paid $37,860 for the *Tonquin*, "a ship of 300 tons mounting twelve guns and mustering a crew of twenty-one men." The plan was to send two groups of men to the Pacific coast to establish a trading post, with one party headed by Hunt, McKenzie, Crooks, McClellan, and Miller going by land (hence the moniker "overland Astorians") and another commanded by McDougall, McKay, and David and Robert Stuart going by sea. Of these nine partners, all but one would return safely to their homes. On September 3, the same day that Hunt and the others reached St. Louis, Astor paid a $10,000 premium to insure the cargo (valued at more than $50,000) then being loaded on the ship. On September 6, the crew, the four partners, eleven clerks, thirteen boatmen, and five mechanics gathered on the *Tonquin*. Ross remembered that "all was bustle and confusion upon deck, and every place in the ship was in such topsy-turvy state, with what sailors call live and dead lumber, that scarcely any one knew how or where he was to be stowed." Amidst this hustle and bustle, "the *Tonquin* set sail, and a fresh breeze springing up, soon wafted her to a distance from the busy shores of New York." The ship was headed around Cape Horn, out into the Pacific to obtain goods and men at the Sandwich Islands, and finally to the mouth of the Columbia River.[9] All of these destinations would be reached. Still, there was nothing ahead for the ill-fated *Tonquin* but trouble.

Toward the end of May, with Andrew Henry preparing to leave the fort at Three Forks and cross the mountains to trap a tributary of the Columbia River, Pierre Menard, accompanied by Thomas James and most of the other American trappers, made his way to the mouth of Clark's Fork of the Yellowstone, where a stock of supplies had been cached (buried) the previous autumn. Although Hidatsa Indians had uncovered the pits and taken the contents of several trunks, the remaining supplies were sent to Henry.

"Here we parted from our companions, who were going to the Columbia," wrote James, "and who returned hence to the Forks with the goods and ammunition for their trip, while we, the homeward bound, continued our course down the river in the canoes and the boat . . . to the Fort on the Big Horn." After repairing a keelboat (which Lisa had left at Fort Raymond in 1808) and loading it with goods, they began their descent of the Yellowstone. As James described it:

> In five days after entering the Missouri, we descended to the Gros Ventre [Hidatsa] village and our Fort [Fort Mandan], and were there joyfully received by our old companions. Whiskey flowed like milk and honey in the land of Canaan, being sold to the men by the disinterested and benevolent gentlemen of the Missouri Fur Company, for the moderate sum of twelve dollars per gallon, they taking payment, beaver skins at one dollar and a half, each, which were worth in St. Louis, six. Their prices for every thing else were in about the same proportion. Even at this price some of the men bought whiskey by the bucket full, and drank.
> 'Till they forgot their loves and debts
> And cared for grief na mair[10]

As noted, Pierre Dorion Jr. was among those who had bought whiskey by the "bucket full," running up a considerable bill with the fine "gentlemen" of the company. And when Menard and his men started down the Missouri a few days later, Dorion went with them, no doubt commiserating with James and the others about how they were now in debt to the company, not the other way around. "They brought me in their debt two hundred dollars, and some of the other Americans, for still larger sums," remembered James. "The reader may ask how this could be. He can easily imagine the process when he is told that the company [making huge profits] charged us six dollars per pound for powder, three dollars for lead, six dollars for coarse calico shirts, one dollar and a half per yard for coarse tow linen for tents, the same for a common butcher knife, and so on."[11]

Whether the debt-ridden Dorion had Marie and the two boys with him at Fort Mandan or picked them up in Yankton country is not clear, but the four of them were all together when Menard's group reached St. Louis in mid-July of 1810. James, however, aptly summed up the quandary of Dorion and several other Missouri Fur Company employees when he said, "they were hopeless of discharging [their debts to the company] by any ordinary business in which they could engage."[12]

On June 5, at Three Forks, Andrew Henry wrote a letter to his friend Francois Vallé, likely at Fort Raymond: "Since you left the fort I was told by Charles Davis that some days past you expressed some regret at going down. If that is the case & you have any wish to stay, you shall have the same bargain which Manuel gave you last fall & better should you desire it." Hinting at his own homesickness and possibly a sense of foreboding about the future, he added, "But on the other hand, if you have really a wish to desind I will by no means advise you to stay but would rather advice you to go home to your family who I know will be extremely glad to see you although the pleasure of your company for a year in the wild country would be to me inestimable."[13]

Vallé chose a reunion with his family over another year in the wild country and went down the Missouri with Menard, James, Dorion, and the others. If Henry had felt a foreshadowing of danger, it quickly developed. "Shortly before his abandoning the fort in the three forks of the Missouri," a second-hand 1811 report read, "there had been a battle between eighteen or nineteen of his hunters, and upwards of two hundred Blackfeet, in which twenty two of the latter were killed, and the hunters enabled to make a safe retreat to the fort with the loss of only one man." A different second- (or third-) hand report from 1819 was not nearly as favorable: "They [Henry and his men] had every prospect of being successful, until their operations were interrupted by the hostility of the Blackfeet Indians. With these people they had several very severe conflicts, in which upwards of 30 of their men were killed; and the whole party were finally compelled to leave that part of the country."[14]

Neither Henry nor any of his men ever recorded the details of a second Blackfoot attack; David J. Wishart balanced the two accounts by estimating that twenty men had been killed. Regardless of the exact number, the conflict apparently convinced Henry to radically change his plans. He had originally planned to reach a branch of the Columbia by ascending the Madison River and crossing over the Continental Divide into present Idaho. As Reuben Lewis had written, the group believed "[t]he upper branches of the Collubmbia are full of beavers, and the rout by the middle fork of the Madisons River is almost without mountains, it is about 5 or 6 days Travel to an illegible place for a fort on that River where the Beaver (from the account of Peter Wisor [Weiser]) is an abundant as in our part of the Country."[15]

Concluding, however, that he would encounter more Blackfoot Indians up the Madison, Henry decided to go east to the Gallatin and Yellowstone Rivers, reaching Crow country as fast as possible. According to the anonymous correspondent who interviewed John Dougherty, one of the Americans with Hoback, Reznor, and Robinson, this was exactly what happened: "Mr Dougherty left the fort [Three Forks post] crossed over to the Yellowstone descend-ed until he met the Rest they then crossed over from the Yellowston to Stinking [Shoshone] River assended to its [word omitted] with the intention of crossing over the mountains onto the Columbia at a place further South below the Blackfeet Indians." When seen in the context of the route taken by Henry's men in March (from Fort Raymond to Three Forks) and combined with the 1819 report that the group "crossed the mountains near the source of the Yellow Stone river," the Dougherty Map and Narrative strongly imply that the men followed Clark's Fork of the Yellowstone into present Wyoming, curved southeast to the Cody area, ascended the Shoshone River and its south fork, crossed Shoshone Pass, made a false start down the Wind River, then headed up that same river, crossed Togwotee Pass—and the Continental Divide—and then crossed the Teton Range into present Idaho to a branch of the Columbia, the Teton River. They followed the Teton downstream, into what is now called the Snake River Valley, and made a jog to the west to reach a branch of the Snake River, now called Henry's Fork, where they built huts and prepared for the coming winter. It would be a hard one.[16]

The year of 1810 also proved to be a fateful year for the two traders who had preceded Lisa into Montana in 1807: John McClallen and Charles Courtin, both of whom had established posts in the area of the present Flathead Indian Reservation north of Missoula. Courtin grew bold in his movements, even though he was still on the fringe of Blackfoot country. The Canadian explorer and trader David Thompson recorded the result: "On the evening of [February 24, 1810] the Indians informed me, that the Peeagans [a division of the Blackfoot Nation] had attacked a hunting party, killed Mr Courter (a trader and Hunter from the U States and one Indian, and wounded several others."[17]

Some time before December of 1810, the Blackfoot launched another raid, this time on McClallen's band, by that time reduced to twelve men and operating somewhere between Three Forks and Great Falls. As with Courtin, news of McClallen's end came from Thompson, who wrote that the Piegan Blackfoot had killed "an officer and 8 soldiers out of a tribe of 12." As Henry Majors has noted, "It would be nearly four decades before American traders could operate successfully in western Montana."[18]

Where Pierre and Marie Dorion and their sons Baptiste (about three years old) and Paul (about one) found shelter in St. Louis is not known. Dorion may have sought out William Clark, who had arrived in St. Louis only two weeks before Menard's group did. Clark had been on a nine-month-trip to the East, returning home for the first time since learning of Lewis's death the previous October (he and his family had been in Kentucky at the time). Clark had already provided Toussaint Charbonneau, Sacagawea, and Baptiste (now five) with a plot of land and horses, cows, and hogs, and he was the kind of man likely to offer the Dorions assistance of some kind. The question naturally arises as to whether Dorion and his family had any contact with Charbonneau and his, for the two families had much in common, but the historical record is silent on the matter.

What is known is that in a letter written on September 12, Clark announced that "P. Dorion The Sac Sub Agent is dead," information likely obtained from Pierre Jr. The elder Dorion's cause of death is unknown, but according to Dorion family tradition, he "died on 23 July 1810 at Petite Rocher, below St. Louis," at seventy years of age.[19]

In the same letter, Clark informed the secretary of war that "Mr Hunt & McKinzey are at this place, prepareing to proceed up the Missouri and prosue my trail to the Columbia. I am not fully in possession of the objects of this expedition but prosume you are, would be very glad to be informed." Clark may not have had a wealth of information, but what he had was accurate—the overland Astorians indeed planned to pursue his trail. In a letter to Albert Gallatin written just a few months earlier, Astor said that he had "made arrangements to send a party of good men up the Missurie for the purpose of exploring the country . . . to assertain whether it afords furrs suficient to carry on an extensive trade." He added that the party intended "to cross the Rockey mountains to columbia's river where it is hoped they will meet" with the men who had sailed on the *Tonquin*.[20]

Neither Clark nor Astor explained the exact route, but based on Lewis and Clark's westbound *and* eastbound journeys, the most efficient path to the Pacific would look something like this: follow the Missouri from St. Charles all the way to the Mandan and Hidatsa villages in present North Dakota; proceed across present Montana, past Great Falls to the mouth of the Dearborn River; follow the Dearborn west to its source; cross (over the Continental Divide) to the Blackfoot River near present Rogers Pass; go west along the Blackfoot to the area near present Missoula; take the Lolo Trail to the Clearwater or one of its branches; and float the Clearwater to the Snake, the Snake to the Columbia, and the Columbia to the Pacific. Which details Hunt understood is not clear, but he likely knew that Lewis and Clark had taken a needless detour by following the Jefferson River to its source, crossing Lemhi Pass into present Idaho, and then heading back north (because the Salmon River was unnavigable) to the Missoula area.

"When Hunt got to St. Louis [from Mackinac]," wrote James Ronda, "he had no reason to doubt that the Lewis and Clark trail was the best highway across the continent. It was a route that Hunt had known about since 1806." Once in St. Louis, however, "Hunt altered his plans [and] it is possible that conversations with Clark were at the heart of such changes." First, Clark's involvement with the Missouri Fur Company, a firm that had established a fort on the Yellowstone River, had quite possibly renewed his interest in that river, which he had found on his return journey to be "large and navigable with but fiew obstructions quite into the rocky mountains." Second, Clark was now hard at work on his master map of the West—"a cartographic masterpiece, a remarkably accurate rendering of the inner continent of North America"—and had obtained new information on the Bighorn and Shoshone Rivers from Drouillard and Colter. Third, Menard had recently returned from the upper Missouri with news of the Blackfoot attack at Three Forks. "Clark might have been the first to tell Hunt about these hazards and the possibility of an attractive Yellowstone detour."[21]

Clark loved to talk about the geography of the West, a subject Hunt had taken a keen interest in as early as 1806, long before he entertained notions of actually going West, but since most of Hunt's letters have been lost, any record he made of getting down on his hands and knees and examining maps with Clark (like Thomas Jefferson did) have been lost as well. But Hunt, who had expressed admiration for Clark, definitely shifted his course southward, soon making plans, according to John Bradbury, who accompanied him for the first leg of his trip west, to "ascend the Missouri to the Roche Jaune [Yellowstone] river, one thousand eight hundred and eighty miles from the mouth, and at that place to commence his journey by land."[22] Exactly what route he hoped to take from the Yellowstone is unknown, but given Menard's disturbing report, he quite possibly expected to follow the Bighorn into present Wyoming. As it turned out, he never made it as far north as the Yellowstone River, but he did find three mountain men to guide him——best they could—across the plains and mountains of Wyoming.

Hunt's immediate need, however, was to recruit men and depart as fast as possible. This was easier said than done, however. Washington Irving, who was furnished with an "abundance of materials in letters, journals, and verbal narratives," when he wrote his classic volume *Astoria*, offered this perspective: "As Mr. Hunt met with much opposition on the part of rival traders, especially the Missouri Fur Company," wrote Irving, "it took him some weeks to complete his preparations." Ross claimed the Missouri Company warned potential recruits of "the horrors, the dangers, and privations that awaited our adventurous friends; that if they were fortunate enough to escape being scalped by the Indians, they would assuredly be doomed, like Nebucahdnezzar, to eat grass, and never would return to tell the sad tale of their destruction." The delays Hunt had experienced in Montreal and Mackinac, when combined with his difficulties in St. Louis, "had thrown him much behind his original calculations, so that it would be impossible to effect his voyage up the Missouri in the present year. This river, flowing from high and cold latitudes, and through wide and open plains, exposed to chilling blasts, freezes early. The winter may be dated from the first of November; there was every prospect, therefore, that it would be closed with ice long before Mr. Hunt could reach its upper waters."[23]

Joseph Miller proved to be the solution to Hunt's recruiting woes. Ross wrote that Miller "had considerable experience among Indians along the route to be followed, and was a great favourite with the people in St. Louis. As soon, therefore, as Mr. Miller joined the expedition, people from all quarters began again to enlist under the banner of the new company. Canoemen, hunters, trappers, and interpreters were no long wanting." Ross was generally correct but a little overoptimistic because, as will be evident, an interpreter was definitely wanting at this point. John Reed carefully recorded the names of recruits (and more particularly the goods and supplies they were changing against their earnings, as well as cash advances), and according to his account book, forty-six Canadians, twenty-six Americans, and a few others of unknown origin had enlisted by this time.[24]

Hunt and the other partners were also busy buying supplies, including the following: a large keelboat, oars, etc., for $275.00; an oilcloth for $30.00; a sail for $15.00; a Schenectady barge for $50.00 and sail for $6.00; an anchor for $20.00; two large awls for $2.00; two handsaws for $2.50; two small padlocks for $1.00; two large copper kettles for $12.50; one hammer for $.50; one drawknife for $.75; one gimlet for $.60; one container of nails for $.25; one caulking iron for $.25; one auger for $.75; one cable for $1.50; nineteen covering bearskins for $9.50; nine linen bags for $3.00; hulled corn for $1.50; one tea kettle for $2.50; four canisters for $2.00; two tin pans for $1.00; 3 tin plates for $.75; six knives and forks for $1.00; three tea cups for $.25; three containers of coffee for $1.50; one container of tea for $2.50; four beaver traps for $18.00. That wasn't all—they bought salt and pepper, bacon, a medicine chest, shoes, socks, combs, hunter's knives, thread, trousers, tobacco, flannel, buttons, blankets, and linen.[25]

Hunt knew he could not reach the upper Missouri before winter came on. "To avoid, however, the expense of wintering at St. Louis, he determined to push up the river as far as possible," noted Irving, "to some point above the settlements, where game was plenty, and where his whole party could be subsisted by hunting, until the breaking up of the ice in the spring should permit them to resume their voyage." The men were in good spirits when they headed west on October 21, 1810.[26]

"Our Canadian voyageurs were now somewhat out of their usual element," wrote Ross. "Boats and oars, the mode of navigating the great rivers of the south, were new to men who had been brought up to the paddle, the cheering song, and the bark canoe of the north. They detested the heavy and languid drag of a Mississippi boat, and sighed for the paddle and song of former days. They soon, however, became expert at the oar."[27] These voyageurs pushed hard, fighting sandbars exposed because of the low water, fighting cold and wet weather. They reached Fort Osage on October 30, and Hunt made straight for George Sibley's store, where he purchased ten kegs of gunpowder for $224. But most of the men were preoccupied with one thing: buffalo robes—the best protection against a Missouri River winter. By the end of the day, twenty-one robes had changed hands at a cost of three or four dollars each.

Leaving the fort on November 1, the boatmen continued their relentless pace, covering 450 miles from St. Louis—upstream miles—in three and a half weeks, about half the time Lewis and Clark had required to go to the same distance in 1804. On November 16, with the traces of ice on the water growing more and more ominous, they stopped at the mouth of the Nodaway River, where Crooks and McClellan and previously built winter quarters. Almost at the same time, McClellan and John Day and their men arrived from the north, bad tempered, with a new tale of misfortune on the Missouri.

During the summer of 1810, with Hunt busy in Canada and Crooks on his way to Mackinac, McClellan and Day had built a trading post in the Council Bluffs area. One day while McClellan and others were out hunting, a group of Sioux Indians had appeared and robbed the remaining men of three thousand dollars' worth of trade goods, quite possibly in revenge for Crooks and McClellan deceiving them the previous summer. Day and several comrades had pursued some of the Sioux but only managed to retrieve a fraction of the plunder. McClellan split what was left among his men and paddled south in a rage, determined to end his bad luck one way or the other. Four years earlier, when he had met Lewis and Clark on their homeward journey, he had been confident that he was on the verge of profitable trading, but one disaster had followed another. Now something had to give.[28]

If McClellan was unhappy about receiving two and a half shares in the new company when Hunt, Crooks, and the other partners had received five, no one left a record of his displeasure. Miller was apparently happy with his two and a half shares—that may have made a difference. McClellan accepted the partnership, and the recruits were pleased, for as always, McClellan's reputation had preceded him. "This gentleman was one of the first shots in America," wrote Ross. "Nothing could escape his keen eye and steady hand; hardy, enterprizing, and brave as a lion: on the whole, he was considered a great acquisition to the party."[29]

In a letter to his brother William, the unpredictable McClellan wrote:

> Six days ago I arrived at this place from my settlement, which is two hundred miles above on the Missouri. My mare is with you at Hamilton, having two

colts. I wish you to give one to brother John, the other to your son James, and the mare to your wife. If I possessed anything more except my gun at present, I would throw it into the river, or give it away, as I intend to begin the world anew tomorrow.[30]

Day also cast his lot with his friends Crooks and Miller. Rather than proclaiming his rebirth in a letter, however, Day took care of more mundane matters, charging a cotton handkerchief, a knife, and a tomahawk to his account on December 21. Like McClellan, he was in his early forties, bringing with him a good reputation as a frontiersman. At this time there was no indication that he had a history of mental illness. That was still in the future.

As the year of 1810 drew to a close, McKay, McDougall, David and Robert Stuart, and all the others aboard the *Tonquin* braced themselves for the voyage around Cape Horn. Ross wrote that on December 19 at 9:00 in the morning they had a full view of the cape. "But adverse winds meeting us here, we were unable to double [circle] it before Christmas morning. . . . While in these latitudes, notwithstanding the foggy state of the weather, we could read common print at all hours of the night on deck without the aid of artificial light." The sky was overcast, the weather "raw and cold," but they saw no ice in the water, despite frequent showers of hail and snow. "Here the snow birds and Cape pigeon frequently flew in great numbers about the ship. After doubling the Cape, a speckled red and white fish, about the size of a salmon, was observed before the ship's bow, as if leading the way." It was christened "the pilot fish" by the sailors. "With gladdened hearts," wrote Ross, "we now bent our course northward on the wide Pacific."[31]

As for Crooks and McClellan, they "must have felt some wryness at starting out once again there at the Nodaway. This was the vicinity of the Black Snake Hills, where they had been isolated two winters earlier by the machinations of the St. Louis Missouri Fur Company." Now, thanks to delays "caused by the same group, the company they were with had been brought up short of its desirings at almost the same spot. But this time, so they may have promised themselves as they . . . settled down for the winter, they were going to show their heels to Manuel Lisa.[32]

Chapter Six

"About Seventy Able Bodied Men, Nerved to Hardship"

Pierre Dorion and his family spent the winter of 1810–1811 somewhere in the St. Louis area, but if any details were ever recorded—which itself seems unlikely—they have been lost. And although Dorion was a native French speaker, spoke enough English to get by, was fluent in number of Sioux dialects, and knew Indian sign language well—and had rudimentary skills in a variety of Indian languages—he is not known to have left any record of himself, not a diary, letter, or note of any kind, not even an *x* for his signature, assuming he was illiterate, a not unreasonable conjecture. So it is quite understandable that the record of his life up to 1804, when he met Lewis and Clark, is a blank slate, and that for the next six years mentions of him are random and fragmentary—he's in Yankton Sioux country; he's in St. Louis preparing to escort a group of Yankton Sioux up the river; he's guiding Lisa through the Dakotas to the Mandan and Hidatsa villages. He appears briefly, then disappears for months or years on end.

That all changed early in 1811. A flurry of recordkeeping tracked Dorion's movements from Missouri to the Great Plains to the Rocky Mountains to the Pacific coast and back to the Idaho wilderness. The thirty-four months from March 1811 to January 1814—the last thirty-four months of his life— are chronicled with careful detail by a variety of diarists. For a third of that period, we know where he was and what he was doing virtually every day; thereafter he is mentioned frequently enough to leave no question about his whereabouts and his activities. One could argue, no doubt, that international markets and competing corporations had initiated the series of events resulting in Dorion's final years being so well documented, but in his practical world the stone that started the avalanche was a simple whiskey bill.

Not staying at the winter camp at the mouth of the Nodaway River, Wilson Price Hunt had returned to St. Louis, arriving on January 20, 1811. Hunt's greatest difficulty, wrote Washington Irving, "was to procure the Sioux interpreter. There was but one man to be met with at St. Louis who was fitted for the purpose, but to secure him would require much management." That man was Dorion, of course. He had presumably provided for his family the last several months by hunting, trapping, and fishing and possibly laboring in a shop that built canoes. But all of this provided a subsistence and nothing more—Dorion knew that his chance to make some real money would come in the spring, when traders heading up the Missouri would remember that he was the one man "fitted for the purpose" of serving as a Sioux interpreter.[1]

Dorion also knew that the fierce competition between the Pacific Fur Company of Astor and the St. Louis Missouri Fur Company of Lisa et al. had made his services more valuable than ever. The Astorians, as was well known in St. Louis, planned to follow Lewis and Clark's route all the way to the Pacific. They were running late and had to get up the Missouri as fast as possible. Lisa and his men were also going up the river, just as they had in 1807 and 1809, but this biannual trip held particular significance. As Irving explained, "What had become of [Henry] and his party was unknown. The most intense anxiety was felt concerning them, and apprehension that they might have been cut off by the savages. At the time of Mr. Hunt's arrival at St. Louis [in January of 1811], the Missouri Company were fitting out an expedition to go in quest of Mr. Henry. It was to be conducted by Mr. Manuel Lisa."[2]

This meant that both groups had to pass the feared Lakota Sioux, Indians that Thomas Jefferson had made special mention of in his instructions to Lewis and Clark. "On that nation we wish most particularly to make a friendly impression," he wrote, "because of their immense power." But when the captains met the Lakota in September of 1804, negotiations quickly broke down, threats were uttered, and the two groups faced off with rifles cocked and arrows drawn. Lewis ordered the cannon loaded with musket balls. "Had that cannon fired," wrote Stephen Ambrose, "there might have been no Lewis and Clark Expedition. The exploration of the Missouri River country and Oregon would have had to be done by others, at a later time." Luckily, a Lakota chief stepped forward and made a conciliatory move, sparing both sides from a good deal of bloodshed. But the indignant Clark hardly forgave and forgot. When he and Lewis came back down the river two years later, he yelled from the boat to a band of Lakota warriors that his men would kill any of them who came too close. When he wrote a lengthy description of several different Indian nations, he called the Lakota "the vilest miscreants of the savage race . . . the pirates of the Missouri."[3]

In his accounts of the near-catastrophe in Lakota country, Clark made it clear that misunderstandings arose immediately because, in his words, "we discover our interpreter do not Speak the language well." The captains had made a major mistake in leaving Pierre Dorion Sr. at the Yankton Sioux villages so he (and presumably Pierre Jr.) could accompany representatives of that nation to St. Louis. The elder Dorion spoke fluent Sioux and had lived among the Sioux for more than two decades—along with translating accurately he could have advised Lewis and Clark on everything from matters of protocol and nuance to Lakota history and tradition. As Lewis and Clark attempted to follow Jefferson's mandate to befriend the Lakota people, nothing could have been more crucial than having an experienced, savvy interpreter. Instead, they called on Pierre Cruzatte, a member of the crew who spoke his mother's Omaha language, to do the impossible and communicate with the Lakota, who certainly didn't understand Omaha. Cruzatte apparently spoke to some Omaha prisoners who did their best to pass on the messages to and from the Sioux, but that failed. "Cap Lewis proceeded to Deliver a Speech which we oblige to Curtail for want of a good interpreter," wrote Clark. In the midst of this chaos, with both the explorers and the Indians quite uncertain about what the other side was saying, patience grew short and tempers flared. Speaking of one of the chiefs, Clark wrote, "his insults became So personal and his intentions evident to do me injurey, I Drew my Sword (and ordered all hands under arms)."[4] A "good interpreter," however, would have been in a position to stop perceived insults from escalating, something well known by Hunt and Lisa. Both had been in St. Louis when Lewis and Clark returned, and both had had ample opportunity to question Clark in the intervening four and a half years. Neither was about to make the same mistake as Lewis and Clark and venture into Lakota territory without a Dorion to rely on.

Hunt and Lisa also knew that Pierre Jr., the undisputed successor to his father, was indeed the one man in St. Louis capable of acting as Sioux interpreter. Dorion's unpaid whiskey tab was hardly a deterrent to Lisa's rehiring him—quite the opposite, it made the prospect more likely because Lisa was the kind of man to leverage the debt in his favor: Dorion could work off part or all of the bill while providing a valuable service at the same time. Hunt, on the other hand, was just as desperate to hire Dorion and, since most of his company was waiting at the mouth of the Nodaway River, would be ready to leave sooner.

Exactly when Hunt first approached Dorion is not known, but he apparently did so not long after his arrival on January 20, no doubt discovering—if he didn't know already—that Dorion's bill with Lisa "remained unsettled, and a matter of furious dispute, the mere mention of which was sufficient to put him [Dorion] in a passion." But, as Irving observed, "the moment it was discovered that Pierre Dorion was in treaty with the new and rival association, [Lisa] endeavored, by threats as well as promises, to prevent [Dorion's] engaging in their service." But Lisa's negotiating strategies—which served him so well in tense encounters with Indians—failed him at this crucial moment: "His promises might, perhaps, have prevailed; but his threats, which related to the whiskey debt, only served to drive Pierre into the opposition ranks." Even then, Dorion was no easy bargain. After negotiating with Hunt for two weeks, he agreed "to serve in the expedition, as a hunter and interpreter, at the rate of three hundred dollars a year, two hundred of which were to be paid in advance."[5]

About that same time, John Bradbury, an English botanist interested in seeing the Missouri River country and collecting plant specimens, expressed an interest in going up the river with the Astorians. "As they were apprised of the nature and object of my mission," wrote Bradbury, "Mr. Wilson P. Hunt, the leader of the party, in a very friendly and pressing manner invited me to accompany them up the River Missouri, as far as might be agreeable to my views." Bradbury accepted the invitation, "to which an acquaintance with Messrs. Ramsey Crooks and Donald M'Kenzie, also principals of the party, was no small inducement."[6] Bradbury was joined by fellow English botanist Thomas Nuttall. Nuttall left no known record of the voyage, but Bradbury's extensive journal has become the primary record relating to the first part of the Astorians' westbound expedition.

Just as Hunt and the others were preparing to make their departure, five American hunters who had signed on with Hunt the previous autumn arrived in St. Louis complaining of ill treatment by the partners at the winter camp. "What was worse," wrote Irving, "they spread such reports of the hardships and dangers to be apprehended in the course of the expedition, that they struck a panic into those hunters who had recently engaged at St. Louis, and when the hour of departure arrived"—on the morning of March 12, 1810— "all but one refused to embark."[7] If that weren't enough, Dorion—at the last minute, according to Irving—refused to board the boat unless Marie and Baptiste and Paul could also come along. Hunt agreed. Like Lewis and Clark, he had planned a journey across the Great Plains and Rocky Mountains to the Pacific Ocean with no intent of taking anyone but adult males, mostly in their twenties and early thirties. But, in a development no one would have prophesied, both expeditions included an Indian woman and her infant son—two sons in Marie's case. And the instant this young Iowa woman boarded the boat with her boys, she formed a permanent link with the unassuming Shoshone woman now known as Sacagawea. The parallels between the two are startling, and the most fascinating parallel still lay in the future.

What was not surprising was that Lisa somehow got word almost immediately that Dorion had left with Hunt. "In the evening," wrote Bradbury, who had delayed his departure to await the mail expected to arrive the next morning from Louisville, "I was informed by a gentleman in St. Louis, that a writ for debt had been taken out against Dorion . . . by a person"—Lisa— "whose object was to defeat the intentions of the voyage."[8] Bradbury further learned that Lisa intended to intercept Hunt's boat at St. Charles and have Dorion arrested.

Knowing that the loss of Dorion could jeopardize the entire mission, Bradbury packed up his things and made arrangements for himself and Nuttall to travel overland on horseback and inform Hunt before he reached St. Charles. Bradbury and Nuttall left St. Louis at 2:00 in the morning, never revealing what obstacles they encountered and how they possibly found the boat. Bradbury simply said he "effected" his plan and warned Dorion. Irving reported that Dorion "immediately landed and took to the woods, followed by his squaw laden with their papooses, and a large bundle containing their most previous effects, promising to rejoin the party some distance above St. Charles." But could Dorion be trusted? After all, he "was at the very time playing an evasive game with his former employers; who had already received two-thirds of his year's pay, and his rifle on his shoulder, his family and worldly fortune at his heels, and the wild woods before him."[9] So Hunt hoped for the best.

They reached St. Charles around noon on March 13, and lawmen presumably sent by Lisa searched for Dorion in vain. Whether they attempted to interrogate Hunt or anyone else is not known, but that was the last official attempt to apprehend Dorion. "We slept on board the boat," reported Bradbury, "and in the morning of the 14th took our departure from St. Charles, the Canadians measuring the strokes of their oars by songs, which were generally responsive betwixt the oarsmen at the bow and those at the stern: sometimes the steersman sung, and was chorused by the men."[10]

A verse from one of their favorite songs, rendered in English, went like this:

> Behind our house there is a pond,
> Fal lal de ra.
> There came three ducks to swim thereon:
> All along the river clear,
> Lightly my shepherdess dear,
> Lightly, fal de ra.[11]

"We soon met with Dorion," continued Bradbury, "but without his squaw, whom it was intended should accompany us. They had quarrelled, and he had beaten her, in consequence of which she ran away from him into the woods, with a child in her arms, and a large bundle on her back." Hunt sent a Canadian voyageur to search for Marie. "The day was very rainy, and we proceeded only nine miles, to Bon Homme Island, where we encamped." The voyageur returned not long after that and reported that his search had been unsuccessful. This left Dorion in an agitated state, reportedly regretting his harsh treatment of his wife and spending a "solitary and anxious night" worrying about her and the boys. But, as Bradbury reported: "About two hours before day, we were hailed from the shore by Dorion's squaw, who had been rambling all night in search of us. She was informed, that we would cross over to her at daybreak, which we did, and took her on board."[12] This was the first—but not the last—mention of Dorion beating his wife. Neither Bradbury nor Irving mentioned what injuries she suffered from the beating, and neither seemed particularly surprised that such a thing should happen.

That same day, an article appeared in the *Louisiana Gazette*:

> Mr. Wilson P. Hunt left this place last Monday, with a well equipped barge, to join his associates, at the Otto village, to proceed on his expedition to the Columbia river. His party amount to about seventy able bodied men, nerved to hardship.
>
> We understand the New-York Fur Company, to whom Mr. Hunt is attached, have dispatched a well furnished ship, to meet the party on the shores of the Pacific.
>
> Mr. Hunt is accompanied by Mr. Bradbury and a Mr. Nuttall, who are deputed to this country, to explore and make known its riches, in the Animal, Vegetal and Mineral kingdoms, for which purpose they are provided with the necessary tests. Mr. B has devoted nearly 12 months to the examination of this neighborhood, and has been enabled to introduce to England, a very considerable number of Plants, before unknown to the Botanic gardens of that country. From the superior advantages which the country of Le baut Missouri furnish, we trust these gentlemen will return with a rich scientific harvest, gratifying to the philosopher, and probably useful to society in general.[13]

On March 17, Hunt's party landed at a French village named La Charette, across the river from where Crooks had met Lewis and Clark in September of 1806 and near where he had met Lisa the next spring. Two more historic meetings were in the offing. "On leaving Charette," wrote Bradbury, "Mr. Hunt pointed out to me an old man standing on the bank, who, he informed me, was Daniel Boone, the discoverer of Kentucky." Bradbury had a letter of introduction from a Colonel Grant, one of Boone's nephews, and went ashore to talk to Boone. The boat went on ahead. "I remained for some time in conversation with him," continued Bradbury. "He informed me, that he was eighty-four years of age; that he had spent a considerable portion of his time alone in the back woods, and had lately returned from his spring hunt, with nearly sixty beaver skins." Either Boone was exaggerating or forgetful or Bradbury misunderstood him—the famed explorer was a mere seventy-seven years old and would live until 1820. We can't say whether his and Bradbury's long conversation touched on his first glimpse of Kentucky, his daring rescue of his daughter, or how he and several other defenders of Boonesboro had withstood a six-month siege by a combined force of British and Indians, but it is doubtful that Boone mentioned the loss of his Kentucky lands, his court-martial, or how his obsession with "elbow room" was a key factor in his son's torture and death.[14]

Leaving Boone to contemplate his incredible life of heroic acts, not-so-heroic acts, triumph, tragedy, and disappointment—or perhaps nothing beyond his sixty beaver pelts or the recent rainstorms—Bradbury made his way through the woods and back to the river. "As the boat had disappeared behind an island, and was at too great a distance to be hailed," he wrote, "I got across [to the south side of the river] by swimming, having tied my clothes together, and inclosed them in my deer skin hunting coat, which I pushed before me. I overtook the boat in about three hours, and we encamped at the mouth of a creek called Boeuf, near the house of one Sullens. I enquired of Sullens for John Colter, one of Lewis and Clarke's party, whom General Clark had mentioned to me as being able to point out the place on the Missouri where the petrified skeleton of a fish, above forty feet long, had been found."[15]

Colter had ventured back to civilization almost ten months earlier, in May of 1810, but his fame had arrived several months before that, in December of 1809, when Dr. Thomas published his article describing Colter's flight from Blackfoot Indians in the *Missouri Gazette*. This was the same month that Bradbury appeared in St. Louis, and he apparently read the article, for he arranged to interview Colter upon his return. "This man [Colter] came to St. Louis in May, 1810," he wrote, "in a small canoe, from the head waters of the Missouri, a distance of three thousand miles, which he traversed in thirty days. I saw him on his arrival, and received from him an account of his adventures after he had separated from Lewis and Clarke's party."[16]

Sullens told Bradbury that Colter lived about a mile away and sent his son to tell Colter of the party's arrival, but Colter did not appear that evening. "At day-break," wrote Bradbury, "Sullens came to our camp, and informed us that Colter would be with us in a few minutes. Shortly after he arrived, and accompanied us for some miles, but he could not give me the information I wished for. He seemed to have a great inclination to accompany the expedition; but having been lately married, he reluctantly took leave of us." Irving added that Colter "had many particulars to give them concerning the Blackfeet Indians, a restless and predatory tribe, who had conceived an implacable hostility to the white men, in consequence of one of their warriors having been killed by Captain Lewis, while attempting to steal horses." Colter was therefore "urgent in reiterating the precautions that ought to be observed respecting" the Blackfoot because "the expedition would have to proceed" through their territory.[17]

Such advice likely strengthened Hunt's resolve to follow the Yellowstone River rather than the Missouri across present Montana; whether it convinced him to avoid the Three Forks area altogether is not known but is distinctly possible. Talking with Colter just a few weeks later, Henry Marie Brackenridge, on his way up the Missouri with Crooks and McClellan's old nemesis Lisa, offered this account:

> The course of the Rocky mountains, is nearly north and south, and about the same length with the Allegheney mountain, but much higher, and more resembling the Alps, or Andes. Immence peaks, and clothed with eternal snows. They subside towards the south, and are lost before they reach the gulf of California. At the head of the Gallatin Fork, and of the Grosse Corne of the Yellow stone, from discoveries since the voyage of Lewis and Clark, it is found less difficult to cross than the Allegheney mountains; Coulter, a celebrated hunter and woodsman, informed me, that a loaded wagon would find no obstruction in passing. [18]

This inconspicuous paragraph, buried in a much longer article by Brackenridge, offered tantalizing clues about things past and things to come. Although Colter descended the Gallatin River for some distance after escaping from his Blackfoot pursuers, he likely passed eastward to Clark's Fork of the Yellowstone before reaching the source of the Gallatin. He had apparently concluded, however, that the head of the Gallatin lay in the same general region as the source of the Grosse Corne, or Bighorn River. He was more correct than he could have realized. The area that Colter ventured into during that memorable winter of 1807–1808, now best known for Yellowstone and Grand Teton National Parks, held not only spectacular mountain ranges and lakes and countless other natural wonders, it was also an astounding and unparalleled source of steams and creeks, supplying and resupplying water to the great rivers of the West, with the Snake River flowing west to the Columbia and on to the Pacific; the Madison and Gallatin flowing northwest and the Yellowstone northeast to the Missouri and on to the Gulf of Mexico; and the Green River flowing south to the Colorado and on to the Gulf of California. But for a band of explorers trying to reach the Columbia and stay clear of Blackfoot Indians at the same time, the key river was the Grosse Corne. It begins at a lake in the Rocky Mountains, flows southeast into a mountainless basin, cuts sharply north through a mountain gap, and then heads north, northwest, and finally northeast, where, 646 miles from its source, it joins the Yellowstone, at the very spot where Lisa constructed Fort Raymond late in 1807. This is the Bighorn River, called the Wind River for its first 185 miles.

Colter may not have seen the source of the Gallatin, but he did see the source of the Wind/Bighorn. He did not, however, follow the Bighorn River south from its mouth—not at all. Instead, he ascended the Yellowstone River toward the present site of Billings, Montana; cut southwest into Wyoming's Bighorn Basin; continued largely south all the way to the Wind River Basin; and ascended the Wind River itself to its head at Brooks Lake, meaning that he had seen the source and mouth of the Bighorn but very little in between. Nor did he have names for the river and lake he had discovered. After his return to St. Louis, however, Colter had consulted with William Clark as Clark created his master map of the west. Clark had also talked with and obtained maps from Drouillard in 1808 or 1809; based on their own explorations and their discussions with Indians, the three men had correctly concluded that Brooks Lake—called Lake Biddle by Clark—was the source of the Bighorn.[19]

As for the pass that was "less difficult to cross than the Allegheny mountains," Togwotee Pass lay just a few miles west of Brooks Lake, offering a passage over the Continental Divide that could indeed accommodate a loaded wagon. Six months after talking to Colter, Hunt had the opportunity to ascend Wind River to its source at Brooks Lake and then cross Togwotee Pass, unaware that this would give him a straight shot to a branch of the Columbia. Instead, he chose Union Pass, southwest of Togwotee Pass, causing him to take a much more roundabout route westward. Hunt soon regretted his decision not to follow Wind River, and though he never said so, he almost certainly regretted not being accompanied by the man who had carefully scouted the area and was in the habit of memorizing crucial details, the man who had been on the verge of dropping everything to go West once more but who had reluctantly taken his leave, standing alone in the rain and watching as the boats faded from view.

On March 21 the incessant rain finally ceased, and Hunt and his men arrived at a French village called Côte sans Dessein. "After we had formed our camp," wrote Bradbury, "the interpreter [Dorion] went into the village, where he had some acquaintance. On his return, he informed us that there was a war party of Indians in the neighborhood, consisting of the Ayauwais [Iowa], Potowatomies, Sioux, and Saukee Nations, amounting to nearly three hundred warriors." Dorion had also learned that the war party "were going against the Osages; but having discovered that there was an Osage boy in the village, they were waiting to catch and scalp him. [Dorion] also informed us, that we might expect to fall in with other war parties crossing the Missouri higher up." The group was alarmed at this "unpleasant news." True, they were "well armed [and] determined to resist any act of aggression," but even with a cannon and much better guns than the Indians likely had, they would be outnumbered more than fifteen-to-one if they met a war party of three hundred.[20]

Dorion gave Marie the bad news: Hunt's party was heading into Osage country, and warriors from her native Iowa nation were about to go to war with the Osage. Not surprisingly, Bradbury said she "appeared to be much afraid of the Osages during our passage up the river." That night and the coming nights, the men slept—or tried to sleep—with their rifles, powder, and ammunition close by and ready. The rain started again and continued for the next three days. "Our bread was now becoming very mouldy, not having been properly baked," noted Bradbury. "Mr. Hunt anxiously waited for a fine day to dry it, together with the rest of the baggage."[21]

The next day, March 25, they met "a boat with sixteen oars" on its way from Fort Osage to St. Louis to pick up fresh supplies. The news from the fort was not good: "The Great Osages had lately killed an American at their village." The weather matched the men's mood—the incessant rain continued. Three days later Bradbury recorded another bad omen: "This evening we had a most tremendous thunder storm; and about nine o'clock, a tree, not more than fifty yards from our camp, was shivered by lightning. Mr. Hunt, Mr. Nuttall, and myself, who were sitting in the tent, sensibly felt the action of the electric fluid." The next morning, Bradbury walked with Hunt and others to a settler's house. "We heard that war had already commenced between the Osages and the confederate nations, and that the former had killed seven of the Ayauways [Iowa]. This determined us to continue our practice of sleeping on our arms, as we had done since the 21st."[22]

But no alarm was sounded the following day, nor the one after that, nor the next, and the partners, hunters, and voyageurs—and the Dorion family—settled into the slow, wearisome, day-to-day life of inching up the river. They watched for Indians but saw none. Bradbury marked the days with details that were interchangeable: a cup of water left "full in the boat, was found to be nearly all solid ice" at dawn; "the carcasses of several drowned buffaloes passed us"; "we had another severe thunder storm"; "the navigation became less difficult." Dorion presumably went out with the hunters, who killed deer and bear. How Marie kept her boys occupied is unknown. Luckily, through careful attention, luck, or both, no serious accident befell either of the boys, even though, as everyone knew, accidents were common. Less than a year earlier, as Clark and his wife and son and others descended the Ohio River on their return to St. Louis, one such accident struck: "A fiew minets after [we] arrived at the Mississippi," he wrote, "rachiel"—apparently the daughter of one of Clark's slaves—"fell between the boats and Drowned."[23]

On April 6 the hunters found a "bee tree" and returned "to the boat for a bucket, and a hatchet to cut it down." Bradbury walked with them back to the tree. "It contained a great number of combs, and about three gallons of honey." Turning philosophical, Bradbury accurately forecast the future, writing that the spread of European bees "has given rise to a belief, both amongst the Indians and the Whites, that bees are their precursors, and that to whatever part they go the white people will follow. I am of the opinion that they are right, as I think it as impossible to stop the progress of the one as of the other."[24]

At 10:00 on the morning of April 8, the group saw Fort Osage, which was six miles away. "We had not been long in sight before we saw the flag was hoisted, and at noon we arrived, when we were saluted with a volley as we passed on to the landing place, where we met Mr. Crooks"—and nine other

Astorians—"who had come down from the river Nauduet to meet us." About three hundred men, women, and children of the Osage Nation had also gathered to greet the party. Hunt, Bradbury, and several others passed through them on their way to meet Lieutenant John Brownson, then commanding the fort in the absence of Captain Eli B. Clemson. Bradbury had a letter of introduction to Dr. Murray, the garrison physician, who gave Bradbury "every information relative to the customs and manners of the Osage nation," as well as an extensive vocabulary of Osage words. "He walked with me down to the boats," wrote Bradbury, "where we found several squaws assembled, as Dr. Murray assured me, for the same purposes as females of a certain class in the maritime towns of Europe crowd round vessels lately arrived from a long voyage, and it must be admitted with the same success."[25]

Early that evening, "an old chief came down, and harangued the Indians assembled about the boats, for the purpose of inviting the warriors of the late expedition to a feast prepared for them in the village." Bradbury was told that a "dance of the scalp" would be performed because the Osage war party had destroyed an Iowa village, killing and scalping two old men and five women and children. "All the rest had fled at their approach; but as rain came on the dance was not performed." The two men walked into the Indian village, which consisted of "about one hundred lodges of an oblong form, the frame of tiember, and the covering mats." One of the chiefs invited them to his lodge and served them "square pieces of cake, in taste resembling gingerbread. "Shortly afterwards some young squaws came in, with whom the doctor (who understood the Osage language) began to joke, and in a few minutes they seemed to have overcome all bashfulness, or even modesty. Some of their expressions, as interpreted by me, were of the most obscene nature," but the chief's wife "did all in her power to promote this kind of conversation," and Dr. Murray said that "similar conduct would have been pursued at any other lodge in the village."[26]

Walking to the lodge of another chief, Bradbury and his host saw the seven scalps, ornamented with raccoons' tails, placed on the roof. A warrior who had distinguished himself in the campaign against the Iowa "came in, and made a speech, frequently pointing to the scalps on the roof, as they were visible through the hole by which the smoke escaped." When the speech concluded, Bradbury and Murray shook hands with everyone present. On their return to the boat they met Marie, who had been so distressed about the Osage Indians as Hunt's party ascended the river. The men shared her concern, and on first meeting Lieutenant Brownson, "it had been debated whether or not it would be prudent to send a file of men to conduct [Marie] from the boat to the fort during our stay." Now, however, Marie had been welcomed into the Osage community. Whether Dorion had acted as an intermediary is not known, but someone had befriended Marie. "She had been invited up to the village by some of the Osages," wrote Bradbury. In a turn of events puzzling to Bradbury and the others of European stock, so conscious of national and ethnic—not to mention class—boundaries, neither Marie nor her new Osage friends were concerned that their two nations were at war and that some of the scalps proudly displayed had been taken from Iowa women. "Of course," noted Bradbury, "according to Indian custom, [Marie] would be as safe with them as in the fort."[27]

On the morning of April 9, before dawn, Bradbury heard a great howling coming from the village and knew that the Osage were lamenting their warriors—and perhaps horses and dogs—slain in one of the battles with the Iowa and their allies. Making himself as inconspicuous as possible, Bradbury tied a black handkerchief around his head, stuck his tomahawk in his belt, and wrapped himself in a blanket. Then he walked into the village. "The doors of the lodges were closed, but in the greater part of them the women were crying and howling in a tone that seemed to indicate excessive grief. On the outside of the village I heard the men, who, Dr. Murray had informed me, always go out of the lodges to lament." Bradbury watched one of the men, who, resting his back against the stump of a tree, "continued for about twenty seconds to cry out in a loud and high tone of voice, when he suddenly lowered to a low muttering, mixed with sobs: in a few seconds he again raised to the former pitch."[28]

That evening, the mourning was replaced with celebration in the dance of the scalp, a ceremony that "consisted in carrying the scalps elevated on sticks through the village, followed by the warriors who had composed the war party, dressed in all their ornaments, and painted as for war." Marie was present with her friends and was "so delighted with the scalp-dance, and other festivities of the Osage village, that she had . . . a strong inclination to remain there." The next morning, however, when the boats departed in the midst of another fierce rainstorm, Marie was onboard one of them. "Our number was now augmented to twenty-six by the addition of Mr. Crooks and his party," wrote Bradbury. "We had not proceeded more than two miles, when our interpreter, Dorion, beat his squaw severely; and on Mr. Hunt inquiring the cause, he told him that she had taken a fancy to remain at the Osages in preference to proceeding with us, and because he had opposed it, she had been sulky every since." Marie's sense of foreboding as she came up the river had thus proved accurate—but the harm she suffered had not come from the Osage or any other Indians but from the man Irving called "her liege lord, . . . perhaps, a little inspired by whiskey, [who] had resorted to the Indian"—and white—"remedy of the cudgel," belaboring "her so soundly, that there is no record of her having shown any refractory symptoms throughout the remainder of the expedition."[29]

About three weeks after Hunt's group left for the Pacific, another expedition was preparing to depart. Just as Bradbury had accompanied Hunt and chroni-

cled his voyage, a lawyer and journalist by the name of Henry Marie Brackenridge did the same for the second party. "It was not known at this time
what had become of Mr. Henry, who had not been heard of for more than a
year," wrote Brackenridge. "It was moreover considered as a duty to carry
relief to their distressed companions, and bring them home. Manuel Lisa was
chosen to undertake this arduous task." There was no doubt, as Brackenridge
noted, that Lisa was "possessed of an ardent mind and of a frame capable of
sustaining every hardship," no doubt that he was the complete "master of the
secret of doing much in a short space of time," but he was also despised by
many. So it was no surprise that Brackenridge added a postscript to his lavish
praise of Lisa, an unintentional touch of humor: "Unfortunately, however,
from what cause I know not, the majority of the members of the company
have not the confidence in Mr. Lisa which he so justly merits; but on this
occasion, he was entrusted with the sole direction of their affairs from necessity, as the most proper person to conduct an expedition which appeared so
little short of desperate."[30]

With some difficulty, a barge of twenty tons was outfitted with a few
thousand dollars' worth of merchandize. "We sat off from the village of St.
Charles, on Tuesday, the 2d of April, 1811, with delightful weather," wrote
Brackenridge. "We are in all, twenty-five men, and completely prepared for
defence. There is, besides, a swivel on the bow of the boat, which, in case of
attack, would make a formidable appearance; we have also two brass blunderbusses in the cabin." Such precautions were absolutely necessary because
of the hostility of the Sioux, "who, of late had committed several murders
and robberies on the whites." To tempt the Indians as little as possible, "the
greater part of the merchandise, which consisted of strouding, blankets, lead,
tobacco, knifes, guns, beads, &c., was concealed in a false cabin, ingeniously
contrived for that purpose." None of this was surprising or unusual, but
Brackenridge then went on to mention something that would make the spring
and summer of 1811 so memorable and so volatile: "Mr. Wilson P. Hunt had
set off with a large party about twenty-three days before us, on his way to the
Columbia, we anxiously hoped to overtake him before he entered the Sioux
nation; for this purpose it was resolved to strain every nerve, as upon it, in a
great measure depended the safety of our voyage."[31]

It had come down to this: Lisa, who had undermined and thwarted first
Crooks and McClellan and then Hunt at every turn, taking every opportunity
to benefit at their expense, now wanted to join with them—for the sake of
numbers and also for the sake of being accompanied by the best Sioux
interpreter in the business—Dorion. Adding irony to irony, Brackenridge
soon learned another "cause of Lisa's anxiety" to catch Hunt: "Lisa was
apprehensive that Hunt would do him some ill office with the Sioux bands;
that in order to secure his own passage through these, he would represent the
circumstances of their own trader being on his way with goods for them."

This was exactly what Lisa had apparently done to Pryor in 1807 and what he was suspected of doing to Crooks and McClellan in 1809. Pryor's misfortune on the river was particularly relevant because Lisa had now switched roles in dramatic fashion: before, Pryor wanted to catch Lisa and combine their forces for added strength—now, Lisa wanted to overtake Hunt for the same purpose, believing that "by this augmentation of Hunt's party, which consisted of eighty men"—a slight exaggeration—"we should be so formidable as to impose respect upon the savages, and compel them to relinquish their designs"; before, Lisa (according to the Mandan woman held as a captive) had told the Arikara that "two boats might be very soon expected," that the crews of those boats "were to remain, for the purposes of trade at [the Arikara] villages"—now, Lisa had used virtually the same language—was he simply quoting himself?—to describe what he feared Hunt would say to the Sioux. What an amazing turn of events. [32]

Brackenridge, however, added another element that made the chain of circumstance that much more fantastic:

> We had on board a Frenchman named Charnoneau, with his wife, an Indian woman of the Snake nation, both of whom had accompanied Lewis and Clark to the Pacific, and were of great service. The woman, a good creature, of a mild and gentle disposition, greatly attached to the whites, whose manners and dress she tries to imitate, but she had become sickly, and longed to revisit her native country; her husband, also, who had spent many years among the Indians, had become weary of civilized life. So true it is, that the attachment to the savage state, or the state of nature, (with which appellation it has commonly been dignified,) is much stronger than to that of civilization, with all its comforts, its refinements, and its security. [33]

Sacagawea and Toussaint Charbonneau, who had come down the river with Pierre Chouteau's armada in the autumn of 1809 (after Sheheke-shote had been safely returned to his village) and had spent a year and a half in St. Louis, were on their way back to Indian territory. This meant that Sacagawea—the first woman known to have journeyed from the Great Plains to the West Coast of America—and her alter ego Marie—about to become the second—had both been caught up in the Great Race up the Missouri. Not only was Lisa chasing Hunt, the young Shoshone woman was chasing the young Iowa woman, though neither knew it and neither would have cared. Their paths, which had crisscrossed in the past, had finally converged (with one key difference: Sacagawea did not have her son, Baptiste, with her—William Clark was providing for his welfare and his education—while Marie was traveling with both of her boys). If the two iconic women had not met at Fort Mandan or in St. Louis, they would yet have another opportunity, for Lisa would soon start gaining ground on Hunt. [34]

By the end of February, 1811, *Tonquin* had reached the Sandwich Islands, where twelve Hawaiians had signed on as crew of the ship and another twelve had signed to labor at the trading post to be built at the mouth of the Columbia. They had agreed "to work for the company for three years and to be paid in goods valued at one hundred silver dollars at the end of their term." *Tonquin* also had "full water casks and a storeroom bulging with yams, taro, and assorted vegetables. The ship's deck resembled a farmyard with one hundred squealing pigs, several goats, poultry, and two sheep." On the first of March, the ship sailed for the coast of North America. When the crew neared that coast three weeks later, the ship's log noted that they had traveled 21,852 miles. But any sense of joy was lost in the deep resentment that virtually every Astorian nursed toward the captain. They agreed with Alexander Ross: "Captain Thorn was an able and expert seaman; but, unfortunately, his treatment of the people under his command was strongly tinctured with cruelty and despotism. He delighted in ruling with a rod of iron; his officers were treated with harshness, his sailors with cruelty, and every one else was regarded by him with contempt."[35]

There was no better example of Thorn's cruelty toward his crew than what he did when *Tonquin* approached the mouth of the Columbia. After leaving the Sandwich Islands, the voyage had been relatively uneventful until March 16, when, according to Gabriel Franchere, "the wind shifted all of a sudden to the S.S.W., and blew with such violence, that we were forced to strike top-gallant masts and top-sails, and run before the gale with a double reef in our foresail. The rolling of the vessel was greater than in all the gales we had experienced previously." Ross wrote that "during this storm, almost everything on deck was carried off or dashed to pieces; all our livestock were either killed or washed overboard; and so bad was the weather, first with rain, and then with sleet, hail, frost, and snow which froze on the rigging as it fell, that there was no bending either ropes or sails, and the poor sailors were harassed to death." In a rare show of caution, Thorn decided to "lay to for two nights successively. At last, on the 22d, in the morning, we saw land. . . . The breakers formed by the bar at the entrance of that river, and which we could distinguish from the ship, left us no room to doubt that we had arrived at last at the end of our journey."[36]

Although the sight of land "filled every heart with gladness," the weather was "cloudy and stormy," the "aspect of the coast . . . wild and dangerous." The wind blew "in heavy squalls, and the sea ran very high," but that did not deter Thorn, who had apparently reached the end of his patience. As soon as he was convinced that they had reached the mouth of the Columbia, he ordered Mr. Fox, the first mate, to "go and examine the channel on the bar." Ross wrote that Thorn assigned "one sailor, a very old Frenchman, and three Canadian lads, unacquainted with sea service—two of them being carters [wagon drivers] from La Chine, and the other a Montreal barber." Franchere, however, identified only four men who accompanied Fox: Basile Lapensée and his brother Ignace Lapensée—presumably the two young carters—Joseph Nadeau, and John Martin, the old man. "Mr. Fox objected to such hands; but the captain refused to change them, adding that he had none else to spare." Fox argued that it was impossible to perform the task, "in such weather, and on such a rough sea, even with the best seamen, adding, that the waves were too high for any boat to live in."[37]

"Mr. Fox," bellowed the captain, "if you are afraid of water, you should have remained at Boston." Fox said no more, simply ordered the boat lowered. But, "if the crew was bad, the boat was still worse—being scarcely seaworthy, and very small. While this was going on, the partners who were all partial to Mr. Fox, began to sympathize with him, and to intercede with the captain to defer examining the bar till a favourable change took place in the weather." Thorn's response? "He was deaf to entreaties, stamped, and swore that a combination was formed to frustrate all his designs. The partners' interference, therefore, only riveted him the more in his determination," and he again ordered Fox to proceed. Ross added that "Mr. Fox was . . . a great favourite among all classes on board; and this circumstance, I fear, proved his ruin, for his uniform kindness and affability to the passengers had from the commencement of the voyage drawn down upon his head the ill-will of the captain." Proof of Thorn's ill will was plainly evident in Fox's "being sent off on the present perilous and forlorn undertaking, with such awkward and inexperienced hands, whose language he did not understand."[38] (Fox apparently did not speak French, the native language of those accompanying him.)

Seeing that the captain was immovable, "turned to the partners with tears in his eyes and said—'My uncle was drowned here not many years ago, and now I am going to lay my bones down with his.' He then shook hands with all around him, and bade them adieu. Stepping into the boat—'Farewell, my friends!' said he; 'we will perhaps meet again in the next world.'"[39]

Although he was convinced he was doomed, Fox had taken "some provisions and firearms, with orders to sound the channel and report themselves on board as soon as possible. The boat was not even supplied with a good sail, or a mast." The partners could do nothing but watch, although one of them offered what he could—"a pair of bed sheets to serve" as a sail, knowing full well, of course, that even a good sail would have meant little.[40]

Ross offered a fitting benediction to the sad scene:

> The moment the boat pushed off, all hands crowded in silence to take a last farewell of her. The weather was boisterous, and the sea rough, so that we often lost sight of the boat before she got 100 yards from the ship; nor had she gone that far before she became utterly unmanageable , sometimes broaching broadside to the foaming surges, and at other times almost whirling round like

a top, then tossing on the crest of a huge wave would sink again for a time and disappear altogether. At last she hoisted the flag; the meaning could not be mistaken; we knew it was a signal of distress. At this instant all the people crowded round the captain, and implored him to try and save the boat; in an angry tone he ordered about ship, and we saw the ill-fated boat no more. [41]

Chapter Seven

"Families, Plantations, and All Vanished"

"We began to notice more particularly the great number of drowned buffaloes that were floating on the river," John Bradbury wrote on April 16, 1811. "Vast numbers of them were also thrown ashore, and upon the rafts, on the points of the islands. The carcases had attracted an immense number of turkey buzzards, (*vultur aura*) and as the preceding night had been rainy, multitudes of them were sitting on the trees, with their backs toward the sun."[1]

The next day, April 17, Wilson Price Hunt's group "arrived at the wintering houses, near the Naduet River, and joined the rest of the party." Neither Bradbury nor Washington Irving said anything about how the men had spent the winter, but Henry Marie Brackenridge offered an opinion when he saw the wooded bluffs and the "log huts" below them a few weeks later: "This is four hundred and fifty miles from the mouth of the Missouri. Here these men must have led the most solitary lives, with no companions but a few hunters and an occasional Indian visitor. Their chief amusement consisted in hunting deer, or traversing the plains."[2]

John Reed's account book revealed one other chief amusement: tobacco. The men bought buffalo robes when the weather turned cold, and as winter wore on they bought everything from shoes, moccasins, needles and thread, deer skins, knives, blankets, and calico, to brass rings, tomahawks, awl blades, kettles, leggings, balls and powder, and hooks and fishing line; but the one constant was tobacco, the most common item mentioned in the log. Second on the list? Tobacco pipes, which went for twenty-five cents apiece. The men frequently bought four at a time.[3] Many a long winter evening was passed around the fire, as the lonely Astorians talked and reminisced, the air thick with the pleasant aroma of tobacco.

Hunt, Donald McKenzie, Ramsay Crooks, Robert McClellan, Joseph Miller, John Day, Reed, and Pierre Dorion—each of whom was about to leave his indelible mark as one of the "overland Astorians" (a group that would eventually include eighty-six men, one woman, and three children)— were about to travel together for the first time.[4] The experiences of these eight strong—sometimes headstrong—personalities over the next few years would run the gamut, from hopelessness and near starvation to conquests over seemingly immovable obstacles to violent death, and yet little was said by them or by others about their inter-relationships. The affection or scorn they felt for each other remains largely a mystery, although a story of profound friendship and loyalty between two of these men does emerge. What is surprising is that the longtime partners Crooks and McClellan are not the protagonists of that story—their relationship is as inscrutable now as it was two hundred years ago. True, they worked together for more than five years, but neither they nor any of their fellow traders left anything in the historical record to indicate whether they felt mutual admiration for each other (as in the case of Lewis and Clark) or mutual contempt (as in the case of Lewis and Frederick Bates). What we do know is that on their long and difficult trek to the coast and back, they gave no sign of being fast friends and made no apparent effort to stay together through thick and thin. The moving tale of comradeship among the overland Astorians involves not Crooks and McClellan but Crooks and Day.

For three days, Hunt and five dozen men packed food and supplies—and the company store; checked arms and ammunition; inspected boats, oars, masts, and sails; and divided into groups. Nature, too, was on the move, as (now extinct) passenger pigeons "were filling the woods in vast migratory flocks." Irving, who had apparently seen the magnificent birds during his trip to Missouri in 1832, wrote: "It is almost incredible to describe the prodigious flights of these birds in the western wilderness. They appear absolutely in clouds, and move with astonishing velocity, their wings making a whistling sound as they fly. The rapid evolutions of these flocks, wheeling and shifting suddenly as if with one mind and one impulse . . . are singularly pleasing."[5]

On April 21, wrote Bradbury, "we again embarked in four boats. Our party amounted to nearly sixty persons: forty were Canadian boatmen, such as are employed by the North West Company, and are termed in Canada *engagés* or *voyageurs*. Our boats were all furnished with masts and sails, and as the wind blew pretty strong from the south-east, we availed ourselves of it during the greater part of the day." The winds continued favorable, and they made impressive progress the next three days. Two days after that, however, the wind changed directions, "and blew so strong that [they] were obliged to stop during the whole day." That night was quite cold, and the next morning, before they "had been long on the river, the sides of the boats and the oars were covered with ice."[6] That was life on the river.

On April 28, the group "breakfasted on one of the islands formed by La Platte Riviere, the largest river that falls into the Missouri. It empties itself into three channels, except in the time of its annual flood, when the intervening land is overflowed; it is then about a mile in breadth." Brackenridge added that the Platte River was "regarded by the navigators of the Missouri as a point of as much importance, as the equinoctial line amongst mariners," or as Irving explained, "The mouth of this river is established as the dividing point between the upper and lower Missouri." To commemorate this crucial passage, the voyageurs had instituted an initiation ritual. "All those who had not passed it before," continued Brackenridge, "were required to be shaved, unless they could compromise the matter by a treat. Much merriment was indulged on the occasion."[7]

Almost four years had passed since John Hoback, Jacob Reznor, and Edward Robinson had come up the river with Manuel Lisa and had crossed to the upper Missouri for the first time, celebrating with "like ceremonials of a rough and waggish nature."[8] Most of the crew had been shaved that day because only the Lewis and Clark veterans and a few others had already traveled beyond the mouth of the Platte. Nor had Hoback and his two friends returned to the Platte to initiate novice sailors—they had not even been close but had spent their days in present North Dakota and Montana before disappearing with Andrew Henry across the Continental Divide into the Columbia River country.

Though they could not have known, the trio was now the object of a search-and-rescue mission to be undertaken by these newly shaved trappers and boatmen. What was never clear, however, was what Lisa intended to do if he reached the Mandan and Hidatsa villages—or Fort Raymond—and found no trace of Henry. Did he intend to ascend the Bighorn River, or the Gallatin, or the Madison, in an attempt to find Henry, or did he have something else in mind?

Lisa never had to answer those questions. Less than two weeks after the party reached the Platte, wrote Brackenridge, "[W]e found a Mr. Benit, the Missouri Company's factor at the Mandan village. He was descending in a small batteaux, loaded with peltry, with five men. . . . He . . . informed us that Mr. Henry is at this time over the mountains, in a distressed situation, that he had sent word of his intention to return to the Mandan village in the spring, with his whole party."[9] How Benit received this "word" from Henry is not clear, but his report was taken seriously, and Henry's "whole party," including Hoback, Reznor, and Robinson, was presumed to be on its way to Fort Mandan. The reality turned out to be something quite different.

Not surprisingly, Bradbury and Crooks struck up a friendship. On May 1, Crooks said he planned to leave the next morning on foot, "for the Ottoes, a nation of Indians on the Platte River, who owed him some beaver. From the

Ottoes he purposed traveling to the Maha [Omaha] nation, about two hundred miles above us on the Missouri, where he should again meet the boats." When Bradbury offered to come along, Crooks was delighted, and they "proceeded to cast bullets and make other arrangements for [their] journey. The next morning, however, as they were preparing to depart, a disturbance in the camp caught their attention. "Amongst our hunters were two brothers of the name of Harrington, one of whom, Samuel Harrington, had been hunting on the Missouri for two years, and had joined the party in the autumn: the other, William Harrington, had engaged at St. Louis, in the following March, and accompanied us from thence." William now informed Hunt that he had enlisted "at the command of his mother, for the purpose of bringing back his brother, and they both declared their intention of abandoning the party immediately." This was particularly disturbing news because the Osage Indians had warned Hunt that the Sioux intended to oppose his progress up the river. The Canadians were superb boatmen but hardly fighters, making the loss of two expert riflemen simply unacceptable. "Mr. Hunt, although a gentleman of the mildest disposition, was extremely exasperated," wrote Bradbury, "and when it was found that all arguments and entreaties were unavailing, they were left, as it was then imagined, without a single bullet or a load of powder, four hundred miles at least from any white man's house, and six hundred and fifty miles from the mouth of the [Missouri] river."[10]

Both Bradbury and Irving drop the narrative at this point, without saying how the Herrington brothers intended to get back to St. Louis or how they hoped to survive without ammunition. Nor is there any picture of the parting. If Samuel and William were "left" in the literal sense, does that mean they stood on the shore and watched as the boats pulled away? Did they show any signs of shame for having deserted their brothers in arms? Or did they simply start walking downstream through the driftwood, grass, and willows lining the shore while the others made ready to leave?

However things unfolded, Hunt was understandably angry, but he was also, as Bradbury said, a gentleman of mild disposition. He was a man of compassion as well and had shown that at Mackinac, when Baptiste Perrault found himself so worried about his family, deeply regretting the three-year commitment he had made. Hunt released him and helped him find work closer to home, but Perrault had not attempted to deceive anyone and had not placed other men in peril by deserting. Hunt's leaving the Herringtons without powder or ammunition was severe but still a world away from Lisa's ordering a deserter shot, something Hunt knew about because he was living and conducting business in St. Louis when George Drouillard and Lisa escaped convictions and prison sentences for Bissonnet's killing. A lesser man might have threatened to shoot the Herringtons but not Hunt.

Three days later, Brackenridge made this note: "In the evening hailed two men descending in a bark canoe; they had been of Hunt's party, and had left him on the 2d of May, two days above the Platte, at Boyer's river." How the Herringtons obtained their canoe is unknown; nor did Bradbury mention if this information was passed on to anyone in Hunt's party, but later records indicate that the brothers safely returned to their mother, whose bold actions may have saved her the fate of the dear mother of the two or three Lapensée brothers.[11]

With the matter resolved—at least from the Herringtons' point of view—Crooks and Bradbury and two Canadians, Gardapie and La Liberte, set out on foot for the Otto village. Over the next nine days—from May 2 to May 11—they wandered one stretch of "vast plain" after another; forded a series of streams; met an American trader named Rogers and temporarily escorted his Omaha wife and child (when it became evident that Crooks spoke the Omaha language); built a raft (after discovering that neither Gardapie or La Liberte could swim) to cross the eight-hundred-yard Platte River; heard rumors of an Indian war party; explored an empty Otto village; found—and lost—a horse belonging to Crooks; endured a night of incessant "thunder, lightning, and rain," the likes of which Bradbury had "seldom witnessed"; visited the grave of a famous Omaha chief named Blackbird; and dined on everything from jerked buffalo and buffalo veal to prairie hens and stalks of plants.[12]

A few days later, Crooks and Bradbury learned that the Otto and Sioux were at war. "It therefore appeared that Mr. Crooks and myself had run a greater risk than we were sensible of at the time," said Bradbury.[13] But even considering that risk and the real but relatively mild discomforts of hunger and wet and cold experienced by the four men as they hiked the Great Plains, they came through it all with their bodies and spirits unharmed, still eager for more adventure. In six months, Crooks, Gardapie, and La Liberte (Bradbury was spared) would endure a trek of genuine hunger and pain, a trek through an alien landscape that sapped them of any notions of adventure and nearly of their lives. The days of roaming the Otto and Omaha country in spring weather would be pleasant but unrecoverable memory.

Hunt and the others with the boats, by contrast, had glimpsed a hint of what was to come. On the night of May 7, wrote Washington Irving, with the men encamped on the shore, "there was a wild and fearful yell, and eleven Sioux warriors, stark naked, with tomahawks in their hands, rushed into the camp. They were instantly surrounded and seized, whereupon their leader called out to his followers to desist from any violence, and pretended to be perfectly pacific in his intentions." Luckily, Dorion was present to interpret, and he advised Hunt that this was a war party that "had been disappointed or defeated in the foray, and in their rage and mortification these eleven warriors had 'devoted their clothes to the medicine,' . . . a desperate act of Indian braves when foiled in war, and in dread of scoffs and sneers." The intent was to "devote themselves to the Great Spirit, and attempt some reckless exploit with which to cover their disgrace."[14]

Learning this, the majority of Hunt's party was for shooting the Sioux "on the spot. Mr. Hunt, however, exerted his usual moderation and humanity, and ordered that they should be conveyed across the river in one of the boats, threatening them, however, with certain death, if again caught in any hostile act." As James Ronda has observed, "It was a wise decision, since killing even a few warriors would have insured violence later."[15]

Hiring Dorion had also been a wise decision. Not only had he assisted Hunt in avoiding violence, he would be counted on in the coming days because three of Dorion's Yankton friends soon arrived at the Omaha village and informed him that "several nations of the Sioux"—particularly the Lakota—"were assembling higher up the river, with an intention to oppose our progress." Vigilance was required, but Hunt had the assurance of knowing that, unlike Lewis and Clark, he would not find himself in a near crisis and conclude "our interpreter do not Speak the language well."[16]

The five days that Hunt and his men spent with the Omaha were pleasant and productive. James Aird, Crooks's former supervisor and the man who, wrote William Clark, "received both Capt. Lewis and my Self with every mark of friendship" on September 3, 1806 (three weeks before Lewis and Clark met Crooks), was present and announced he was leaving for St. Louis in a few days. "I therefore availed myself of this opportunity to forward letters," wrote Bradbury, "and was employed in writing until the 12th [of May] at noon." Hunt also made the most of the opportunity and wrote a letter to Astor, likely giving a detailed description of the trip up the Missouri. The letter is no longer extant, but Washington Irving, who apparently saw it when he visited Astor in the mid-1830s, wrote: "In his correspondence with Mr. Astor, from this point of his journey, Mr. Hunt gives a sad account of the Indian tribes bordering on the river. They were in continual war with each other," their wars involving not only the "sackings, burnings, and massacres of towns and villages, but of individual acts of treachery, murder, and cold-blooded cruelty." No one was safe, not "the lonely hunter, the wandering wayfarer," or "the squaw cutting wood or gathering corn"—anyone was "liable to be surprised and slaughtered. In this way tribes were either swept away at once, or gradually thinned out, and savage life was surrounded with constant horrors and alarms."[17]

Bradbury's encounters with the Omaha were leaving him in a much lighter frame of mind. He was searching for interesting plants when an old Indian galloped toward him. "He came up and shook hands with me, and pointing to the plants I had collected, said, '*Bon pour manger*?' to which I replied, '*Ne pas bon*.' He then said, '*Bon pour medicine*?' I replied '*Oui*.' He again shook hands and rode away, leaving me somewhat surprised at being addressed in French by an Indian." But Bradbury was just as surprised when he met two

Indians who had seen him in St. Louis and gave "satisfactory proofs of it," even though he had no memory of them. "The Indians are remarkable for strength of memory in this particular," explained Bradbury. "They will remember a man whom they have only transiently seen, for a great number of years, and perhaps never during their lives forget him."[18]

Passing through the village, Bradbury was stopped by a group of Omaha women, who, he said, "invited me very kindly into their lodges, calling me *wakendaga*, or as it is pronounced, wa-ken-da-ga (physician)." He declined the invitation, saying that he needed to get back to the boats. "They then invited me to stay all night; this also I declined, but suffered them to examine my plants, for all of which they had names."[19]

Many of the men, however, eagerly accepted the hospitality of the Indian women, a fact that could easily be seen by the entries in Reed's account book. In the days prior to the arrival at the Omaha village, normal charges followed one after another—tobacco, pipes, strouding, cotton shirts, powder horns, fire steels, knives, and blankets. After the arrival, however, vermilion jumped to the top of the list and was easily the most purchased commodity for the next few days. Produced by grinding minerals into a pigment, vermilion was a powdered dye highly prized by Indian women, who moistened it and used the mixture to paint their faces. (Men also used vermilion as body paint, and both men and women used it to paint objects.) Vermilion was an essential trade item; virtually every group of traders took a good supply up the river, just as Lewis and Clark had done. It could be traded for virtually anything—including horses, food, buffalo robes, or female companionship.[20]

As James Ronda has said, "Omaha women, like their Arikara and Mandan sisters, used their contact with the traders as a means to enhance their own material status." Such sexual activity among Indian women was hardly looked down on. To the contrary, many Indian men offered their wives or daughters to visiting trappers or explorers, both as a token of good will and also in an effort to partake of the white man's special powers or *medicine*. "To modern eyes, the idea of women being given to others may seem like prostitution, but the Indians in question—male and female—did not view it this way. Women fully understood and accepted their roles and were often as eager to engage in sexual relations as the solders [speaking specifically of Lewis and Clark's men] were." Not only that, but refusing the advances of the Indian women could be seen as an insult. Lewis and Clark increased the tension between them and the Lakota by declining to accept sexual favors.[21]

By May 14, the run on vermilion had ceased, and Reed got back to normal business. "We embarked early [on the morning of May 15]," wrote Bradbury, "and passed Floyd's Bluffs, so named from a person of the name of Floyd (one of Messrs. Lewis and Clarke's party) having been buried there." (Charles Floyd, a twenty-two-year-old sergeant with Lewis and Clark, had died at this spot, near present Sioux City, Iowa, on August 20,

1804, probably of appendicitis). The winds were favorable, and they made good progress the next few days. Then they were "stopped all day by a strong head wind" and also found "that the river was rising rapidly" from the spring thaw: "It rose during this day more than three feet." As the river took them west rather than north, they changed their hunting philosophy: "As we were now arriving at the country of our enemies, the Sioux, it was determined that [our hunters] should in a great measure confine themselves to the islands, in their search for game." Although confined to islands, the hunters still killed three buffalo and two elk on the morning of May 22. "We dined at the commencement of a beautiful prairie," wrote Bradbury. "Afterwards I went to the bluffs, and proceeded along them till evening. On regaining the bank of the river, I walked down to meet the boats, but did not find them until a considerable time after it was dark." The boats had not gone as far as Bradbury expected because "they had stopped early in the afternoon, having met with a canoe, in which were two hunters of the names of Jones and Carson."[22]

Jones and Carson. Twenty days after William and Samuel Herrington had disappeared downstream, leaving Hunt exasperated, their replacements had appeared from upstream, restoring Hunt's optimism. They were experienced hunters, and Bradbury's note that they "had been two years near the head of the Missouri" was good evidence they had worked for the Missouri Fur Company and had been present at Three Forks a year earlier with Pierre Menard and Henry, apparently returning with Menard to Fort Mandan. Some time in the few months after that, they had traveled south into present South Dakota and had spent the winter among the Arikara nation. "These men agreed to join the party," wrote Bradbury, "and were considered as a valuable acquisition; any acquisition of strength being now desirable."[23]

Jones and Carson were a superior acquisition to the Herringtons because both were Missouri Company men, both hunters with experience fighting Indians, and Carson was also a gunsmith. They had seen their share of peril, it is true, but each of them would see plenty more. Both would reach the Pacific, but they would take different paths and arrive at different times. Both would safely return east, but one would go though the United States and one through Canada. One would be attacked and robbed by Indians and would wander the Rockies destitute and starving and would barely survive; the other would become one of four key founders of the Oregon Trail. Jones and Carson would both live relatively long lives, one dying in 1835 and the other a year later, one dying in Missouri and one in Oregon, one from sickness and the other from a shotgun blast.[24]

Any pleasure Hunt took in the enlistment of Jones and Carson was short-lived. Two days later, actually less than two days, on the morning of May 24, two men arrived at Hunt's camp near the Ponca village "with a letter to Mr. Hunt from Mr. Lisa." According to Bradbury, "Mr. Lisa had arrived at the

Mahas some days after we left, and had dispatched this man by land. It appeared he had been apprised of the hostile intentions of the Sioux, and the purport of the letter was to prevail on Mr. Hunt to wait for him, that they might, for mutual safety, travel together on that part of the river which those blood thirsty savages frequent."[25]

The proud Lisa, the man who had ordered Bissonnet shot and had berated him while he was dying, the man who had made certain he reached the Arikara before Nathaniel Pryor and Pierre Chouteau, not caring what happened afterwards, had reduced himself to begging his competitors to wait for him, for "mutual safety" of all things. His exact words are not known—and won't be until someone discovers the letter itself in an old trunk in the old attic of an old house, or somewhere else. Nor can the immediate reactions of Hunt and Crooks and McClellan be reconstructed because Bradbury suddenly and inexplicably dropped the subject. But Irving hinted that it must have been a scene to behold, especially the wrath of McClellan.

Exactly what Hunt had been thinking about Lisa is not clear. Before Lisa's messenger arrived, Bradbury had made no mention of Hunt worrying that Lisa might catch him, indicating that Hunt believed he had left early enough in the season not to be concerned. His stays at Fort Osage and the Omaha village where both rather leisurely. But during this same period, Lisa's men were rowing furiously. "Lisa himself seized the helm, and gave the song, and at the close of every stanza, made the woods ring with his shouts of encouragement. The whole was intermixed, with short and pithy addresses to their fears, their hopes, or their ambition." At every opportunity, Lisa asked Indians who had seen Hunt when he had passed. By April 26, the group knew they were eighteen days behind, meaning they had gained three days (though they thought they had gained five). Brackenridge was aware, however, that "there existed a reciprocal jealousy and distrust" between the two men, knowing that "Hunt might suppose, that if Lisa overtook him, he would use his superior skill in the navigation of the river, to pass by him, and (from the supposition that Hunt was about to compete with him in the Indian trade) induce the Sioux tribes, through whose territory we had to pass . . . , to stop him, and perhaps pillage him." That was, of course, exactly what Hunt feared. "Lisa had strong reasons, on the other hand, to suspect that it was Hunt's intention to prevent us from ascending the river; as well from what has already been mentioned, as from the circumstances of his being accompanied by two traders, Crooks and M'Clelland, who had charged Lisa with being the cause of their detention by the Sioux, two years before; in consequence of which they had experienced considerable losses." Brackenridge nevertheless hoped that the two groups could unite and "present so formidable an appearance, that the Indians would not think of incommoding [them]."[26]

Lisa pushed his men mercilessly; he had gained several more days by May 4. Warming himself near the fire that night, Brackenridge overheard several of the boatmen talking. "'It is impossible for us,' said they, 'to persevere any longer in this unceasing toil, this over-strained exertion, which wears us down. We are not permitted a moment's repose; scarcely is time allowed us to eat, or to smoke our pipes. We can stand it no longer, human nature cannot bear it; our bourgeois has no pity on us.'" Trying to ease their minds, Brackenridge reminded them that they were approaching open country, where they could be carried by the wind. "I exhorted them to cease these complaints, and go to work cheerfully," he wrote, "and with confidence in Lisa, who would carry us through every difficulty. The admonitions had some effect, but were not sufficient to quell entirely the prevailing discontent."[27]

Two weeks later, Lisa's party discovered they were only six or seven days behind Hunt. "Our men feel new animation on this unexpected turn of fortune," said Brackenridge. On May 19 they launched their boats at first sunlight, "with the hope of reaching the Maha village in the course of the day. Here we entertained sanguine hopes of overtaking the party of Hunt, and with these hopes the spirits of our men, almost sinking under extreme labor, were kept up; their rising discontents, the consequences of which I feared almost as much as the enmity of the Indians, were by the same means kept down." Around noon, the Omaha village came in sight. "We anxiously looked towards the place, and endeavoured to descry the party of Hunt; but as we drew near we found, alas! they were not there."[28]

Hunt, they were told, had left four days earlier. As if that weren't bad enough, the Sioux had learned "that a number of traders are ascending the river, in consequence of which, instead of going into the plains as is usual at this season of the year, they are resolved to remain on the river, with a determination to let no boats pass; that they had lately murdered several white traders, and were exceedingly exasperated at the conduct of Crooks and M'Clelland [in 1809]." So, if Crooks and McClellan were correct in concluding that Lisa had been the cause of their troubles with the Sioux, Lisa's treachery had now come full circle to haunt him. Hardly one to express—or even contemplate—such irony, Lisa resolved to leave the Omaha village immediately, breaking etiquette by not even stopping to pay respects to a prominent chief by the name of Big Elk (as all traders were expected to do). Lisa also decided to "despatch a messenger by land, who might overtake [Hunt] at the Poncas village, about two hundred miles further by water and about three days journey by land. For this purpose a half Indian was hired [as a guide], and set off immediately in company with Toussaint Charbonneau. As Lavender has explained, "the Missouri twisted prodigiously. By short-cutting its bends (as Crooks and Bradbury had done after their side jaunt to the Oto village), good walkers could overtake Hunt before he reached Sioux."[29]

Lisa had chosen Sacagawea's husband, Lewis and Clark's interpreter, as his emissary, but Bradbury had no idea who Charbonneau was. Hunt and Charbonneau communicated in French, with Hunt giving his assurances that his group would remain at the Ponca village and wait for Lisa. Charbonneau and his Indian guide immediately obtained a canoe and set off downstream to deliver the good news to Lisa. (Whether Charbonneau and Dorion interacted is not known.) "It was judged expedient to trade with the Indians for some jerked buffalo meat, and more than 1000 lbs. was obtained for as much tobacco as cost two dollars," wrote Bradbury. Hunt wanted the meat to save travel time. Urged on by Crooks and by McClellan—who had "renewed his open threat of shooting [Lisa] the moment he met him on Indian land"— Hunt had lied to Charbonneau, hoping his promise would encourage Lisa to cut back on his hectic pace. He had no intention of waiting for Lisa but wanted to get upriver as fast as possible, preferring an encounter with the Sioux, even with his limited force of riflemen, to any involvement with Lisa, who was liable to sabotage the Astorian enterprise at the first opportunity. At noon the expedition set off in great haste. The real race was now on. [30]

Bad news followed bad news. Early the next morning, wrote Bradbury, it was discovered that "two men who had engaged at the Mahas, and had received equipments to a considerable value, had deserted in the night. As it was known that one of them could not swim, and we had passed a large creek about a league below, our party went in pursuit of them, but without success."[31] Once again, however, two deserters would be replaced through a quirk of circumstance.

The next morning, May 26, Hunt's men were eating breakfast on a beautiful stretch of the Missouri when someone spotted two canoes descending on the opposite side of the river. "In one," wrote Bradbury, "by the help of our glasses [telescopes], we ascertained there were two white men, and in the other only one. A gun was discharged, when they discovered us, and crossed over. We found them to be three men from Kentucky." These three, said Bradbury, "had been several years hunting on and beyond the Rocky Mountains, until they *imagined* they were tired of the hunting life; and having families and good plantations in Kentucky, were returning to them; but on seeing us, families, plantations, and all vanished; they agreed to join, and turned their canoes adrift."[32]

More than four years after leaving St. Louis and one year after leaving Three Forks, Hoback, Reznor, and Robinson had made it back, almost back, that is. From their position in present southeast South Dakota they were close—three weeks or less from St. Louis, where they could board boats bound for their Kentucky homes via the Mississippi and Ohio Rivers. But, as Bradbury said, *all vanished* with the prospect of working for John Jacob

Astor. Nor was their original contract with Lisa the issue. They had fulfilled their three-year agreement by the time Menard had left Three Forks in the spring of 1810 and could have gone home then.

The scene was a virtual reenactment of what had happened four years earlier, when Lisa's group, including Hoback and his two friends, had seen John Colter canoeing his way down the Missouri, two or three weeks from home and family. When offered a contract, Colter had not hesitated, turning his back on home sweet home for the siren song of the Rocky Mountains. Now, the trio of trappers had followed in Colter's footsteps, even though they had been present at Three Forks when Colter had expressed his deep regret at returning west and told of his vow to his Maker.[33]

The pronouncement that all three men had families and plantations in Kentucky, however, was not the whole truth and nothing but the truth. While the sketchy historical record indicates that was true for Hoback and Robinson, Reznor had taken a different path, apparently leaving his family in 1797—the last year his name shows up in the Kentucky records. According to Reznor family tradition, he had gone "off west to the mountains with a party of trappers and hunters and was never heard from again." He left at least three children—Solomon, seven; William, one; and Nancy, age unknown. Early in 1804, his wife, Sarah, remarried, with the marriage record calling her "the widow of Jacob Reizoner." He had apparently been gone long enough to be declared dead, although an official declaration has not been found. Reznor's missing decade remains a mystery—we don't know where he wandered or if he learned that his parents had died, his mother in about 1805 and his father in 1807. He may have settled in present Illinois, for a Jacob Reznor turns up in the Indiana Territory census in 1807.[34] But where he was headed before meeting the Astorians is hazy, like his recent past.

There is little doubt, however, that before being hailed from the shore, Hoback and Robinson had every expectation of seeing their families soon, every hope of walking unannounced down a familiar path and watching as someone in the old house recognized them and came running; savoring the embrace of a wife, feeling young and green again at the prospect of spending a night together for the first time in fifteen hundred days and counting; seeing sons, daughters, or even grandchildren transformed from children to adolescents, or from adolescents to young men and women; and enjoying a pipe stuffed with fresh tobacco in a real house, with a fire in the old hearth, and a faithful dog sitting close by.

All that vanished, perhaps as soon as the scene along the riverbank came into focus. "The sight of a powerful party of traders, trappers, hunters, and voyageurs, well armed and equipped, furnished at all points, in high health and spirits, and banqueting lustily on the green margin of the river," wrote Irving, "was a spectacle equally stimulating to these veteran backwoodsmen with the glorious array of a campaigning army to an old soldier; but, when they learned the grand scope and extent of the enterprise in hand it was irresistible."[35]

The arrival of the three wanderers gave Jones and Carson a chance to renew old friendships, to reflect on the attacks at Three Forks, to ask about the men who had gone south with Henry. One name likely to come up was that of Pelton. Sometime in the last year—although the exact time and location were apparently never recorded—the jovial Yankee had lost his mind and disappeared into the dreary wilderness, gone forever, or so it seemed.

For Hoback, Reznor, and Robinson, there were at least two other familiar faces among the Astorians—Crooks and McClellan, who had both met Lisa's contingent in the spring of 1807. But most of the other men were strangers, French speakers, Canadians, not Kaintucks. And this group took a particular interest in the old man.

"Robinson was sixty-six years of age," wrote Bradbury, "and was one of the first settlers in Kentucky. He had been in several engagements with the Indians there, who really made it to the first settlers, what its name imports, 'The Bloody Ground.' In one of these engagements he was scalped, and has since been obliged to wear a handkerchief on his head to protect the part."[36]

If Robinson offered further details, Bradbury did not record them, but the sexagenarian had been present at the siege of Fort Henry in September of 1777, at the future site of Wheeling, West Virginia. Before attacking the fort itself, three or four hundred Wyandot, Shawnee, and Mingo Indians—armed and encouraged by the British—had gathered in the woods, staging a series of ambushes on small groups of soldiers who ventured from the safety of the garrison. Robinson could have been scalped, or "wounded," in one of these encounters, when the Revolutionary War was two years old and Robinson thirty-two. "Where scalping only is inflicted, it puts the person to excruciating pain, though death does not always ensure," a contemporary of Robinson's had written in 1791. "There are instances of persons of both sexes, now living in America . . . who, after having been scalped, by wearing a plate of silver or tin on the crown of the head, to keep it from cold, enjoy a good state of health, and are seldom afflicted with pain."[37]

In the autumn of 1810, Robinson had found himself at another Fort Henry, this one quite different from the one he had known thirty-three years earlier. The first had been constructed near the Ohio River by four hundred men, bordered by a bluff and a ravine, complete with blockhouses, a palisade of eight-to-ten-foot pickets, cabins, horse corrals, and storehouses. The second was hardly worthy of being called a fort, nothing more than a collection of huts thrown together on a stretch of the Snake River plain overgrown with sagebrush. This time Robinson was on the Pacific side of the Continental Divide, near a river known ever since as Henry's Fork. Leaving the Wyandot and Mingo far behind him, Robinson's most recent scrapes with Indians had involved the Blackfoot, who had killed several of his fellow trappers, and the

Crow, who had stolen many of the group's horses as they crossed the mountains. And although Brackenridge would later write that "Mr. Henry wintered in a delightful country, on a beautiful navigable stream,"[38] that was hardly the whole truth and nothing but the truth.

"The sufferings of Mr. Henry and his party on the Columbia, and in crossing the mountains, have been seldom exceeded," the *Louisiana Gazette* reported. "A great part of his time he subsisted principally on roots, and having lost his clothes, like another Crusoe, dressed himself from head to foot in skins." Thomas Biddle offered a similar report in 1819, writing that Henry's group "wintered in 1810–1811 on the waters of the Columbia. At this position they suffered much for provisions, and were compelled to live for some months entirely upon their horses." He added that the party became "dispirited, and began to separate: some returned into the United States by way of the Missouri, and others made their way south, into the Spanish settlements, by the way of the Rio del Norte."[39]

Hoback, Reznor, and Robinson had been among those returning east by way of the Missouri—actually branches of the Missouri. As far as is known, they had no compasses, sextants, maps, or anything of the sort, and arrived at Hunt's camp without any written record of their trek. Still, they were about to have a dramatic impact on westward expansion.

"As we had now in our party five men who had traversed the Rocky Mountains in various directions," wrote Bradbury, "the best possible route in which to cross them became a subject of anxious enquiry. They all agreed that the route followed by Lewis and Clarke was very far from being the best, and that to the southward, where the head waters of the Platte and Roche Jaune [Yellowstone] rivers rise, they had discovered a route much less difficult." Hunt, who had originally planned to follow the Missouri River across present Montana, as Lewis and Clark had done in 1805, now rejected his second choice, "which had been to ascend the Missouri to the Roche Jaune river, one thousand eight hundred and eighty miles from the mouth, and at that place to commence his journey by land." The more southerly course, noted Irving, would allow Hunt to "pass through a country abounding with game, where he would have a better chance of procuring a constant supply of provisions than by the other route, and would run less risk of molestation from the Blackfeet." Taking the recommended path also meant that Hunt should "abandon the river at the Arickara town, at which he would arrive in the course of a few days. As the Indians at that town possessed horses in abundance, he might purchase a sufficient number of them for his great journey overland, which would commence at that place." After consulting with McKenzie, Crooks, McClellan, and Miller, "Hunt came to the determination to follow the route thus pointed out, to which the hunters [Hoback, Reznor, and Robinson] engaged to pilot him."[40]

None of Lisa's former employees could have been surprised at the bad blood between him and Hunt or that Hunt wanted to keep his distance. For the moment, however, there were other concerns. The weather had turned pleasant and should have been perfect for rowing, but there were so many carcasses of drowned buffalo lining the shore of the twisting river that the stench was overwhelming. The men—and Marie and her boys—endured the best they could, and a favorable wind got them to a straight, clear stretch of water. They made thirty miles on May 30 but the next morning saw something more alarming than dead bison: "We discovered two Indians on a bluff on the north-east side of the river," wrote Bradbury. "They frequently harangued us in a loud tone of voice. After we had breakfasted, Mr. Hunt crossed the river to speak with them, and took with him Dorion, the interpreter."[41]

When Hunt and Dorion returned, they informed the group "that these Indians belonged to the Sioux nations; that three tribes were encamped about a league from us, and had two hundred and eighty lodges." Any doubts about hiring Dorion were instantly dispelled, for the nearby Indians included both Yankton and Lakota Sioux. Dorion had lived among the Yankton, spoke fluent Sioux, and was the best man to negotiate. Even so, the news was not good: "The Indians informed Mr. Hunt that they had been waiting for us eleven days, with a decided intention of opposing our progress, as they would suffer no one to trade with the Ricaras, Mandans, and Minaterees [Hidatsa], being at war with those nations." Since it was normal to estimate two warriors to a lodge, Hunt and his men faced the prospect of facing almost six hundred warriors intent on blocking the way. Not only that, but "it had also been stated by the Indians that they were in daily expectations of being joined two other [Lakota] tribes."[42]

Hunt's group proceeded cautiously upstream, but a large island blocked their view of the opposite shore for almost thirty minutes. "On reaching the upper point we had a view of the bluffs, and saw the Indians pouring down in great numbers, some on horseback, and others on foot. They soon took possession of a point a little above us, and ranged themselves along the bank of the river." Watching the Indians through their telescopes, Hunt and the other partners "could perceive that [the Sioux] were all armed and painted for war. Their arms consisted chiefly of bows and arrows, but a few had short carbines: they were also provided with round shields. We had an ample sufficiency of arms for the whole party, which now consisted of sixty men; and besides our small arms, we had a swivel and two howitzers."[43]

The choice was simple: either fight or retreat down river, effectually abandoning Astor's enterprise. "The former was immediately decided on," and the group landed on the shore opposite the main body of warriors. Every man checked his rifle and ammunition. Next the cannon and the howitzers were filled with powder and fired, making Hunt's intentions clear. "They were then heavily loaded, and with as many bullets as it was supposed they would bear, after which we crossed the river. When we arrived within about one hundred yards of them, the boats were stationed, and all seized their arms." Apparently stunned that their bluff had been called, "the Indians now seemed to be in confusion, and when we rose up to fire, they spread their buffaloe robes before them, and moved them from side to side." At least one of Hunt's men understood what this meant: "Our interpreter called out, and desired us not to fire, as the action indicated, on their part, a wish to avoid an engagement, and to come to a parley."[44]

Hunt instantly agreed and requested that McKenzie, Crooks, McClellan, and Miller—along with the indispensable Dorion—join him in smoking the calumet with the Sioux chiefs. Bradbury accompanied the partners while the men in the boats stood by their arms. "We found the chiefs sitting where they had first placed themselves, as motionless as statues; and without any hesitation or delay, we sat down on the sand in such a manner as to complete circle. When we were all seated, the pipe was brought by an Indian, who seemed to act as priest on this occasion: he stepped within the circle, and lighted the pipe." The pipe was at least six feet long and was elaborately decorated with tufts of horse hair that had been dyed red. The priest lifted it toward the sun, then pointed it in different directions. "He then handed it to the great chief, who smoked a few whiffs, and taking the head of the pipe in his hand, commenced by applying the other end to the lips of Mr. Hunt, and afterwards did the same to every one in the circle. When this ceremony was ended, Mr. Hunt rose, and made a speech in French, which was translated as he proceeded into the Sioux language, by Dorion." Hunt made it clear that his purpose was not to trade with enemies of the Sioux but to go his brothers who "had gone to the great salt lake in the west, whom [he] had not seen for eleven moons." He and his men would rather die than not go to their brothers, and they would kill anyone opposing them. But, Hunt adeptly added, to show his good will to the Sioux, he had brought gifts. "About fifteen carrottes of tobacco, and as many bags of corn, were now brought from the boat, and laid in a heap near the great chief, who then rose and began a speech, which was repeated in French by Dorion." Not only did the chief accept the gift, he advised Hunt to camp on the opposite side of the river to avoid trouble from overzealous Indians. "When the speech was ended, we all rose, shook hands, and returned to the boats."[45]

Over the next few days, Hunt successfully negotiated with two hostile groups of Indians who were enemies of each other. The first was the same group of Sioux guilty of "plundering and otherwise maltreating" Crooks and McClellan the previous two years. The second was a war party, three hundred men strong, of Arikara, Mandan, and Hidatsa warriors intent on attacking the Sioux. On meeting Hunt, however, they decided to accompany him to the Arikara villages in hopes of obtaining more arms and ammunition. On the morning of June 3, one of the chiefs overtook Hunt on horseback and "said that his people were not satisfied to go home without some proof of their having seen the white men." Hunt agreed, and the chief was "much pleased" at receiving a cask of powder, a bag of balls, and three dozen knives. Just as this was happening, an Indian ran up and informed Hunt that a boat was coming up the river. We immediately concluded that it was the boat belonging to Manuel Lisa, and after proceeding five or six miles, we waited for it."[46]

Lisa's boat arrived, and Brackenridge came over to greet Bradbury. "It was with real pleasure I took my friend Bradbury by the hand," noted Brackenridge, adding this cryptic aside: "I had reason to believe our meeting was much more cordial than that of the two commanders." Nor did Bradbury offer any information on what happened between Hunt and Lisa, merely reporting that he took advantage of the increased security to take a walk along the bluffs. "On my return to the boats," he wrote, "I found that some of the leaders of the party were extremely apprehensive of treachery on the part of Mr. Lisa, who being now no longer in fear of the Sioux, they suspected had an intention of quitting us shortly, and of doing us an injury with the Aricaras. Independent of this feeling, it had required all the address of Mr. Hunt to prevent Mr. McClellan or Mr. Crooks from calling him to account for instigating the Sioux to treat them ill the preceding year." Brackenridge hardly described McClellan's attitude as wanting to call Lisa "to account"—instead reporting that McClellan had "pledged his honor" to shoot Lisa on sight "if ever he fell in with [him], in the Indian country" and that it was only through Hunt that McClellen "was induced not to put his threat in execution."[47]

Bloodshed was avoided—for the moment—but Hunt and the other partners were convinced that Lisa, although giving the appearance of being friendly, was determined to sabotage Astor's enterprise and would do so at the first opportunity. Moreover, Lisa had twenty expert oars on his keelboat, and—as shown by the way he had caught Hunt—could get away cleanly upstream if needed. "It was determined," wrote Bradbury, "to watch [Lisa's] conduct narrowly."[48]

An uneasy truce persisted for two days, but on June 5, after he and Brackenridge had been out hunting and exploring, Bradbury wrote that "a circumstance happened that for some time threatened to produce tragical consequences. We learned that, during our absence, Mr. Lisa had invited Dorion, our interpreter, to his boat, where he had given him some whiskey, and took that opportunity of avowing his intention to take him away from Mr. Hunt, in consequence of a debt due by Dorion to the Missouri Fur Company, for whom Lisa was agent." This strategy promptly backfired. As Irving wrote, "The mention of this debt always stirred up the gall of Pierre Dorion, bringing with it the remembrance of the whiskey extortion. A violent

quarrel arose between him and Lisa, and [Dorion] left the boat in high dudgeon," returning to his own camp to tell Hunt what had happened. He had
hardly reached his own tent when Bradbury and Lisa arrived by pure coincidence at the same time, Lisa on the pretext of borrowing a *cordeau*, or
towing line from Hunt. Hearing Lisa, the rabid Dorion "instantly sprang out
of his tent, and struck him. Lisa flew into the most violent rage, crying out,
"*O mon Dieu! ou est mon couteau!*"—"O my God! Where is my knife!"
Then he ran toward his own camp.[49]

Picking up the narrative, Brackenridge related what happened when he set
foot in Lisa's camp: "I found Mr. Lisa furious with rage, buckling on his
knife, and preparing to return: finding that I could not dissuade him, I resolved to accompany him." Lisa's honor had been offended, and he was
primed for a duel, but why he went out to face Dorion with a knife rather
than a pistol is not clear. Predictably, Dorion armed himself with a pair of
pistols, "and took his ground, the party ranging themselves in order to witness the event."[50]

Neither Bradbury nor Brackenridge mentioned whether Marie was watching from the sidelines, but both of them were determined to stop the affair of
honor. Dorion had a pistol in each hand, and Brackenridge stood between
him and Lisa. "As Dorion had disclosed what had passed in Lisa's boat,"
wrote Bradbury, "Messrs. Crooks and M'Clellan were each very eager to
take up the quarrel, but were restrained by Mr. Hunt."[51] Seconds later, however, Lisa cast an insult in Hunt's direction, and the man who had kept a tight
rein on his passions through more than a year of quandaries and frustrations
as the leader of the overland Astorians finally hit his limit. He announced that
the mater would be settled between him and Lisa and told the Spaniard to go
fetch his pistols.

"I followed Lisa to his boat, accompanied by Mr. Brackenridge" said
Bradbury, "and we with difficulty prevented a meeting, which, in the present
temper of the parties, would certainly have been bloody one."[52] Bradbury
and Brackenridge had great powers of persuasion because Lisa was not the
kind of man to back down from a challenge. He stayed in his camp, however,
escaping the wrath of Dorion, Crooks, McClellan, and Hunt like he had that
of Rose, Cheek, James, and any number of others.

"Having obtained, in some measure, the confidence of Mr. Hunt, and the
gentlemen who were with him" wrote Brackenridge, "and Mr. Bradbury that
of Mr. Lisa, we mutually agreed to use all the arts of mediation in our power,
and if possible, prevent any thing serious." The mediation worked, and the
boats proceeded up the river one after another but maintained separate
camps. "Continued under way as usual," Brackenridge wrote two days later.
"All kind of intercourse between the leaders has ceased."[53]

By June 11, however, the Astorians and Missouri Fur Company men were
approaching the Arikara villages and had to communicate with each other.

These were the same Indians who in 1807 had meted out such harsh treatment to Charles Courtin, who had attacked Pryor and Chouteau, killing four
men and wounding several others. "This evening I went to the camp of Mr.
Hunt to make arrangements as to the manner of arriving at the village, and of
receiving the chiefs," wrote Brackenridge. "This is the first time our leaders
have had any intercourse directly or indirectly since the quarrel. Mr Lisa
appeared to be suspected; they supposed it to be his intention to take advantage of his influence with the Arikara nation, and do their party some injury
in revenge. I pledged myself that this should not be the case."[54]

The next day, two Arikara chiefs came onboard Lisa's boat, accompanied
by an interpreter, none other than Joseph Gravelines, who had assisted Lewis
and Clark in 1804 and had attempted to assist Courtin in 1807. "The leaders
of the party of Hunt were still suspicious that Lisa intended to betray them,"
noted Brackenridge. "M'Clelland declared that he would shoot him the moment he discovered any thing like it."[55] But Lisa did nothing to provoke
McClellan or anyone else. When the chiefs finally assembled later in the day
with the traders, a pipe was sent around, and one chief declared he was happy
to see his friends in his village.

Next came one of the most remarkable speeches known to have passed
from Lisa's lips. "Lisa in reply to this, after the usual common-place, observed that he was come to trade amongst them and the Mandans, but that
these persons, (pointing to Hunt and his comrades,) were going on a long
journey to the great Salt lake, to the west, and he hoped would meet with
favourable treatment; and that any injury offered them, he would consider as
done to himself; that although distinct parties, yet as to the safety of either,
they were but one." This said Brackenridge, "at once removed all suspicion
from the minds of the others."[56] Whether that was true or not, the dispute
with Lisa was put to rest, and apparently not even McClellan made any more
threats. On June 18, Lisa agreed to buy Hunt's boats, offering horses from
Fort Mandan as part of the deal. At the same time, Hunt attempted, with
limited success, to purchase horses from the Arikara.

About this same time, Hunt added one more recruit to his roster, a man
well known to Hoback, Reznor, and Robinson—and to Lisa: Edward Rose.
After joining Lisa's 1809 expedition, he had apparently gone with Henry to
Fort Raymond and Three Forks, but had vanished at some point, probably
living among the Indians until reappearing—a pattern typical of his entire
career. As Irving wrote, he had arrived at an opportune time: "The dangers to
be apprehended from the Crow Indians had not been overrated by the camp
gossips." The Crow, "through whose mountain haunts the party would have
to pass, were noted for daring and excursive habits, and great dexterity in
horse stealing. Mr. Hunt, therefore, considered himself fortunate in having
met with a man who might be of great use to him in any intercourse he might
have with the tribe." Rose, of course, had lived among the Crow, becoming a

feared warrior and chief among them (by his own account) and was perfectly at home with their language and culture. And although Irving consistently described "the Five Scalps" (Rose's Crow name) in negative terms, the fur trade historian Hiram Martin Chittenden properly pointed out "that everything definite that is known about him is entirely to his credit."[57]

Rose's purchases from Reed's company store were likely typical of the other men. He bought powder, balls, scalping knives, a coffee kettle, pipes, tobacco, a shirt, and a bridle for the journey; to enjoy female companionship during his stay at the Arikara villages he bought blue beads, a yard of blue flannel and another of green cloth. "Our common boatmen soon became objects of contempt, from their loose habits and ungovernable propensities" wrote Brackenridge. "To these people, it seemed to me that the greater part of their females, during our stay, had become mere articles of traffic; after dusk, the plain behind our tents was crowded with these wretches, and shocking to relate, fathers brought their daughters, husbands their wives, brothers their sisters, to be offered for sale at this market of indecency and shame." The Indian women, it seemed, had been seized by an "inordinate passion . . . for our merchandize," and the "silly boatmen . . . in a short time disposed of almost every article which they possessed, even their blankets, and shirts. One of them actually returned to the camp, one morning entirely naked, having disposed of his last shirt—this might truly be called *la derniere chemisse de l'amour.*"[58]

But Brackenridge also experienced peaceful times among the Arikara. "In the evening, about sundown," he wrote, "the women cease from their labors, and collect in little knots, and amuse themselves with a game something like jack-stones: five pebbles are tossed up in a small basket, with which they endeavor to catch them again as they fall."[59] Whether the Indian women present with Hunt and Lisa—Marie Dorion and Sacagawea—joined in the game is not known. Nor did Bradbury or Brackenridge say a single word about them. Their French Canadian interpreter husbands, however, had much in common and no reason to quarrel, so it is possible that during the peaceful week from June 12 (when Lisa argued for Hunt's safe passage before the Arikara chiefs) to June 19 (when Lisa and no doubt Charbonneau and his family departed for the Mandan villages) Marie and Sacagawea had a chance to meet, even converse through their husbands, for they shared no common language. Playing with Marie's boys would have made Sacagawea lonely for her own son, now six years old and living under William Clark's care in St. Louis, the son she would never see again.

One day before Lisa left, Crooks, Bradbury, and others headed overland for the Mandan villages to collect the horses promised by Lisa. They were guided by Benjamin Jones. They reached Fort Mandan on June 22 and obtained approximately fifty horses. Crooks and his companions began driving the horses south on June 27, taking pains to keep their plans secret (and the horses safe) from local Indians. Bradbury waited several days, then returned by boat with Lisa to the Arikara towns. "I had the pleasure of meeting my former companions," he wrote on July 7, "and was rejoiced to find that Mr. Crooks arrived safely with the horses, and that Mr. Hunt had now obtained nearly eighty in all. Soon after my arrival, Mr. Hunt informed me of his intention to depart from the Aricaras shortly." Ten days later, on July 17, Bradbury, now traveling with Brackenridge, added a benediction to his memorable time with the Astorians: "I took leave of my worthy friends, Messrs. Hunt, Crooks, and M'Kenzie, whose kindness and attention to me had been such to render the parting painful; and I am happy in having this opportunity of testifying my gratitude and respect for them." Waving goodbye, Bradbury boarded one of Lisa's boats, and as the boat swung out into the Missouri, "Mr. Hunt caused the men to draw up in a line, and give three cheers, which we returned; and we soon lost sight of them."[60]

**Ramsay Crooks. Jules Emile Saintin painted this portrait in 1857, two years be-
fore Crooks's death. Courtesy of Wisconsin Historical Society, WHS-2593**

Voyageurs in Camp for the Night, Frederic Remington, 1892. Courtesy of Wisconsin Historical Society, WHS-3776

A Blackfoot Indian on Horseback, Karl Bodmer, ca. 1832. Courtesy of Wisconsin Historical Society, WHS-6732

In a Stiff Current, Frederic Remington, 1892. Courtesy of Wisconsin Historical Society, WHS-6961

Bear River, James F. Wilkins, 1849. Miller, Hoback, Reznor, Robinson, and Cass trapped Bear River in the autumn of 1811. Courtesy of Wisconsin Historical Society, WHS-31554

View of the Canyon, photographer unknown. Hunt's group traveled along this part of the Snake River, downstream from Caldron Linn, early in November, 1811. Courtesy of Wisconsin Historical Society, WHS-68543

Celilo Falls (Columbia River), Benjamin A. Gifford. McClellan, Reed, and others were attacked by Indians—and Crooks and Day robbed—near the falls in the spring of 1812. Celilo Falls was submerged by The Dalles Dam in 1957. Courtesy of the Oregon Historical Society

Astoria as it was in 1813. Courtesy of the Oregon Historical Society

Crow Indians, Karl Bodmer, ca. 1832. Courtesy of Wisconsin Historical Society, WHS-6745

First View of Rocky Mountains, James F. Wilkins, 1849. This was the last view of the Rockies for Stuart's group as they headed east through present Wyoming in late October of 1812. Courtesy of Wisconsin Historical Society, WHS-31293

Sweetwater River, photographer unknown. Stuart's group first saw the Sweetwater on October 28, 1812. Courtesy of Wisconsin Historical Society, WHS-68541

Catholic Church at St. Louis, Marion County, Oregon, ca. 1910. Marie Dorion was buried inside the old church in 1850. That structure burned down in 1880 and was replaced by this one. Courtesy of the Oregon Historical Society

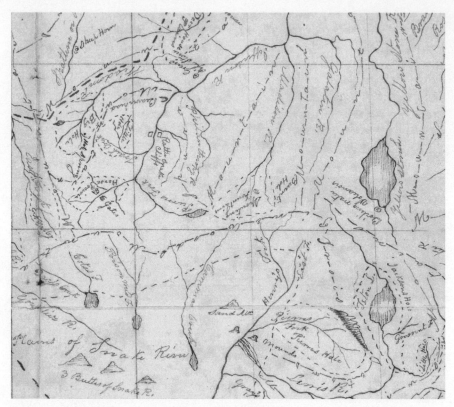

Detail from "Map of the Northwest Fur Country," Warren A. Ferris, 1836. Key sites in this portion of Ferris's masterful map include the convergence of the Gallatin, Madison, and Jefferson Rivers (the three forks of the Missouri River), where Blackfoot Indians attacked Missouri Fur Company men in 1810; and the Teton Range, Lewis River (south fork of the Snake River), and Pierre's Hole, important landmarks for Andrew Henry in 1810, Wilson Price Hunt in 1811, and Robert Stuart in 1812. Courtesy of L. Tom Perry Special Collections, Harold B. Lee Library, Brigham Young University, Provo, Utah

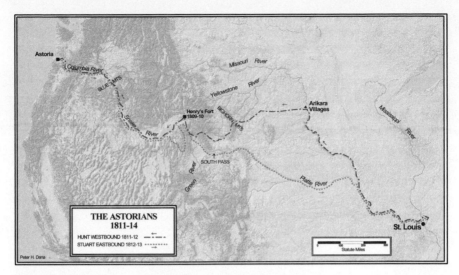

Used by Permission of Peter H. Dana and Robert M. Utley

Chapter Eight

"A Very Sad Recollection"

"On July 18, 1811," wrote Wilson Price Hunt, "Messrs. Hunt, Mackenzie, Crooks, Miller, McClellan, and Reed, who were accompanied by fifty-six men, one woman and two children, and had gone by water from Saint Louis to the Arikaras' village on the Missouri, left there with eighty-two horses laden with merchandise, equipment, food and animal-traps. All traveled on foot except the company's partners and the woman or squaw."[1] Pierre Dorion, who apparently did not hesitate to beat his wife when she talked back, had made sure that she and the boys had a horse. Whether Dorion knew that she was about four months pregnant is unknown.

From the Arikara villages eight or ten miles north of the mouth of the Grand River (north of present Mobridge, South Dakota), Hunt headed southwest, along the Grant River and its tributaries. Over the next week the group made sixty-seven miles, "bearing a little more toward the west in the prairies where grass was knee-deep and the horses could graze to their satisfaction. The country was bare. Only a few cottonwoods grew along the rivers."[2]

Progress halted suddenly because several members of the party were sick, "Mr. Crooks, especially, [who] was so unwell that he could not keep on his horse. A rude kind of litter was, therefore, prepared for him, consisting of two long poles, fixed, one on each side of two horses, with a matting between them, on which he reclined at full length, and was protected from the sun by a canopy of boughs."[3] For Ramsay Crooks, this was a portent of the chronic poor health that would plague him almost continuously over the next twenty-one months, and on and off for the rest of his life.

While hunting, John Day and Benjamin Jones had already discovered an Indian camp nearby. Concluding the Indians were the friendly Cheyenne, they approached the camp and were warmly welcomed. "There I bought thirty-six horses," wrote Hunt, "at a much better price than at the Aricaras'

village. The camp was in the middle of the prairie near a little stream. . . .
These indians are honest and cleanly; they hunt bison; they raise many horses
which every year they exchange at the Aricaras' village for corn, beans,
squashes and merchandise."[4]

Departing again on August 6, the Astorians now had enough horses to
allow every two men to walk and ride alternately and make six horses available to buffalo hunters. "We travelled 42 miles on the 6th and 7th," wrote
Hunt. "Later we somewhat slowed our pace in order that our hunters, who
were behind us, might rejoin us. The country became mountainous and the
water scarce. . . . We made fires on the summit to guide our hunters." The
missing men were Dorion, Alexander Carson, and Baptiste Gardapie, all
veteran hunters, and Hunt was confident they were simply on a prolonged
hunt and would return soon. When he had not seen them by August 10, he
"caused a huge pyre of pine wood to be made, which soon sent up a great
column of flame that might be seen far and wide over the prairies. This fire
blazed all night, and was amply replenished at daybreak; so that the towering
pillar of smoke could not but be descried by the wanderers if within the
distance of a day's journey."[5] Still, there was no sign of the hunters.

"The route now became excessively toilsome, over a ridge of steep rocky
hills, covered with loose stones. These were intersected by deep valleys,
formed by two branches of Big [Grand] River, coming from the south of
west, both of which they crossed. These streams were bordered by meadows,
well stocked with buffaloes."[6] Any pleasure at the plentiful buffalo, however, was offset by concern over the missing men. Hunt and the other partners
began to fear that the trio had been attacked by Indians. What was said to
Marie is not known, but she spoke French and likely asked Hunt about her
husband.

On August 13, "Hunt varied his course, and inclined westward, in hopes
of falling in with the three lost hunters; who, it was now thought, might have
kept to the right hand of Big River. This course soon brought him to a fork of
the Little Missouri, about a hundred yards wide, and resembling the great
river of the same name in the strength of its current, its turbid water, and the
frequency of drift-wood and sunken trees." Hunt had thus left present Hard-
ing County, South Dakota, and crossed into Carter County, Montana. "The
weather was overcast and rainy, and a general gloom pervaded the camp; the
voyageurs sat moping in groups with their shoulders as high as their heads,
croaking their foreboding[s], when suddenly towards evening came slowly
lagging into the camp, with weary looks, and horses jaded and wayworn."
Dorion, Carson, and Gardapie were all unhurt but dead tired. They had rid-
den so far in search of game that their own tracks were soon covered by
tramping buffalo, and they lost their way, the monotonous landscape offering
them no clues of navigation. They did not see any of the smoke signals sent
their way. Finally, on August 11, they had found Hunt's trail, following it

faithfully until they found their friends huddling in the rain. "Those only, who have experienced the warm cordiality that grows up between comrades in wild and adventurous expeditions of the kind can picture to themselves the hearty cheering with which the stragglers were welcomed to the camp," wrote Washington Irving, who enhanced Hunt's spare account through interviews with eyewitnesses. "Every one crowded round them to ask questions, and to hear the story of their mishaps; and even the squaw of the moody half-breed, Pierre Dorion, forgot the sternness of his domestic rule, and the conjugal discipline of the cudgel, in her joy at his safe return."[7]

Mid-August brought extremes in temperature and terrain. "The evening [of August 14] was very cold. At the north were mountains covered with pines. They were crossed on the 15th. The country was extremely rugged; it became more so on the 17th, and a way out of these mountains [apparently the southern foothills of the Powder River Range] could not be found." The men saw bighorn sheep "running and jumping on the edge of the precipices," and Jones got close enough to bring one down. "The flesh is good and much resembles mutton." On August 18 "it was necessary to leave the mountains and return to the broken country." They camped to the left of a mountain range, and Hunt and Donald McKenzie climbed two of the nearest peaks. "Their view extended in all directions. They saw far off in the west mountains which appeared white in several places,"[8] a profound omen of things to come.

The night of August 20 was cold; the men woke to find ice on the nearby stream as thick as a dollar. They followed an Indian trail for two days, into a country of rough hills and broken gullies, the weather suddenly hot and oppressive, with no trace of water. They trekked on for twenty-five miles, finally arriving at a small stream. They quenched their thirst, but McKenzie drank out of duty rather than enthusiasm—the water had come too late to save his faithful dog, which had died of thirst several miles back. How long the dog had been with him is not known; perhaps he had brought it with him from his home in Canada.

Now in present northeastern Wyoming, Hunt met a group of Absaroka (Crow) Indians on August 30. "They were all on horseback," he wrote. "Even the children do not go afoot. These indians are such good horsemen that they climb and descend the mountains and rocks as though they were galloping in a riding school." Hunt gave the Crow warriors tobacco, knives, and a variety of trinkets, reserving a piece of scarlet cloth, some powder and balls, and other gifts for the chief. Hunt was also able to trade some weary horses for fresh ones, and some of the men bought horses for themselves, increasing the total number of horses to 121—"most of them well behaved and capable of crossing the mountains."

Despite the favorable reception from the Crow, something was nagging at Hunt. "We had in our party," he wrote, "a hunter by the name of Rose; he was a very bad fellow full of daring. We had been warned that he had planned to desert us as soon as we should be near the Absarokas, take with him as many of our men as he could seduce, and steal our horses. Wherefore, we kept close watch during the night." Hunt did not say who had warned him, but he was determined to forestall him. Robert McClellan was so agitated that he threatened to shoot Rose the minute a conspiracy unfolded. Nothing unusual happened, but the men continued their surveillance of Rose. On September 2, Hunt's camp was visited by a different band of Crow than those they had traded with a few days earlier. Seeing this as the perfect opportunity to rid himself of Rose, Hunt made an offer that any trapper would have found hard to refuse. "I suggested to Rose," he said, "that he remain with these indians, offering him half of his year's wages, a horse, three beaver-traps and some other things. He accepted these terms and immediately quitted his confederates, who, no longer having a leader, continued the journey."[9]

Rose was gone, but was he? On September 4 he was back, sent by a Crow chief who realized from Rose's description that Hunt had taken the wrong road. Rose directed them to a different trail, "which was shorter and better."[10] Then he was gone again. Hunt did not say if his opinion of the Five Scalps had changed.

"We soon met the Absarokas," added Hunt, "who were going the same way as we; this gave me a chance to admire the activities of these indians on horseback. It was really unbelievable. There was, among others, a child tied to a two-year-old colt. He held the reins in one hand and frequently plied his whip. I inquired his age; they told me that he had seen two winters. He did not talk as yet."[11]

Hunt was soon clear of the Bighorn Mountains and followed a plain to the southwest, reaching the Wind River near present Shoshoni, Wyoming, on September 9. He now began relying on John Hoback, Jacob Reznor, and Edward Robinson, who had traveled this road in reverse about five months earlier. Hunt had presumably tried to follow the path of the three Kentuckians ever since leaving the Arikara villages, but he never stated that explicitly. Indeed, he had not mentioned them at all during the vexing journey through present northeastern and central Wyoming, indicating that any directions they gave turned out to be of little value, if not misleading. Now, however, they recognized one landmark after another, assuring Hunt that ascending the Wind River to its source would allow him to cross to a tributary of the Columbia with relative ease. Taking this route, Hunt would have stayed on the Wind River until reaching present Brooks Lake, then crossed the Continental Divide at Togwotee Pass. "For five succeeding days," wrote Irving, "Mr. Hunt and his party continued up the course of the Wind River, to the distance of about eighty miles, crossing and recrossing it, according to its windings, and the nature of its banks; sometimes passing through valleys, at other times scrambling over rocks and hills. The country in general was destitute of trees, but they passed through groves of wormwood, eight and ten feet in height, which they used occasionally for fuel."[12]

Hunt grew increasingly concerned because of the winding, rugged trail and the scarcity of game. He soon decided to abandon the Wind River near present Dubois, Wyoming, and the group cut to the southwest and followed an Indian trail over the Continental Divide at Union Pass. "One of our hunters," wrote Hunt, "who had been on the shores of the Columbia, showed us three immensely high and snow-covered peaks which, he said, were situated on the banks of a tributary of that river." As the men gazed at the magnificent mountains on the western horizon for the first time, Hunt named them the Pilot Knobs, but they would later be called *les Troi Tetons*, the three teats or breasts.[13] Whether it was Hoback, Reznor, or Robinson who pointed them out, Hunt did not say, but the entire group was pleased to be this close to a branch of the Columbia River, which they expected to take them in short order to their "brothers in the west." What they could not realize was that the scenic river on the banks of the three peaks, not visible from their present position, was not navigable and in short order would nearly prove their doom.

"On the 16th," wrote Hunt, "snow was frequently encountered. . . . Halt was made beside Spanish River, a large stream on the banks of which, according to indian report, the Spaniards live. It flows toward the west and empties supposedly into the Gulf California. We were surrounded by mountains in which were disclosed beautiful green valleys where numerous herds of bison graze."[14] The group had reached the Green River, and the Indian report was amazingly accurate. There were no doubt Spaniards living along this river (although much farther away than the Indians suspected), and it did indeed flow into the Gulf of California—after merging with the Colorado River. It flowed west only briefly, however, then headed south.

Two days later, Hunt, McKenzie, and McClellan saw a few Indians hunting buffalo. The Indians immediately took flight, but the three partners finally caught up with two of them whose horses were not as fast as the others. "They seemed at first very disquieted," reported Hunt, "but we soon reassured them. They led us to their camp. It was a band of Snake (Shoshone) who had come into the neighborhood to dry meat; they had a large quantity of it which was very fat." Many of the Indians had never seen whites and gave the men a hearty welcome. Hunt was able to buy nearly two thousand pieces of dried bison meat, which he added to the four thousand pieces prepared by his own men. He wrote that the total "will load all our horses except six."[15]

Hunt had every reason to be optimistic—he had a good supply of jerked buffalo meat and a large, healthy herd of horses, and the Columbia River, which he assumed would quickly take him to the Pacific coast, was just over a nearby pass. But he was also seeing constant reminders of the late season. "Having . . . climbed a small mountain," he wrote, "we arrived by a good road at a tributary of the Columbia"—. "We had snow on all the heights to each side of us and in front of us." They frequently forded the Hoback on September 25 and 26. "Its rapidity is so great that nobody could walk there without assistance. Our road has been very winding amidst small mountains and on the edge of the precipices which surround us. One of our horses fell from a height of nearly two hundred feet, but was uninjured."

Hunt seldom mentioned Marie, likely because she persevered much like the men, even while caring for her boys. As Irving had commented, "nor did any of the men show more patience and fortitude than this resolute woman in enduring fatigue and hardship."[16]

The party emerged from the mountains on September 27, where the Hoback flows into a larger and a south- and swift-running river, one that Andrew Henry's men had named "Mad River"—the south fork of the Snake. They were now south of present Jackson, Wyoming, at Hoback Junction, and Hunt acknowledged that they could have saved time by continuing up the Wind River and then crossing over to this point, apparently the route east taken by Hoback, Reznor, and Robinson, but a lack of provisions had forced them to detour to the Green River.

"On the banks of Mad River," wrote Irving, "Mr. Hunt held a consultation with the other partners as to their future movements. The wild and impetuous current of the river rendered him doubtful whether it might not abound with impediments lower down, sufficient to render the navigation of it slow and perilous, if not impracticable. The hunters who had acted as guides, knew nothing of the character of the river below." The question was whether they should abandon their horses and hope to navigate the river, casting "themselves loose in fragile barks upon this wild, doubtful, and unknown river; or should they continue their more toilsome and tedious, but perhaps more certain wayfaring by land?"[17]

The men were consulted, and no one was surprised that they voted almost unanimously to proceed by water. After all, the great majority were boatmen, adept with currents and oars, virtually born in the water, but disoriented, ill at ease, and footsore when hiking over mountain passes. They were promptly "set to work to fell trees, and the mountains echoed to the unwonted sound of their axes." At the same time, Hunt sent John Reed, Day, and Dorion downstream, "with orders to proceed several days' march along the stream, and notice its course and character."

Hunt had one other thing in mind: the entire Columbia River system was considered Astor's domain, and there were frequent signs of beaver in these parts. "Here, then, it was proper to begin to cast loose those leashes of hardy trappers that are detached from trading parties in the very heart of the wilderness. The men detached in the present instance were Carson, Louis St. Michel, Pierre Detayé, and Pierre Delaunay," with Carson and St. Michel forming one team and Detayé and Delaunay another. "They were fitted out with traps, arms, ammunition, horses, and every other requisite, and were to trap upon the upper part of Mad River, and upon the neighboring streams of the mountains."[18] Then they left with high hopes, bidding farewell to their friends, who would never see one of them again.

The four men had hardly left when two Shoshone Indians appeared. When they saw several men building canoes they shook their heads, giving every indication that any attempt to navigate the river would be a lost cause. Determined to embark, the boatmen scoffed and kept on working. When Reed, Day, and Dorion returned on October 2, however, they confirmed the Indians' warning. "At the end of two days' march [Reed] had been obliged to quit his horses, which were of no help to him in climbing the mountains and rocks. After an hour's effort to proceed afoot along the river, he had been forced to relinquish his undertaking. An attempt to get through by means of travel across the highlands would have been an endless task."[19]

For Hunt, the only reasonable decision was to ford Mad River, scale the mountains on the other side, and make their way to the post established by Henry a year earlier. Hoback, Reznor, and Robinson assured him it was not far away, close to a branch of the Columbia. The partners concurred in this decision, except Joseph Miller, that is, who wanted to embark by canoe regardless of the risk. He was afflicted with a physical ailment of some kind that made riding a horse quite painful and was also in a morose state of mind, upset that he had received half as many shares as the other partners (except McClellan, that is). He could not be reasoned with, and Hunt and the other partners simply had to overrule him.[20]

Presumably communicating with Dorion via sign language, the two Shoshone Indians made it clear that they knew the site of Henry's Fort and the surrounding area perfectly well and volunteered to act as guides. Hunt accepted—to Miller's disgust— likely concluding that the Indians would know the way better than Hoback and his companions. "All day long on the 3rd," wrote Hunt, "rain and sleet fell. Everything was in readiness for crossing the mountain which was regarded as the last." The notion that the Teton Range presented the last obstacle between them and the Pacific seems to have been widely held among the men, along with the assumption that the river near Henry's Fort "would be easy to navigate in canoes."[21] These were curious conclusions, apparently based more on wishful thinking than anything else. The interviews of Hunt, Crooks, and McClellan with Lewis and Clark were no help at all because the captains had traveled far to the north and any information they offered on the rivers and mountains of western Montana and northern Idaho may well have been descriptions of Africa. Nor could Hoback, Reznor, and Robinson point the way, making it plain from the start that they had not ventured west of Henry's Fort. They had no idea how far the fort was from the coast or whether the river was navigable. The Astorians thus found themselves in the midst of an untracked wilderness, with a Rocky Mountain winter coming on fast. They were undeniably on the verge of a potential or even probable disaster, but if anyone uttered that thought, Hunt did not record it.

"We crossed Mad River," he continued, "—the water being up to the horses' bellies—and camped at the foot of the mountains." They passed the cold night a few miles south of present Wilson, Wyoming. "On the 5th, the mountain was crossed by an easy and well-beaten trail; snow whitened the summit and the northerly slope of the heights." They had crossed Mosquito Pass into present Idaho, stopping near a stream in a picturesque valley later known as Pierre's Hole, where the likes of Jedediah Smith, Kit Carson, Jim Bridger, and many others would wander—and gather for rendezvous in coming years.[22]

The group followed the Teton River north and then west as it rapidly took in one stream or river after another. "Numerous bands of antelope were seen. Wild cherries were common, they are the size of ordinary red cherries: they were not yet ripe. A dozen miles northwest of our camp is a hot spring. I went there with Mr. Mackenzie. It is not erupting, but constantly emits steam." Whether the two took the opportunity to soak in a hot pool—a popular activity among both Indians and trappers—Hunt did not say.[23]

"It was very cold all day on the 8th," wrote Hunt; "the wind from the west blew with force, a little snow fell. We arrived at the fort of Mr. Andrew Henry. It consists of several small buildings which he had erected so as to spend last winter there on a tributary [Henry's Fork of the Snake River] of the Columbia, 300 to 400 feet wide. We hoped that we could navigate it. We found some trees suitable for making canoes. On the 9th, we had already begun eight, all of cottonwood."[24]

Hunt likely did not realize that his situation was remarkably similar to that of Lewis and Clark. During the first part of October of 1805, in present northern Idaho, after experiencing harsh weather and difficult marches through the Rocky Mountains, Lewis and Clark had built canoes to ascend a tributary of the Snake River, the Clearwater, not knowing what lay before them. Now, six years and a few days later and in southern Idaho, after enduring snow in the Rockies, Hunt and his men had built canoes and were preparing to navigate a branch of the Snake River never before explored by white men. There was one key difference between the two: Lewis and Clark were lucky and Hunt was unlucky, although *jinxed* would be a more appropriate word. One month after they boarded their canoes, the captains and all their men reached the mouth of the Columbia River in reasonably good health and prepared to build a winter camp. Hunt's decision to leave seventy-seven horses behind and depart in canoes would prove disastrous—a month later he would still be in Idaho, with many of his supplies—and one of his men—lost in the raging river, and the prospect of starvation looming ahead.

Hunt left the horses in the care of the two Shoshone guides, hoping that Fort Henry could become an Astorian trading post. Four trappers would be left to trap beaver—Hoback, Reznor, Robinson, and Martin Cass, who had joined Hunt at the Arikara village. They were outfitted with horses and all the supplies they would need, with the intent of bringing their beaver pelts either to Fort Henry or Astor's post on the Pacific. Robinson was the leader of the group. But, as Irving relates, "When they were about to depart, Mr. Miller called the partners together and threw up his share in the company, declaring his intention of joining the party of trappers. This resolution struck every one with astonishment, Mr. Miller being a man of education and of cultivated habits, and little fitted for the rude life of a hunter. Besides, the precarious and slender profits arising from such a life were beneath the prospects of one who held a share in the general enterprise."[25]

Hunt—and presumably Crooks and McClellan—did everything possible to persuade Miller to reconsider. Hunt argued at length, promising Miller that once they reached Astoria, if Miller desired, he would be guaranteed passage to New York on one of Astor's ships. "To all this Miller replied abruptly, that it was useless to argue with him, as his mind was made up. They might furnish him, or not, as they pleased, with the necessary supplies, but he was determined to part company here, and set off with the trappers." The inexplicable thing was that at Mad River he had wanted desperately to travel by boat rather than horse but was now opting for a painful horse ride while the others boarded boats. Hunt's account of this incident was surprisingly understated—or possibly redacted by a French translator: "On the 10th, Mr. Miller, with four hunters and four horses, left to go beaver-trapping. They took with them the two Snakes, and descended along the mountains in the hope of finding a baned of indians from whom they trusted to obtain information useful for their hunt."[26]

On October 19, the group embarked in fifteen canoes. The strong current took them swiftly downstream. Perhaps one of the partners played with Marie's sons the way William Clark had sometimes done with Sacagawea's son, Pomp, during canoe journeys. Hunt saw signs of bear along the shore, which was lined with cottonwood trees. Beaver, ducks, and geese frequently appeared. The weather was cold: snow fell the entire day. When a large river flowed in from the east, merging with Henry's Fork by way of a delta, Hunt correctly identified it as Mad River, the same river they had crossed near the Tetons. (The confluence of Henry's Fork and the South Fork of the Snake is near present Menan.) He called the new river *Canoe River*, but the name *Snake River* was firmly in place by the time Washington Irving wrote his account of the Astorians.

The next day came a portent of things to come: "The bed of the river was intersected by rapids," Hunt wrote. "There were two others a little further down. In passing there, two canoes filled with water. It was necessary to stop forthwith. I sent my canoe and one other to their assistance. The men were rescued. Many goods and provisions, as well as one canoe, were lost. . . . It was cold." The next day, October 21, the group made a series of portages around several stretches of rough water at present Idaho Falls. Even so, "one of the small canoes filled and capsized, some goods were lost."[27]

On October 23, when several of the men pursued a band of Shoshone Indians who had fled at seeing them, came another portent: "We found in their camp some small fish not more than an inch long, some roots and seeds which they were drying for winter, some vessels woven of flax or nettle." Back on the river, said Hunt, "[we] encountered three of these indians who were on a flimsy raft of reeds, we accosted them. They were wholly naked, except for a piece of rabbit-skin robe over their shoulders. Their bows and arrows were skillfully fashioned. The bow is of pine-wood, cedar-wood or bone, reinforced with sinews of animals. The arrow is of reed or of well-trimmed wood, and is tipped with a green stone."[28] These Indians, surviving without the bison staff of life that had saved the Plains Indians, eked out their living on the edge of extinction, making use of every odd and end of nature. Hunt may have replenished his supplies by trading with the Osage, the Omaha, and the Arikara, but such was not tenable with the impoverished Shoshone.

"Halt was made at a waterfall thirty feet high," Hunt wrote at present American Falls. Now for the first time, Hunt and his men were traveling on what would become the Oregon Trail, and the scene on either side of the river would grow hauntingly familiar: lava rock and sagebrush. Words written three decades later by John C. Fremont aptly described what lay ahead—for the Astorians and for the Oregon Trail pioneers—in Idaho's expansive Snake River Valley:

> Water, though good and plenty, is difficult to reach as the river is hemmed in by high and vertical rocks and many of the streams are without water in the dry season. Grass is only to be found at the marked ramping places and barely sufficient to keep strong animals from starvation. Game, there is none. The road is very rough by volcanic rocks detrimental to wagons and carts. In sage bushes consists the only fuel. Lucky that by all these hardships the traveler is not harassed by the Indians, who are peaceable and harmless."[29]

Fremont's assessment proved to be accurate, except the final sentence.

On October 25, Hunt's group made a six-mile portage to avoid white water; then they had to lower the canoes back to the river by way of a towline. They had not been back on the water for long when they hit more rapids. "We lost some more goods. The river was winding, the country uneven and rocky. The mountains crowded to the water's edge on the left or south bank."[30] The lost *goods*, of course, inevitably included food—the huge stock of jerked buffalo meat obtained near the Green River, likely considered a bland, monotonous meal by the boatmen and hunters, was vanishing, and no longer unappetizing.

Hunt stopped to visit an Indian camp on October 26. "These poor fellows fled at our approach," but Hunt convinced one to return. "He was on horseback and seemed better equipped than those I previously had seen . . . but his fear was so great that I could not persuade him to indicate by signs the route I ought to take. He was concerned only in begging me not to deprive him of his fish and meat, and in consigning himself to the protection of the good spirit."[31]

That same day, the *Louisiana Gazette* ran a notice that would have been of particular interest to the partners and Hoback, Reznor, and Robinson: "Arrived on last Monday, Mr. Manuel Lisa from the Mandan village, and the upper part of the Missouri. We are happy to find him accompanied by Messrs. Reuben Lewis [returning to St. Louis two years after his brother's death] and Andrew Henry, members of the company, who have been absent from civilized life for nearly three years." Although the article depicted Henry's sufferings as extreme, he had returned with forty packs of beaver, which, as Jim Hardee notes, was "a fairly significant accomplishment, considering a typical pack weighs nearly one hundred pounds, and had a value of about five dollars per pound—roughly $20,000 for the winter's efforts. It would have taken fifteen to twenty pack animals to get the hides to market," meaning that Henry had somehow obtained a sizeable group of horses after losing many to Crow rustlers and killing others for food.[32]

But Hunt hardly had time or inclination to ponder what the news might have been back in the old and lost world of St. Louis. As Irving put it, October 28 "was a day of disaster. The river again became rough and impetuous, and was chafed and broken by numerous rapids. These grew more and more dangerous, and the utmost skill was required to steer among them." Crooks was seated in the second canoe of the fleet, and the steersman was the experienced and skilled Canadian voyager Antoine Clappin. "The leading canoe had glided safely among the turbulent and roaring surges, but in following it, Mr. Crooks perceived that his canoe was bearing towards a rock. The canoe was split and overturned. There were five persons on board. Mr. Crooks and one of his companions were thrown amidst roaring breakers and a whirling current, but succeeded, by strong swimming, to reach the shore." Clappin and two others clung to the splintered canoe, catapulted toward another boulder. "The wreck struck the rock with one end, and swinging round, flung poor Clappine off into the raging stream, which swept him away, and he perished. His comrades succeeded in getting upon the rock, from whence they were afterwards taken off."[33]

Clappin's drowning, the first death among the overlanders, "brought the whole squadron to a halt, and struck a chill into every bosom. Indeed they had arrived at a terrific strait, that forbade all further progress in the canoes, and dismayed the most experienced voyageur." Robert Stuart, a partner who had reached Astoria on the *Tonquin*, would see the site of Clappin's death, dubbed "Caldron Lin" by the men, ten months later and described it thus: "The whole body of the River is confined between 2 ledges of Rock somewhat less than 40 feet apart & Here indeed its terrific appearance beggars all description—Hecate's caldron was never half so agitated when vomiting even the most diabolical spells, as is this Linn in a low state of [*the*] water."[34]

Not surprisingly, "many goods" were lost in the accident. "I went scouting with three men to investigate whether we could pass our canoes down the northerly side," wrote Hunt. "For 35 miles, I followed the shores of the river, . . . Its bed is not more than from sixty to ninety feet wide, is full of rapids and intersected by falls from ten to forty feet high. The banks are precipitous everywhere. . . . We returned to our camp on the 29th, very tried and very hungry." The catastrophe, looming in Hunt's peripheral vision for weeks, now hit him head on: "Our situation had become critical, we had food for not more than five days." He sent Reed and three others downstream to obtain horses—every man hearing that request must have regretted the seventy-seven horses left at Fort Henry—and food and garner any information possible about the river ahead. Meanwhile, another group had explored the south side of the river, finding a spot "about six miles from the camp, where they thought it possible that the canoes might be carried down the bank and launched upon the stream, and from whence they might make their way with the aid of occasional portages." Sixteen men consequently left with four of the best canoes to attempt the passage.[35]

The first day of November brought bad weather and bad news: "Our sixteen men had lost one of their canoes, as also their goods, in trying to pass it down the rapids by means of a rope. The other three were stuck fast in the midst of the rocks. Seeing no means of continuing our journey by water, we made ready to go in various directions in quest of indians." So that was that. Hunt's descent of the great Columbia River had lasted fourteen days—and he had still stopped hundreds of miles short of the Columbia proper. Now, in the constant rain, he and the other partners made a plan: "Mr. Mackenzie with four men headed northerly toward the plains in hope of finding the Big River [the Columbia]. Mr. McClellan and three men descended along Canoe River; Mr. Crooks and three men ascended toward its headwaters. I remained with thirty-one men, one woman and two children. We spread a net. Only one fish was found in it."[36]

Crooks, who apparently had five men with him rather than three, intended to walk along the river toward Henry's Fort, returning all the way to the fort if they did not find help from Indians. Hunt, meanwhile, "now set to work with all diligence, to prepare caches, in which to deposit the baggage and merchandise, of which it would be necessary to unburden themselves, preparatory to their weary march by land." The hunters brought in eight beaver, "a slight relief."[37]

Three days after the various groups departed, those remaining were thrilled to see Crooks approaching from the east—surely a sign that friendly Indians had offered food or horses or both. But their joy "was soon dispelled. Mr. Crooks and his companions had been completely disheartened by this retrograde march through a bleak and barren country; and had found, computing from their progress and the accumulating difficulties besetting every step, that it would be impossible to reach Henry's Fort, and return to the main body in the course of the winter. They had determined, therefore, to rejoin their comrades, and share their lot." Nor did two of Reed's men who returned give a favorable report. They had explored the river upstream "but had met with no Indians from whom to obtain information and relief. The river still presented the same furious aspect, brawling and boiling along a narrow and rugged channel, betwixt rocks that rose like walls." Compounding the discouragement, on November 7 Hunt found himself right back at the spot where the group had camped on October 28, "having thus wasted nine days in fruitless efforts."[38] Any lingering hopes of going by water were now dashed. There was no choice: they had to proceed on foot, but they held out hope that they would soon reach the Columbia River nevertheless.

Eleven men sent out exploring had not returned—Reed and one companion, McKenzie and four others, and McClellan and three others. Knowing they could nothing more than hope to meet those eleven, Hunt and Crooks decided to divide into two groups, with Hunt's party of twenty men, one woman, and two children setting out on the north bank of the Snake and Crooks's contingent of twenty men marching along the south bank. "On the 8th, I again had goods cached and I distributed among all the people whatever of our provisions remained," wrote Hunt. "Each person had five and a quarter pounds of meat. We had in addition forty pounds of corn, twenty pounds of grease and nearly five pounds in bouillon tablets. That was what must serve for the subsistence of more than twenty people."[39] What they did not realize—and it was better that they didn't—was that they were one thousand miles from Astoria.

The two groups parted the next day. The day after that, Hunt's people traveled all day with no water to drink besides what they found in the hollows of rocks. At dusk they finally found a spot where they could descend safely to the river for water, something that had generally been impossible because of the steep cliffs lining the river. Over the next two days they visited two Indian villages. In one, "the women fled so precipitately that they had not time to take with them such of their children as could not walk. They had covered them with straw. . . . The men trembled with fear." Hunt calmed their fears, and they gave him some dried fish and sold him a dog. Two more dogs were bought at the next village—all three were promptly slaughtered and eaten. Hunt continued to meet small bands of Indians, buying dogs whenever possible. The Indians were clad like paupers; no bison had been seen in the area for a long time. On November 15, they saw a snow-covered mountain before them; then "the indians told us of some of our people who had passed by this spot." Two days later Hunt obtained a horse in exchange for an old kettle. "The country was devoid of wood, even the sagebrush had disappeared. . . . There remained to us one quart of corn and a little morsel of grease for each man." On November 18 they camped opposite of present Grand View, Idaho, changing their route the next day on the advice of the Indians, who indicated they would find water. They did not. "Everything seemed to indicate that we would be no more fortunate on the following day. What vexation for men whose food consisted principally of dried fish!"[40]

It rained on November 20, giving them a little water to drink. "This alleviation was timely," wrote Hunt, "as several Canadians had begun to drink their urine. It continued to rain all night." The next day they saw a westerly flowing river—now called the Boise—and met some Indians who were more prosperous than those seen earlier and had many horses. One of the Indians, however, claimed that the horse Hunt was riding had been stolen from him. As Irving commented, "There was no disproving a fact supported by numerous bystanders, and which the horse-stealing habits of the Indians rendered but too probable; so Mr. Hunt relinquished his steed to the claimant; not being able to retain him by a second purchase." That night Hunt's group feasted on fish and dogs, marching ten miles the next day and stopping only because of rain. At another Indian camp they obtained more fish and dogs, "and two of the men were fortunate enough each to get a horse in exchange for a buffalo robe." One of these men was Pierre Dorion, added Irving, "the half-breed interpreter, to whose suffering family the horse was a timely acquisition. And here we cannot but notice the wonderful patience, perseverance, and hardihood of the Indian women, as exemplified in the conduct of the poor squaw of the interpreter. She was now far advanced in her pregnancy, and had two children to take care of; one four, and the other two years of age." Since the party had set out on foot, Marie had carried her younger son, Paul, on her back, "in addition to the burden usually imposed upon the squaw, yet she had borne all her hardships without a murmur, and throughout this weary and painful journey had kept pace with the best of the pedestrians." Indeed, said Irving, "on various occasions in the course of this enterprise, she displayed a force of character that won the respect and applause of the white men."[41]

Marie would have good reason to remember this area near the Boise River, the site of present Caldwell, Idaho, and she would return here two years later.

On November 24 the group crossed the Boise River "a little above our Canoe River, which continued to flow toward the north. The mountains in front of us were everywhere covered with snow." The next day, "despite the severe weather, our fatigue and our weakness, we forded another river"—the Payette—"which came from the east. The water was waist-deep." They approached a series of hills that stretched along the snow-covered mountains, crossing the Weiser River before reaching "a defile so narrow as to leave scarcely space enough to pass through. We frequently were obliged to remove the baggage from our horses and to travel in the water. On the previous evening, a beaver had been caught, which furnished us a scanty breakfast. We had supped off bouillon tablets." In one of Hunt's most memorable passages, he added: "I therefore had a horse killed. My men found the flesh very good. I ate it reluctantly because of my fondness for the poor beast."[42]

Early on November 28 they arrived at a Shoshone camp, purchasing some flax and horse meat to eat. Hunt attempted to buy a horse from the Indians, but they refused. "When the women saw that I insisted, they shrieked frightfully as though I had wanted to rob them." In spite of his efforts, Hunt was unsuccessful. "The indians told me of white men who had taken the same route as ours, and of others who had passed on a different side." This was the first news Hunt had received of Crooks since they parted two and a half weeks earlier—he was "greatly assured . . . concerning Mr. Crooks and his company, especially when I learned that he still had one of his dogs, as I concluded that he had not suffered too much from lack of food." But Crooks himself later told quite a different story, saying he saw few Indians during this period and they were too poor to offer him much help. He and his men had subsisted on half a meal every twenty-four hours for eighteen days.[43]

The Indians told Hunt that three more days in the mountains and an additional six days on the trail would take him to the falls of the Columbia. "However," he said, "I had little confidence in this talk, because it appeared to me that they were impatient to see me depart." Depart Hunt did, the next day, but the bad trail forced him to unload the horses. He was approaching the confluence of the Snake and Oregon's Powder River, north of present Weiser, Idaho, and the Snake's bed was rapidly narrowing. "We climbed mountains so high that I would never have believed our horses could have got over them. On the 30th, the mountains still further narrowed the bed of the river. The summits displayed some pine trees and were covered with snow. We experienced the greatest difficulty in going onward because the steep rocks and the precipices projected to the very edge of the river. . . . A black-tailed deer was killed, which made us a sumptuous repast."[44]

The first day of December brought more snow, now knee deep. Luckily, the chokecherries still clinging to the bushes were excellent because the cold had taken away their tartness. "Snow fell so densely on the mountains where we had to go that we could see nothing a half-mile ahead of us. Accordingly, it was necessary to remain encamped on the 2nd. The previous evening, a small beaver was caught. We had nothing more to eat. I killed another horse."[45] A similar pattern was repeated the next few days: excessive cold, slow marches through snow and up and down rocky hills, camping in the cold, killing a horse for food.

"On the 6th," wrote Hunt, "we had just started out, when—What was my astonishment and distress!—I beheld Mr. Crooks and his party on the other side of the river." Hunt ordered a canoe made from the skin of the horse killed the previous night and sent food over to the starving men. "Mr. Crooks and one of party came to us. Poor man!—he was well-nigh spent from fatigue and want." According to Crooks's later account, in the last nine days he and his men had eaten nothing but one beaver, a dog, a few wild cherries, and some old moccasin soles. "He told me that he had gone three days' march further down; that the mountains there [the present Wallowa Range] are even higher and come closer to the river, which at that spot is compressed into a canal not more than sixty to a hundred feet wide between precipitous rocks; and that it was impossible for men in their condition to proceed." Crooks also said that he had seen Reed and McKenzie and their men a few days earlier—they in turn said that McClellan "had crossed the mountains with the hope of falling in with the Flatheads [Salish Indians]."[46]

Hunt spent the night contemplating the crisis he found himself in, concluding—to his "great regret"—that he had no alternative but to backtrack all the way to the three rivers—the Weiser, Payette, and Boise—they had crossed two weeks earlier. "I counted on buying from [Indians] a sufficient quantity of horses to feed us until we should reach the Big River, which I flattered myself to be able to accomplish this winter" said Hunt. "I feared nevertheless that Mr. Crooks and some of his men would not be able to follow us. What an outlook! We must expect having nothing to eat for several days: because, on this side of the indian huts which we left November 29th, we have found only cherries; and perhaps there would be no more of them in the same places."[47]

The skin canoe had somehow been lost during the night. Some of the men built a raft so that Crooks and his companion, apparently Francois Le Clerc, could cross to the other side. "The attempt failed," wrote Hunt. "On the 7th, we were reduced to marching slowly, because Mr. Crooks was so feeble that he had great difficulty in keeping up with us. Most of my men"—as well as Marie and Dorion and their sons—"had gone on ahead." They made another raft the next day, but the current of the Snake was so violent that repeated trials brought no success. More of the men went ahead. "Mr. Crooks was quite ill in the night. . . . I left three men with him; and departed on the 9th with two others to rejoin my party. I had three beaver skins, two of which I left with them. We supped on the third. The weather was extremely cold."[48]

Hunt overtook his men on December 10. Dorion's horse was the only one remaining, "skin and bones" at this point, and Hunt wanted to kill it for food—"to which the half-breed flatly refused his assent, and cudgeling the miserable animal forward, pushed on sullenly, with the air of a man doggedly determined to quarrel for his right."[49] Hunt gave in, on the pretext that it was best to wait and make sure the Indians were still in the same camp, but no one, especially the thoughtful Hunt, could fault Dorion for insisting on keeping the horse for Marie and the boys to ride. On a stroke of luck the group soon afterwards met a band of Shoshone who had twenty horses and were willing to sell five of them. Hunt had one killed on the spot and sent a man on horseback to take some meat back to Crooks. Several of the men had not eaten anything for three days.

Crooks arrived the next day and, according to Irving, was shocked to find that none of the fresh horsemeat had been sent to his men across the river. "He immediately caused a skin canoe to be constructed, and called out to his men to fill their camp-kettles with water and hang them over the fire, that no time might be lost in cooking the meat the moment it should be received. The river was so narrow, though deep, that everything could be distinctly heard and seen across it." Crooks attempted to navigate the river himself but found that he was far too weak. Most of Hunt's men were wary of trying it themselves, but "the good feelings of Ben Jones, the Kentuckian, at length overcame his fears, and he ventured over. The supply was received with trembling avidity." A Canadian by the name of Baptiste Provost, however, "whom famine had rendered wild and desperate, ran frantically about the bank, after Jones had returned, crying out to Mr. Hunt to send the canoe for him," declaring that he would otherwise would lie down and die.[50]

Apparently to appease Provost, Joseph Delaunay was soon sent back across the turbulent Snake with additional supplies. Provost "immediately pressed forward to embark. Delaunay refused to admit him, telling him that there was now a sufficient supply of meat on his side of the river." Provost replied that he was starving and the meat was not yet cooked. "Finding the canoe putting off without him, he forced himself aboard. As he drew near the opposite shore, and beheld meat roasting before the fire, he jumped up, shouted, clapped his hands, and danced in a delirium of joy." The result was predictable. He upset the canoe, and "the poor wretch was swept away by the current and drowned." Delaunay almost drowned himself before reaching the shore.[51]

Hunt now sent all his men forward except two or three. When the skin canoe was sent over with more provisions for Crooks's men, John Day returned in it to join Crooks. "Poor Day, once so active and vigorous, was now reduced to a condition even more feeble and emaciated than his companions," wrote Irving. "Mr. Crooks had such a value for the man, on account of his past services and faithful character, that he determined not to quit him; he exhorted Mr. Hunt, however, to proceed forward, and join the party, as his presence was all important to the conduct of the expedition. One of the Canadians, Jean Baptiste Dubreuil, likewise remained with Mr. Crooks."[52]

Hunt had set out from the Nodaway winter camp seven months earlier with four other partners—McKenzie, Crooks, McClellan, and Miller. Now he was leading what remained of the main group by himself, and he had good reason to question whether he would, in this life, ever see any of the others again.

On December 16, Hunt's party finally emerged from the mountains. "Thus," wrote Hunt, "for twenty days, we had uselessly tired ourselves in seeking a route along the lower part of the river. . . . The river contained drifting ice. The weather was extremely cold." To Hunt's good fortune, however, he found Indians willing to sell a horse, some dried fish, some roots, and some pulverized cherries. They told Hunt that he and his men would have died had they tried to push farther down the river. Then, although Hunt offered a gun, some pistols, and a horse to whomever would serve as a guide, "they all replied that we would freeze and urged me to remain with them during the winter." Such communication presumably happened with Dorion and Hunt using sign language. Hunt said the Indians spoke with a forked tongue and called them women, using "expressions most likely to pique them. Finally one of them proved resolute enough to undertake guiding us as far as to the Sciatogas [an Indian nation living to the northwest, in present northeastern Oregon]," who reportedly had many horses.[53]

Two additional Indian guides joined the first, and on December 21, Hunt and his men prepared to cross the Snake. They killed two horses to make a new skin canoe to take Marie and her sons, the weaker men, and whatever supplies remained across. On the other side they met sixteen of Crooks's men, who said they had seen no trace of Crooks or his two companions. Three of those men—Baptiste Turcotte, André La Chapelle, and Francois Landry—wanted to stay with the Shoshone Indians; Hunt gave them a canoe and some goods and hoped they would soon meet up with Crooks. The crossing was completed on December 23, and the men regained their courage as they entered present Oregon. "My party now consisted of thirty-two whites, a woman more than eight months pregnant, her two children and three indians," wrote Hunt. "We had only five wretched horses for our food during the passage of the mountains. On the 24th, I quitted the Canoe River, of which we all shall keep a very sad recollection."[54]

Out of the mountains now, the party traveled west and northwest over a long series of huge rolling hills, making reasonably good progress. They were following the Powder River as the year of 1811 drew to a close. At dawn on December 30, in a long, pleasant valley where the Powder River flows from the mountains in the north (near present North Powder, Oregon),

Marie gave birth to her baby. Hunt did not say whether the child was a boy or a girl. "As the fortitude and good conduct of the poor woman had gained for her the good-will of the party, her situation caused concern and perplexity," wrote Irving. "Pierre, however, treated the matter as an occurrence that could soon be arranged and need cause no delay. He remained by his wife in the camp, with his other children and his horse, and promised soon to rejoin the main body, who proceeded on their march." Hunt said that Dorion "rejoined us on the 31st. His wife was on horseback with her newborn infant in her arms; another, aged two years, wrapped in a blanket, was slung at her side. One would have said, from her air, that nothing had happened to her." One week later, Hunt added this postscript: "The snow had entirely disappeared. Dorion's baby died."[55] There was no mention of how Marie reacted, whether any sort of service was held, or whether it was possible to bury the child in the frozen ground. Perhaps the body was left on a scaffold, in the tradition of the Plains Indians.

As was typical of this part of the trek, joy and sorrow intermixed in baffling ways.

"January 8 marked a memorable milestone in what had become an endless journey," wrote James P. Ronda. "On that day, near present-day Pendleton, Oregon, the Astorians stumbled into a large encampment of Cayuse and Tushepaw Indians. Hunt guessed that these Indians had more than two thousand horses. Surely there would be some available for both food and transportation. The famished Astorians found a ready welcome with these Indians. Once again western explorers had been saved by native generosity."[56]

Hunt stayed six days at the camp, buying eight horses and two colts and rewarding his Shoshone guides with two of the horses. Several of the men also bought horses. The days of starvation appeared to be over—so much so that some of the men got sick from overeating. In better spirits than he had been for months, Hunt wrote: "I cannot sufficiently express my gratitude to Providence for having let us reach here; because we all were extremely fatigued and enfeebled."[57]

The mix of joy and sorrow continuing, the peace at the Indian camp was dampened by the disappearance of a Canadian voyager by the name of Michel Carriere. He had last been seen the afternoon before Hunt entered the camp, "mounted behind a Snake Indian on a horse." A number of men straggled into the camp in the coming days, but Carriere was not among them. Then, as the men made themselves moccasins and prepared for the last leg of their journey, Hunt sent two men to look for Carriere. "They did not find him," reported Hunt. "This poor fellow had perhaps taken a hunting-trail of the indians and thus lost his way. The Snakes having moved their lodges to another place, my men could learn nothing about him."[58] In this unsettled state of affairs, Hunt did what he had to do: he left. The voyager was never seen or heard from again.

Hunt traveled along the Umatilla River for several days, losing three horses in a flash flood. He bought four others as soon as he could, wishing "to have a certain number because the indians told me that, on the Big River, I could obtain a canoe in exchange for one of these animals." Another group of Indians gave Hunt "some very reassuring particulars concerning the whites who had earlier descended the river."

On January 21, Hunt made another monumental entry in his journal: "We at last reached the banks of the Columbia, for so long the goal of our desires. We had travelled 1751 miles, we had endured all the hardships imaginable. With difficulty I expressed our joy at the sight of this river. It was three-fourths of a mile wide. Its shores were bare of trees; and were formed of pebbles and in some places, of steep rocks." The weather soon turned mild, the terrain mountainous, and the Indians prosperous. The group passed "the falls of the Columbia" on January 31, later known as Celilo Falls but now submerged by The Dalles Dam. "The bed of the river is blocked by rocks, across which the water plunges by several channels. . . . This is the great fishery of the Columbia," wrote Hunt. It resembles one of the small fishing ports on the eastern coast of the United States. On both sides of the river are to be seen large flakes well made of interlaced sticks for drying fish. . . . In the springtime, when the waters of the river are high, the salmon come in schools, so large that the indians catch them with dip-nets attached to the end of poles."[59]

Hunt talked with an Indian who spoke limited English. "He recounted to me," said Hunt, "the catastrophe of Mr. Mackay and of the ship *Tonquin*. The news wire was alive and well on the Columbia. In the next few days Hunt heard two more reports of "the distressing news" of "Mr. Mackay's disaster"—as well as a request for news of Lewis and Clark and their men from an Indian who already knew of Lewis's death.[60]

The fate of *Tonquin* was distressing indeed. In June of 1811, not long after Hunt and Lisa had nearly faced off in a duel, *Tonquin* sailed for Vancouver Island to trade with Indians. According to the sole survivor of the calamity, an Indian interpreter named Jack Ramsay, when one chief complained about trade prices, "[Captain] Thorn exploded in a characteristic rage and rubbed the headman's face in the furs. Such an insult could not go unavenged," and the Indians planned an attack under the guise of trade. After a large group of them boarded the ship and began trade negotiations, a second group arrived via canoe and "were on deck before [Thorn] could stop them." Alexander McKay, the only partner present, and Ramsay knew something was wrong and urged Thorn to set sail immediately, but the captain had hardly given orders when "the Indians drew knives, clubs, and hatchets from beneath furs and attacked the crew. McKay died first, his skull crushed by a war club. Thorn soon fell defending himself to the last with a small knife." Ramsay escaped by leaping overboard, but the rest of the crew—or so the

Indians thought—were killed. The next day, with a throng of Indians celebrating on the decks, a survivor or group of survivors set off the ship's powder magazine and blew up the ship. Ramsay said that "arms, legs and heads were flying in all directions and this tribe of Indians lost nearly 200 of its people in this unfortunate affair."[61]

Given the extreme loss of life on *Tonquin* and his own ordeal along the Snake River, Hunt likely considered the end of his trip west unextraordinary. He bought horses and exchanged them for canoes, embarking in a canoe himself with all his goods and sending the mounted men ahead on February 3. A week later, after fighting weather and Indians intent on stealing his goods, Hunt was joined by the rest of his party. They made a series of troublesome portages to avoid rapids, and Hunt had time to describe the scenery, the fish, and the seals. They saw Indian huts everywhere, with the Indians selling dogs, dried salmon, beaver skins, and wapato—a potato-like root that Sacagawea had been quite fond of.

"On the 16th, we started early. It had rained all night," Hunt wrote on the last page of his journal. "The fog was so thick that we could see only the lowlands and some small islands; all was covered by it. It disappeared in the afternoon at high tide. I found that we were navigating along a large bay, and shortly afterward I saw the fort of Astoria on the southerly bank."

Never one to neglect details, Hunt noted that his dating was somehow a day off—it was really February 15. Then, with typical understatement, he concluded his record: "It was a very real pleasure for travellers harassed by fatigue to rest in quiet and be surrounded by friends after so long a journey in the midst of savages of whom it is always prudent to be wary.

"We had covered 2073 miles since leaving the Aricaras' village."[62]

Chapter Nine

"The Inscrutable Ways of Providence"

Almost one month before Hunt reached Astoria, on January 18, 1812, Duncan McDougall, the partner in charge of the post, had made this entry in the headquarters log of the Pacific Fur Company:

> About 5 P. M. we were agreeably surprized by the arrival of Messrs. Donald McKenzie, Robert McClellan & John Reed (clerk), with 8 hands, viz.:
> William Cannon
> Joseph L'Andrie
> Andrez Defresne
> Eitenne Leucier
> Michel Samson
> Andrez Vallé
> Prisque Felax
> Guillaume Le Roux, dit Cardinal
> in two canoes, they having left Messrs. Hunt & Crooks with 36 men on the 2nd November last, on this side the R Mountains, among the Snake nation. [They separated from the party to search for horses, but being unable to bring them any assistance they continued on their way here.] They encountered considerable hardships, and suspect that should the latter Gentlemen pursue their route this Winter, they must seriously suffer for want of provisions, etc. [1]

Although they had left the camp near Caldron Linn separately, Donald McKenzie, Robert McClellan, and John Reed and their companions had united. "After wandering for several days without meeting with Indians, or obtaining any supplies," wrote Washington Irving, "they came together fortuitously among the Snake River Mountains, some distance below that disastrous pass or strait which had received the appellation of the Devil's Scuttle Hole [Caldron Linn]." They were all in the same predicament—without horses or supplies—and agreed that returning to Hunt would be useless.

"Their only course was to extricate themselves as soon as possible from this land of famine and misery and make the best of their way for the Columbia."[2]

Following the "rugged defile" found impassable by Hunt and Crooks, the eleven men continued to follow the Snake but, repeating a pattern from weeks earlier, found that "its banks were so high and precipitous, that there was rarely any place where the travellers could get down to drink of its waters." Nor could they find any game, and they survived for a time on broiled strips of beaver skin, "doled out in scanty allowances, barely sufficient to keep up existence." When a blizzard brought them to a halt, they huddled under the edge of a mountain and steeled themselves for death. At that moment McClellan spotted a bighorn sheep on the side of the hill above them. He grabbed his rifle and "made a cautious circuit; scrambled up the hill with the utmost silence, and at length arrived, unperceived, within a proper distance. Here leveling his rifle he took so sure an aim, that the bighorn fell dead on the spot." He rolled the carcass down to this fellow nomads, who, showing incredible restraint, saved the meat for subsequent days, supping now on soup made from the bones.[3]

"At length, after twenty-one days of toil and suffering, they got through these mountains, and arrived at tributary stream of that branch of the Columbia called Lewis River. . . . In this neighborhood they met with wild horses, the first they had seen west of the Rocky Mountains." More important, the men fell in with a band of friendly Indians, who fed them and sold them canoes. In the midst of this good fortune, they experienced one of the most astounding events of the entire Astorian adventure. "They also encountered, in these parts, a young American, who was deranged, but who sometimes recovered his reason," wrote Gabriel Franchere, a clerk present at Astoria when McClellan and the others arrived. "This young man told them, in one of his lucid intervals, that he was from Connecticut, and was named Archibald Pelton; that he had come up the Missouri with Mr. Henry; that all the people at the post established by that trader were massacred by the Blackfeet; that he alone had escaped, and had been wandering, for three years since, with the *Snake* Indians."[4]

The jovial friend of Thomas James and of John Hoback, Jacob Reznor, and Edward Robinson had somehow survived and somehow found fellow trappers. His own account, which contained obvious errors of fact, made it hard to determine what had happened to him. It had only been a year and a half, for example, since the attacks at Three Forks—nor had he been the sole survivor. He had most likely disappeared from Fort Henry a year earlier—in a setting where there would have been Shoshone Indians to help him. Still, it was miraculous that an insane white man could end up safe near the convergence of the Clearwater and Snake Rivers, three hundred miles from either Three Forks (to the east) or Fort Henry (to the southeast).[5]

"Our people took this young man with them," added Franchere, "and so arrived at the establishment [Astoria], safe and sound, it is true, but in a pitiable condition to see; their clothes being nothing but fluttering rags."[6]

After reaching Astoria, McClellan had busied himself with such useful activities as hunting and making salt. He and McKenzie enjoyed a reunion with Hunt's group a month after their own arrival, and, like everyone else, wondered if and when Crooks would ever appear. By March, however, McClellan was growing restless and discontent. Alexander Ross offered this account: When plans were announced for one group to go back to Caldron Linn to retrieve Hunt's cached goods and for another group led by John Reed to accompany them and continue all the way to New York with dispatches for Astor, "Mr. M'Lellan, following the example of his colleague, Mr. Miller, abruptly resigned, and joined the party for New York." Showing how well he understood McClellan, Ross added: "This gentleman possessed many excellent qualities, but they were all obscured and thrown into the shade by a fickle and unsteady mind." Like Joseph Miller, McClellan could not be convinced to reconsider. He left with Reed, Robert Stuart (on his way to a trading post), and several others on March 22.

"Everything went on smoothly till the party reached the long narrows [Celilo Falls]," wrote Ross. "While in the act of making the portage, the party being unavoidably divided, they were furiously attacked by Indians. Mr. Reed, the bearer of the express for New York, was knocked down in the scuffle, and severely wounded; and had not M'Lellan, with a bravery and presence of mind peculiar to himself, leaped dexterously over a canoe, he could have been felled to the ground"—a sure sign that McClellan's jumping ability had not been the stuff of mere legend. "His agility saved him, and in all probability saved the whole party" continued Ross, "for he instantly shot the man who aimed the blow, then drawing a pistol from his belt, shot him who had assailed Reed dead at his feet; then clapping his hand to his mouth, in the true Indian style, he gave the war whoop, fired his rifle, and the Indians fled."[7]

Robert McClellan was back in his element.

They were not yet out of harm's way, but the men managed to get clear of the falls and head upriver. Not only was Reed wounded, he had lost the papers scheduled for delivery to Astor. He had been carrying them in a shiny tin box in an effort to protect them, but the box had attracted the attention of the Indians, who grabbed it in the confusion because they thought it valuable. The overland trip was thus canceled, but the entire party proceeded to Fort Okanogan, situated on the Columbia River above its confluence with the Snake, in present north central Washington. "Here they remained for five days, when the party left for Astoria, in four canoes, carrying off with them 2500 beaver skins."[8]

As if McClellan's encounter with Pelton on his first voyage to Astoria had not been astonishing enough, he was about to experience another on his second voyage. "On their way down, one morning a little after sunrise, while near the [Umatilla River]," wrote Ross, "where a crowd of Indians were assembled together, they were hailed loudly in English to 'come on shore.' . . . To shore the canoes instantly steered; when, to the surprise of all, who should be there, standing like two spectres, but Mr. Crooks and John Day, who, it will be remembered, had been left by Mr. Hunt among the Snake Indians the preceding autumn." The two friends were "so changed and emaciated . . . that our people for some time could scarcely recognise them to be white men."[9]

Ross next offered an account of what had befallen the two ghosts, in Crooks's own words: "We remained for some time with the Snakes, who were very kind to us. When they had something to eat, we ate also; but they soon departed, and . . . we had to provide for ourselves the best way we could." They collected some brushwood and coarse hay and made themselves a wigwam; then they collected firewood, but Day grew so weak that he could not stand without help, and they were unable to start a fire. For a day they went without food, water, or drink, but "Providence is ever kind. Two straggling Indians happening to come our way, relieved us. They made us a fire, got us some water, and gave us something to eat." The Indians also warned Crooks and Day that the roots they had intended to cook when they could get a fire going were poison. "Who can tell but the hand of a kind and superintending Providence was in all this?" asked Crooks. He added that their Indian friends stayed for two days and left them with two pounds of venison. "We were really sorry to lose them."[10]

The next day, in a scene reminiscent of McClellan's killing the bighorn sheep, Day shot a large wolf that came prowling around their hut. "To this fortunate hit I think we owed our lives. The flesh of the wolf we cut up and dried, and laid it by for some future emergency, and in the mean time feasted upon the skin." Again, like McClellan, they pounded the bones between stones, "and with some roots made a kind of broth, which, in our present circumstances, we found very good." They began to regain their courage. "For two months we wandered about, barely sustaining life with our utmost exertions. All this time we kept travelling to and fro, until we happened by mere chance, to fall on the [Umatilla River]; and then following it, we made the Columbia about a mile above this place, on the 15th day of April, according to our reckoning."[11]

They found another group of kind Indians. "This man," said Crooks, pointing to an old Indian called Yeck-a-tap-am, "in particular treated us like a father. After resting ourselves for two days with the good old man and his people, we set off, following the current," in hopes of reaching Astoria. They traveled for nine days and were not far from the falls when a considerable number of Indians gathered round them and stole their rifles. "The Indians"—who intimated that some of their people had been killed by whites—"then closed in upon us, with guns pointed and bows drawn, on all sides, and by force stripped us of our clothes, ammunition, knives, and everything else, leaving us naked as the day we were born." Certain they were going to be killed, Crooks and Day were relieved when the Indians did not prevent them from walking away. "All that day we travelled without tasting food, and at night concealed ourselves among the rocks—without fire, food, or clothing." The next day they found some fish bones and tried unsuccessfully to eat some. Now they headed back upriver, toward Yeck-a-tap-am's camp. "Providence still guarded us," said Crooks. [12]

They found an Indian wigwam, where the inhabitants, quite frightened at first, gave them fish, broth, and roots. "This was the first food we had tasted, and the first fire we had seen, for four days and four nights. Our feet were severely cut and bleeding, for want of shoes; yet we lost no time, but set off, and arrived here three days ago, and our good old friend, Yeck-a-tap-am, received us again with open arms, and gave us these skins to cover our nakedness, as ye now see." The old man had given them a good supply of dried horsemeat, and the two had resolved to retrace their steps to St. Louis. "When you came in sight we were just in the act of tying up our bundles," Crooks told them. [13]

Stuart rewarded the old Indian by clothing him from "head to foot for his friendly services. Mr. Crooks and his fellow-sufferer then cordially shaking hands with Yeck-a-tap-am, the party pushed off, and continued their voyage. . . . From the long narrows the party met with no interruption, but continued on their route till they reached Astoria, on the 12th of May, where Crooks and all the party were greeted with a hearty welcome." [14]

"In the afternoon of Monday the 29th day of June 1812 we sailed from Astoria," wrote Robert Stuart, a Canadian partner who had fought Indians at the falls of the Columbia with McClellan and who had rewarded Crooks's friend Yeck-a-tap-am with a fine suit of clothes. After describing the boats and men headed for "the interior parts of the Country above the Forks of the Columbia," Stuart noted that "the other" canoe "contained R. McClellan, R. Crooks, John Day, Benjamin Jones, André Vallé, Francois Leclairc . . . and myself with the necessaries for the prosecution of this voyage." [15]

The "voyage" was a mission to follow Hunt's route in reverse and deliver letters to Astor in New York. Like McClellan, Crooks had given up his shares in the company and was returning to St. Louis. Despite their ordeal reaching Astoria, it seems that neither of them could leave the place soon enough. For the upteenth time, their partnership had been dissolved. They were now part of the "eastbound" Astorians, joining Day, Jones, and Vallé as the only men to go overland to the coast and back. Neither Crooks nor

McClellan ever offered a detailed account of how they felt about their experience with the Pacific Fur Company and why they had given in or given up so quickly.

Trouble came much sooner for the eastbound team than it had for the westbound. On July 1, Stuart wrote: "Between the hour we stopped here, and dusk, evident symptoms of mental derangement made their appearance in John Day one of my Hunters who for a day or two previous seemed as if restless and unwell but now uttered the most incoherent absurd and unconnected sentences—several spoke to him, but little satisfaction was obtained, and he went to bed gloomy and churlish." Day was worse on July 2, with his disorder becoming "very alarming"—"several times he attempted getting possession of some of our arms, with the intention of committing suicide." After lulling the others into false security, Day fired too pistols at his head, "but fortunately too high to take effect, he was instantly Secured & placed under a guard." On July 3, only four days out, Stuart concluded that "Day's insanity amounted to real madness I agreed with some Indians . . . for a few articles to carry him back to the Fort." The other men concurred with this decision, Crooks no doubt regretfully because Day had been such a good friend to him. Failing to make the journey both east- and westbound, Day was safely escorted back to Astoria.[16]

The voyage settled into routine. "Had a strong fair wind all day which enabled us to sail 40 miles," Stuart wrote on July 22. They were near the spot where Crooks and Day had been rescued in May. "The Country is without a stick of wood, and the soil an entire desert of sand even on the tops of the Bluffs."[17]

Now on horseback, the Astorians reached the Boise River on August 15, getting a hint that they might soon meet members of the company. They met one of the Indians who had guided Hunt "over the Mad River Mountain last Fall—He said that he parted ten nights ago with 3 of our Hunters, who had caught a great many Beaver, but that the Absarokas . . . had discovered the place where this hunt was concealed and carried off every thing." The guide also said "that the others had lost their Horses & were stripped by the same nation with whom they at present were—the three whom he lately saw were on their way down, had only a horse each & but one Gun among them their names he said are Alexis, Michel & Makan."[18]

That same guide told Stuart that "there is a shorter trace to the South than that by which Mr. Hunt had traversed the R Mountains," and that he knew the route well.[19] Stuart immediately hired him to guide the group east. The Indian accepted, and although his tenure as a guide was brief, his claim turned out to be accurate.

By August 20, the six men had reached a lazy stretch of river near present Grand View, Idaho. "Went East by South 12 Miles across two Bends," wrote Stuart, "where going to drink we found John Hobough fishing and in an instant Mr. Miller[,] Edward Robinson & Jacob Reznor who had been similarly employed came out of the Willows & joined us." The three Kentuckians and the former partner had not been heard from in almost a year, and they finally had a chance to relate their adventures and sufferings. Mounting their horses at Henry's Fort, they rode two hundred miles south, where they trapped the Bear River along the borders of present Idaho, Utah, and Wyoming for a season. Next they rode another two hundred miles due east, across the lower valley of Green River to Wyoming's Sierra Madre Mountains, where they found an Arapaho village of sixty lodges. Those Indian robbed them of several horses and most of their clothing. They traveled another fifty miles, to extreme southern Wyoming or northern Colorado, where they wintered, but "early in the Spring were overtaken by the same Rascals," who robbed them of all their horses and nearly everything else.[20]

With half their remaining ammunition, they "purchased of them two of their own Horses and after travelling about 950 miles in which they suffered greatly by Hunger, thirst & fatigue," until being almost in a state of nature when they met Stuart, "without even a single animal to carry their Baggage." They also reported that their other companion, Martin H. Cass, had "villainously left them with one of the Horses," while on the headwaters of the Bighorn River, "and the other was stolen by some Indians on this side of the Rocky Mountains—For the greater part of their route, scarcely either quadruped or Bird came within reach of their Guns, and the Inhabitants of the Waters were their only means [of] subsistence during this long and tedious journey." They had come in contact with the Shoshone, Arapaho, and Ute nations; the southern watercourses they had visited were "abundantly stocked with Beaver of the largest size & best quality they have ever seen."[21]

By this report, the pilgrimage of Hoback, Reznor, Robinson, and Miller had been every bit as harrowing as that of Hunt, McKenzie, Crooks, McClellan, Reed, and Pierre and Marie Dorion. After providing the wanderers from Henry's Fort with the best possible meal, the entire group proceeded about three miles along the river, to a good fishing and grazing spot, where they took up their lodgings for the night.

Despite their sufferings, Hoback and his fellows had forged back west, clinging to the elusive dream of "making a fortune before they return," but now, on meeting the well-supplied and eastbound Stuart, they changed their minds and announced their "determination to accompany [Stuart] to St. Louis." The Doomed Trio was finally going home. At every Indian camp the group passed, Stuart tried to buy horses. "Strong were the inducements we held out for a few Horses," he wrote on August 22, "but they withstood . . . our temptations, saying they had not a sufficency for themselves, consequently we were obliged to content ourselves by exchanging two that were worn out for a couple of . . . fresh ones."[22]

On August 29, wrote Stuart, "we again struck the main River at the Caldron Linn, where one of the unfortunate Canoes was lodged among the Rocks." They continued on to the area of Hunt's caches, and, "finding good grass we unloaded and took up our quarters." When they checked some of the caches, however, "we found six of them open and except a few Books which lay scattered by the wind in every direction, the whole of the contents had vanished." As they proceeded up the river, they passed "a very long & bad Rapid, where [Clappine] was drowned."[23]

The resolve of Hoback, Reznor, and Robinson to return to Kentucky lasted ten days. On Sunday, August 30, without explaining further details of how or why the three changed their minds, Stuart simply said that he found a few dry goods, traps, and ammunition in the remaining caches and that he furnished the trio "as far as lay in my power with every thing necessary for a two years hunt, which they are to make on this River below Henry's Fort as they preferred that, to returning in their present ragged condition to civilized society." Miller, on the other hand, had "fully satisfied" his desire to travel through Indian country and was going back with Stuart. The party now consisted of seven men, just as it had on departure, with Miller essentially replacing Day. Whatever farewells were said to Hoback, Reznor, and Robinson were left unrecorded, with Stuart noting that Miller and McClellan went fishing and caught thirteen trout.[24]

Stuart reached American Falls on September 5, having roughly followed Hunt's route in reverse since leaving Astoria. Soon their paths diverged, however, as Miller led the group to the southeast, through areas he had seen with Hoback, Reznor, and Robinson, toward the Bear River, which starts in Utah before winding through parts of Wyoming and Idaho and draining in the Great Salt Lake, the longest river in North America not ultimately flowing to the sea. Between them, Robinson's and Stuart's groups had now laid the foundation for another section of the Oregon Trail—leading from American Falls to the Idaho/Wyoming border southeast of Montpelier, Idaho. On September 9, the men rode past dusk, where they found "grass enough to satisfy [their] hungry Horses for the night; having come in all this day 42 miles nearly East." Stuart did not mention the water, but they were at the site of present Soda Springs, Idaho, a region of springs and geysers and cones and craters renowned among future pioneers. "These soda springs are well worth a notice, possessing all the properties of pure soda water," Samuel Hancock wrote in 1845. Rufus B. Sage, who saw the springs three years earlier advised: "The draught will prove delicious and somewhat stimulating, but, if repeated too freely, it is said to produce a kind of giddiness like intoxication."[25]

On September 12, Stuart and his companions met a band of Crow Indians, who were friendly at first but soon turned hostile. "To prevent an open rupture we gave them about twenty loads of Powder and left them happy at getting off on no worse terms." On September15 they saw a multitude of pronghorn antelope but could not get close enough to shoot any. The next day, now in present Wyoming, they lost their bearings, unable to find the "intended track" they expected to take them through the Rocky Mountains to the south. This was combined with "the great probability of falling in again with the Crows," who would undoubtedly steal their horses. They therefore concluded to go north and "pass the first spur of mountains by the route of [Hunt's] party who came across the Continent last year."[26]

Leaving what would become the Oregon Trail, Stuart followed Greys River north, running low on food as he and his men continued to see antelope too swift to hunt. Finally, on September 17, he wrote: "Killed a buck Antelope today which was in fine order, and proved an agreeable addition to our stock of provisions, now become very low." Two days later, camped near the confluence of Greys River and the south fork of the Snake River—"Mad River"—close to the site of present Alpine, Wyoming, Stuart wrote:

> We were all up soon after the dawn and I had just reached the river bank, when I heard the Indian yell raised in the vicinity of our Camp, and the cry "To Arms" "There's Indians" echoed by all of our Party—We had just time to snatch our arms when two Indians at full gallop passed 300 yards to one side of our station driving off [by their yells] every horse we had [notwithstanding their being tethered & hobbled], towards them we rush, and got [almost] within shot of the nearest when repeated yells in the direction from which they came, made us desist from the pursuit in order to defend ourselves and Baggage; for there being only two Indians after the Horses, we very readily imagined that the main body were in reserve to attack our rear did we follow the foremost, or to Plunder the Camp if opportunity offered.[27]

Joining William Clark and Andrew Henry and a host of others, Stuart had lost his horses to the unparalleled horsemen of the Rockies—the Crow Indians. But even Stuart acknowledged his loss as "one of the most daring and intrepid actions" he had ever heard of among the Indians. He was also convinced that it would have been virtually impossible for such a small group of men to prevent the determined and patient Crow from eventually capturing their horses. Resigned to their gloomy situation, the men made preparations to follow Mad River west on foot, "along the Plains of which below Henry's Fort, we have hopes of meeting with some of the Snakes, from whom if we can procure a couple of Horses, we shall continue our former determination and if possible reach the Cheyenne River before the Winter sets in." Then he added: "We have just food enough for one meal, and rely with confidence on the inscrutable ways of Providence to send in our road wherewith to subsist from day to day."[28]

The resourceful men built two rafts to descend the Snake River, and they were soon back in present Idaho, making twenty miles by water on September 23. Four men navigated one raft and three the other. They suddenly found game, including a deer and an elk that had earlier been shot by what appeared to be a Blackfoot arrow. Convinced that Blackfoot warriors would kill them on the spot, they kept a careful watch and stopped using their rifles. A few miles northwest of the present site of Heise Hot Springs they dried the elk meat, sewed new moccasins, and prepared to go overland on foot. Each man would carry twenty pounds of jerked elk meat.

Apparently concluding they had no chance of finding any of the horses left behind by Hunt a year earlier, Stuart decided not to travel to Fort Henry, instead cutting toward Pierre's Hole to cross the Teton Range as soon as possible. A nineteen-mile march on the last day of September, wrote Stuart, "brought us to our nights lodgings in a deep gulley near a boiling spring [present Green Canyon Hot Springs, visited by the westbound party]. Mr. Crooks is a good deal indisposed and . . . has a considerable fever." The next day, McClellan refused to carry the group's trap any farther; "neither would he pack an equivalent in dried meat but leaving us said he could kill enough for his daily subsistence and when informed that we would cross the mountain to the right the better to avoid the Blackfeet . . . his answer was, that he must consult the ease of his sore feet and went on, round the mountain"—in open view of any Indians in the area.[29]

So the unpredictable but quite predictable McClellan was gone when his old partner Crooks needed him most. As the half-dozen men hiked through deep snow up the mountain, they could see McClellan making his way across the plain below them. Reaching the Teton River, Stuart's company stopped after a march of eighteen miles. By that time Crooks had a "violent fever" and was so weak that even attempting to walk the next day was out of the question. The other four men argued that they had to leave Crooks behind to save their own lives, "very justly representing the imminent dangers we exposed ourselves to by any delay in this unknown and barren tract," wrote Stuart, "among most inveterate enemies to whites, and in the midst of impervious mountains of snow, at such an advanced season, without one days provision, and no very favourable appearances of procuring an addition here."[30]

Stuart "at length prevailed on them" to stay with Crooks. They agreed with extreme reluctance. Not judging them, the eloquent Stuart commented:

> The sensations excited on this occasion, and by the view of an unknown & untravelled wilderness, are not such as arise in the artificial solitude of parks and gardens, for there one is apt to indulge a flattering notion of self sufficien-

cy, as well as a placid indulgence of voluntary delusions; whereas the phantoms which haunt a desert, are want, misery, and danger, the evils of dereliction rush upon the mind; man is made unwillingly acquainted with his own weakness, and meditation shows him only how little he can sustain, and how little he can perform. [31]

The next morning Jones was out searching for a spot to set a trap for a grizzly bear when one suddenly appeared and rushed toward him. He saved himself by shooting it—the bear wandered away wounded. With Crooks still sick and their food gone—and any Blackfoot in the area already aware of the gunshot—Stuart sent Jones out hunting. "He returned having killed five elk." In weather "piercingly cold" they carried Crooks "six miles south up the Fork to where the dead animals lay and encamped in the vicinity. The food and an "Indian Sweat" had a good effect on Crooks—he began to slowly mend, and they started east again. On Wednesday, October 7, they crossed the pass over the Teton Range—where there was little snow—and crossed the south fork of the Snake as well—at a point where there were "Five channels of from 30 to 60 yards wide each and from 11/2 to 3 feet water a very rapid current." Continuing to follow Hunt's path in reverse, they reached the Hoback River the next day and the Green River on October 12. [32]

Their food supply gone again, the men left camp on October 13 on the edge of despair. Le Clerc had gone ahead, but they soon met him coming up the river with the news that he had found McClellan "fishing but without success." McClellan told Le Clerc that "he had been very much indisposed and lived on little or nothing . . . since he parted with us." Stuart wrote that when they arrived, "we found him lying on a parcel of straw . . . worn to a perfect skeleton" and hardly able to speak or raise his head "from extreme debility." McClellan said "it was as well for him to die there as any where else, there being no prospect of our getting any speedy relief." The others, "by much persuasion . . . prevailed on him to accompany us"; he reluctantly agreed. [33]

They prepared to sleep on empty stomachs, but the drama for the day had not ended. One of the Canadians came to Stuart with his rifle in his hand and announced that since they had no hope of securing any provisions for at least three or four days, "he was determined to go no farther, but that lots should be cast and one die to preserve the rest, adding as a farther inducement for me to agree to his proposal that I should be exempted." The proposal, of course, was for the man drawing the short stick to be killed and eaten by the others. "I shuddered at the idea & used every endeavor to create an abhorrence in his mind against such an act," wrote Stuart, "urging also the probability of our falling in with some animal on the morrow but, finding that every argument failed . . . I snatched up my Rifle cocked and leveled it at him with the firm resolution to fire if he persisted." The unnamed Canadian—

apparently either Le Clerc or Vallé—was so terrified that he fell to his knees and begged the party's forgiveness, "swearing he should never again suggest such a thought." Contemplating all of this with increasing despair, "I at length became so agitated and weak that it was with difficulty I crawled to bed," wrote Stuart, "and after being there I for the first time in my life could not enjoy that repose my exhausted frame so much wanted."[34]

Hunt had reached the Green River by descending Wind River and crossing to the Pacific side of the Continental Divide at Union Pass. To take that route in reverse, Stuart would have gone north, but he was seeking a more southerly path across the Rockies, and he headed southeast, reaching the site of present Pinedale, Wyoming on October 16. By October 21, a sense of normalcy was returning to the caravan—they had a good store of food because McClellan had killed a buffalo the previous night. "The cold continued," wrote Stuart, "and was accompanied by Snow soon after we left the drain which compelled us to encamp at the end of 15 miles E N E on the side of a Hill . . . where we found a sufficiency of dry Aspen for firewood, but not a drop of water."[35]

Stuart did not realize it, but he had reached his southerly crossing of the Rocky Mountains, now called South Pass. As James P. Ronda has written, "Surely the most notable geographic accomplishment for the Astorians came in 1812 when Robert Stuart and his eastbound party came upon South Pass in Wyoming's Wind River range. South Pass became an essential part of the Oregon Trail. It was rediscovered in the 1820s by Jedediah Smith, but the Astorians deserve credit as the initial European discovers."[36]

Over the next six months, Stuart, Crooks, McClellan, and the others would see the same sights and sites seen by Oregon Trail, Mormon Trail, and California Trail pioneers—the Wind River Range, the Sweetwater River, Devil's Gate, Independence Rock, the Laramie Mountains and the North Platte River, Scotts Bluff, Chimney Rock, and the Platte River. Traversing present Wyoming with a single, reliable, faithful pack horse, they made a reasonably comfortable winter camp on the last day of 1812, near present Torrington, Wyoming. No one was lost; no one drowned; no one was left behind. They traveled along water routes, seeing more and more buffalo, meeting friendly Indians. Crooks and McClellan reached their old friend the Missouri River on April 18, 1813, at a spot they had last seen two years and ten days earlier, when they were so full of hope and enthusiasm. Traveling by canoe now, they passed their old winter camp at the mouth of the Nodaway River four days later.

"A little before sunset we reached the Town of Saint Louis," Stuart wrote on Friday, April 30, 1813, "all in the most perfect health after a voyage of ten months from Astoria during which time we had the peculiar good fortune to have suffered in one instance only by want of provisions." A week later, the *Missouri Gazette* announced the news: "Arrived here a few days ago from the mouth of the Columbia river, Mr. Robert Stuart, one of the partners of the Pacific Fur Company, accompanied by messrs. R. Crooks, Jos. Miller and Rob. M'Clellan, with three hunters. . . . Next week we shall present our readers with an account of their journey from the Pacific Ocean to this place, a short narrative which will evince to the world that a journey to the Western Sea will not be considered (within a few years) of much greater importance, than a trip to New York."[37]

Within a few months the enterprising Crooks had gone East to re-enlist with John Jacob Astor; within a few days the hapless McClellan had been thrown in jail for nonpayment of debt.[38]

Epilogue

"Desolation and Horror Stared Me in the Face"

"About the middle of August [1813]," Marie explained to the Astorians, "we reached the Great Snake River, and soon afterwards, following up a branch to the right hand, where there were plenty of beaver, we encamped." Here, near the confluence of the Snake and Boise Rivers (near present Parma, Idaho) John Reed and his men built a cabin and went to work trapping beaver. The Snake was wide and slow at this point, with small islands everywhere, offering an inviting habitat for gadwalls, mallards, and Canada geese. There were also mule deer, pheasants, and rabbits darting in and out of the marshy wetlands, giving the group a steady and varied diet. Or they could catch catfish or trout in the rivers and streams. Not only that, but "the Indians about the place were very friendly."

The Indians were part of the Snake—or Shoshone—Nation, which ranged from Wyoming to Nevada. These were the western Shoshone, and like Sacagawea's people, the Lemhi Shoshone, whose home lay two hundred miles to the northeast, they were small in stature and subsisted largely on roots, dried berries, and fish, dwelling in conical huts constructed of willows and bark. They had seen white men for the first time when the overland Astorians passed through the area a year and a half earlier, greeting them with good will but too poor themselves to offer much help in the way of food or horses.

"About the latter end of September," said Marie, "Hoback, Robinson, and Reznor came to us; but they were very poor, the Indians having robbed them of everything they had about fifteen days before." The company (now grown to ten men, one woman, and two children) included another trio of friends—André La Chappelle, Francois Landry, and Jean Baptiste Turcotte—Canadian voyagers who had survived a tumultuous year in the Idaho wilderness before being rescued by none other than Reed. Like their fellow French speakers, they had taken to calling the Snake River "*La maudite riviere enragèe*"—the accursed mad river. But the first casualty among La Chapelle, Landry, and Turcotte came not from the hazardous river but from a simple accident. "Landry got a fall from his horse, lingered for a while, and died of it," reported Marie. About that same time, a second member of the trio was lost when Turcotte died of the "King's Evil," or scrofula, a form of tuberculosis that affects the lymph nodes of the neck.[1]

The bad luck persisted: Pierre Delaunay, a man "of violent temper, who had taken an Indian woman to live with him," apparently deserted. He was never seen again, but, said Marie, "my husband told me that he saw his scalp with the Indians, and knew it from the color of the hair." The son of a French trader and an Indian mother, Delaunay had trapped the upper Missouri for years before signing on as a hunter with the Astorians and had possibly met Lewis and Clark in 1806. He too had wandered the Idaho country in desperation before being rescued by Reed.[2]

The remaining seven men tried to carry on but found themselves harassed not by local Indians but by "strange tribes"—perhaps Delaunay's murderers—who were "troublesome, and always asked Mr. Reed for guns and ammunition." Tension heightened when the Indians stole a hooded cloak from La Chappelle and "drove an arrow into one of our horses." Concluding it was best to abandon the first post, Reed moved further up the Boise River, on the opposite side, and built a second cabin there. The area was "well stocked with beaver, of which they succeeded in trapping a considerable quantity." As winter came on, the men continued trapping, "sometimes sleeping out for several nights together at a time. Mr. Reed and one man generally stayed at the house," where Marie remained, taking care of her sons, fixing meals, and dressing skins.[3]

Late one night about January 10, said Marie, "a friendly Indian came running to our house, in a great fright, and told Mr. Reed that a band of the bad Snakes, called the Dog-rib tribe, had burnt the first house that we had built, and that they were coming on whooping and singing the war-song." John Hoback and Edward Robinson were camping and trapping nearby, but the four others were working out of a rude hut several miles farther up the Boise River. Marie immediately volunteered to go upriver and warn her husband, Jacob Reznor, La Chappelle, and a voyager by the name of Giles Le Clerc. Meanwhile, Reed had to find Hoback and Robinson, get back to the cabin, and prepare for battle.

"I took up my two children, got upon a horse, and set off to where my husband was trapping," said Marie, "but the night was dark, the road bad, and I lost my way." When a storm blew in the next morning, Marie and her boys sheltered themselves in the brush and "did not stir." The next day she set out again but saw smoke in the direction she had to travel. "Thinking it might proceed from Indians, I got into the bushes again and hid myself."[4]

On the third day, late in the evening, Marie finally reached the hut. "But just as I was approaching the place, I observed a man coming from the opposite side, and staggering as if unwell." The man was Le Clerc, "wounded and faint from loss of blood." He told Marie that her husband, La Chappelle, and Reznor had been robbed and murdered that morning. The Indians had "suddenly fallen on them while they were at their traps." Taking in this life-altering news, Marie kept her head. "I did not go into the hut; but putting Le Clerc and one of my children on the horse I had with me, I turned round immediately [and] took to the woods." Going back the same way she had come, she concentrated on saving Le Clerc and warning the others.[5]

But Le Clerc was badly injured and "could not bear the jolting of the horse, and he fell once or twice, so that we had to remain for nearly a day in one place." As night came on, Marie tried to make him comfortable. Rather than speak of his family in Canada, whom he had not seen since signing on with Astor almost four years earlier, Le Clerc gave Marie "directions as to the best means of effecting her escape, but ere he had concluded"—sometime before dawn—he died.[6]

"I covered him over with brushwood and snow," she reported. Next, determined to make it back to Reed's cabin, she put her sons, Baptiste, six, and Paul, four, on the horse, "I myself walking and leading the animal by the halter."[7] Whether he heard and understood what Le Clerc had said about his father, Baptiste knew the small family was facing a crisis—with Marie taking extreme measures to avoid Indians, rationing what little food they had, and huddling with the boys in a buffalo robe to endure the endless nights.

On the fourth day, Marie saw "a number of Indians on horseback galloping in an easterly direction." She immediately got the boys off the horse and "was fortunate enough to escape unnoticed." Late in the evening of the fourth day, she reached a bluff overlooking the cabin but saw no signs of life. Then, with mettle that proved so characteristic over the coming months, Marie "determined to ascertain whether any of the party were still living."[8]

First, she hid her boys and the horse in a grove of trees, knowing that the horse might be gone—that the boys might be gone—when she came back. Both of her sons lived to adulthood, but neither left a record of what was said in the midst of this crisis. Then, armed with a large knife, "she cautiously crept towards the scene of carnage. All was silent and lonely, and at every step fresh traces of blood met her view. Anxious to ascertain if any had escaped the massacre, she repeatedly called out the various names of the party, but no voice responded."[9]

Marie now knew for certain, if she had not earlier, that no one had survived.

"Sad was the sight!" she said. "Mr. Reed and the men"—Hoback and Robinson—"were all murdered, scalped, and cut to pieces. Desolation and horror stared me in the face."[10]

Three or four decades after his first encounter with Indians, Edward Robinson had used up the last of his nine lives and had been scalped a second and final time. He and Hoback had gone down together, separated from their friend Jacob Reznor because the others had needed an old hand to guide them. Hoback, Robinson, and Reed had died first, probably the day after Marie fled. Dorion, Reznor, La Chappelle, and Le Clerc had been attacked two days later, before Marie could reach them. The irony was that Marie's arriving too late to warn them had probably saved her and the boys.

"I turned from the shocking sight in agony and despair," she said, "took to the woods with my children and horse, and passed the cold and lonely night without food or fire. I was now at a loss what to do: the snow was deep, the weather cold, and we had nothing to eat. To undertake a long journey under such circumstances was inevitable death." Had she been alone, Marie said, she "would have run all risks" and taken flight. "But the thought of my children perishing with hunger distracted me. At this moment a sad alternative crossed my mind: should I venture to the house among the dead to seek food for the living?"[11]

Marie and her boys had not eaten for two days, and she knew the cabin contained a good stock of fish, unless it "had been destroyed or carried off by the murderers." It was also possible that the Indians were still lurking about, yet, she said, "I thought of my children. Next morning, after a sleepless night, I wrapped my children in my robe, tied my horse in a thicket, and then went to a rising ground, that overlooked the house, to see if I could observe anything stirring about the place." She saw nothing and resolved to enter the cabin after dark. "So I returned back to my children, and found them nearly frozen, and I was afraid to make a fire in the day time lest the smoke might be seen; yet I had no other alternative, I must make a fire, or let my children perish." She made the fire and warmed the boys, then wrapped them in the buffalo robe, put out the fire, and "set off after dark to the house," where she found the welcome sight of dried fish. "I gathered, hid, and slung upon my back as much as I could carry, and returned again before dawn of day to my children."[12]

The boys were "weak with hunger. I made a fire and warmed them, and then we shared the first food we had tasted for the last three days. Next night I went back again, and carried off another load; but when these afflictions were over, I sank under the sense of my afflictions, and was for three days unable to move, and without hope. On recovering a little, however, I packed all up, loaded my horse, and putting my children on top of the load, set out again on foot, leading the horse by the halter as before."[13] In this sad and hopeless condition, she forded the freezing Snake River and traveled through the deep snow and rugged paths for nine days, perhaps following the long valley where she had given birth to her third child two years earlier.

She traveled until she and the horse could travel no more. "Here I selected a lonely spot at the foot of a rocky precipice in the Blue Mountains, intending there to pass the remainder of the winter. I killed my horse, and hung up the flesh on a tree for my winter food. I built a small hut with pine branches, long grass, and moss, and packed it all round with snow to keep us warm, and this was a difficult task, for I had no axe, but only a knife to cut wood. In this solitary dwelling, I passed fifty-three lonely days!"[14]

She then left the hut and set out with her children to cross the mountains, but, like James and his companions in 1810, found herself snow blind, forced to stay in the same spot for three days while she used most of her food. "Having recovered my sight a little, I set out again, and got clear of the mountains, and down to the plains on the fifteenth day after leaving my winter encampments; but for six days we had scarcely anything to eat, and for the last two days not a mouthful." Not long after reaching the plains, she spotted smoke in the distance; "but being unable to carry my children farther, I wrapped them up in my robe, left them concealed, and set out alone in hopes of reaching the Indian camp, where I had seen the smoke; but I was so weak that I could hardly crawl, and had to sleep on the way." At noon the next day she arrived at the camp, which belonged to the Walla Walla, who treated her kindly. "Immediately on my arrival the Indians set off in search of my children, and brought them to the camp the same night." Marie and her boys stayed with the Walla Walla for two days. Then they had boarded canoes, hoping to meet white people on their way up or down the river.

"Thus ended the woman's story of hardships and woe," wrote Alexander Ross, the only eyewitness who recorded her story in detail. "That it was the Snakes who killed the party there is not the least doubt. The Dog-ribbed tribe have always passed for bad Indians." Ross ended his account of Marie's rescue by "recapitulating the number of casualties or disasters which befell the Pacific Fur Company during its short existence. . . . The tragical list stands thus:—

Lost on the bar	8
Land expedition	5
Tonquin	27
Astoria	3
Lark	8
Snake Country	9
Final departure	1
Total	61

"Well might we, with Virgial, say, 'Who can relate such woes without a tear!'"[15]

But John Jacob Astor perhaps said it best in a letter to Ramsay Crooks: "Was there ever an undertaking of more merit, or more hazard and more enterprising, attended with a greater variety of misfortune?"[16]

Chronology

September 12, 1806 Returning to St. Louis after a twenty-eight-month expedition, Lewis and Clark meet Robert McClellan, who is on his way up the Missouri River on a trading mission.

September 14, 1806 Lewis and Clark meet three keelboats, one commanded by French-Canadian trader Charles Courtin.

September 17, 1806 Lewis and Clark meet former U.S. Army officer John McClallen, commanding a keelboat.

September 20, 1806 Lewis and Clark meet Ramsay Crooks and several other traders.

September 23, 1806 Lewis and Clark arrive in St. Louis.

Winter 1806/1807 Crooks and McClellan form a fur-trading partnership.

March 1807 Meriwether Lewis is appointed governor of Louisiana Territory; William Clark is appointed chief Indian agent and brigadier general of territory militia.

April 1807 From a camp in Omaha country, McClellan writes a letter to Lewis, informing him of the situation on the Missouri River.

Manuel Lisa's party, including Hoback, Reznor, and Robinson, heads up the river.

May 1807 Nathaniel Pryor's party, including Pierre Dorion Sr. and Jr., departs St. Louis in attempt to return Mandan chief Sheheke and family to Mandan villages in present North Dakota.

Under orders of Lisa, George Drouillard shoots deserter Antoine Bissonnet, who dies of his wounds the next day.

June 22, 1807 Courtin writes a letter from the Arikara villages, reporting that those Indians have robbed and detained him.

Late June 1807 John Colter meets Lisa's men near the mouth of the Platte River and goes back upriver with them.

Late July 1807 Crooks and McClellan leave St. Louis with two keelboats and eighty men.

August 13, 1807 North West Company trader David Thompson receives a July 10 letter signed by "Zachary Perch" (John McClallen's alias) warning him not to interfere with U.S. trading operations in present northwestern Montana.

September 1807 Pryor's party is attacked by Arikara Indians, several men killed; returning to St. Louis, Pryor meets Crooks and McClellan near Council Bluffs; they decide to winter downstream, near the mouth of the Nodaway River.

Aaron Burr is acquitted of treason.

Courtin apparently establishes a trading post in the Three Forks area of present Montana.

November 1807 Lisa's group reaches the mouth of the Bighorn River and begins building Fort Raymond.

Winter 1807/1808 Drouillard and Colter make separate explorations of Wyoming's Bighorn Basin, with Colter likely traveling to Brooks Lake and then north along the western edge of Yellowstone Lake, in present Yellowstone Park; both men contribute to Clark's seminal map of the West.

January 1808 In a letter to De Witt Clinton, John Jacob Astor outlines his plans for the Western fur trade.

April 6, 1808 Astor's American Fur Company is organized.

Summer 1808 Crooks travels to Mackinac Island to obtain trade goods.

August 1808 Thomas Jefferson writes Lewis about a "powerful company" being formed by Astor.

Clark establishes Fort Osage about three hundred miles from St. Louis, on a bluff overlooking the Missouri River.

Late summer 1808 Colter escapes from Blackfoot Indians near Three Forks and makes famous run back to Fort Raymond.

Autumn 1808 Courtin apparently moves to area near Jocko River (in present northwestern Montana).

September 1808 George Drouillard is acquitted of the murder of Antoine Bissonnet; no charges are filed against Lisa.

By order of government agents, Crooks and McClellan winter near present site of St. Joseph, Missouri, not on upper Missouri as planned.

February 17, 1809 Crooks and McClellan sign statement dissolving their partnership; it is published in the *Missouri Gazette* on April 12.

March 4, 1809 James Madison inaugurated as fourth president of United States.

March 7, 1809 St. Louis Missouri Fur Company formally organized; the new company has already received a contract from Governor Lewis to escort Sheheke to his village.

May 1809 Crooks, apparently contacted by Wilson Price Hunt about joining Astor's westbound expedition, once again travels to Mackinac to obtain goods.

Representing the Missouri Fur Company, Pierre Chouteau departs St. Louis with 160 men; Lisa leaves with a large group of men, including Thomas James and John Dougherty, in June.

July 1809 Crooks, making excellent time from Mackinac, encounters Lisa at Fort Osage, then proceeds upriver to meet McClellan.

August 1809 Pierre Dorion Jr. and father join Missouri Fur Company men at Omaha villages.

September 1809 On their way to the Mandan and Hidatsa villages, Crooks and McClellan are halted by hostile Lakota and winter near the mouth of the Platte River.

Lewis and Clark leave on separate trips east.

September 22, 1809 Chouteau's group safely returns Sheheke and family to their home.

October 11, 1809 Meriwether Lewis dies of self-inflicted wounds at Grinder's Stand, Tennessee.

November 20, 1809 Chouteau, Lisa, their crew, and their passengers— Charbonneau, Sacagawea, and Pomp—arrive in St. Louis.

February 1810 Courtin killed by Blackfoot Indians east of present Missoula, Montana.

March 1810 Colter guides Pierre Menard and Andrew Henry and their men, including Hoback, Reznor, and Robinson, from Fort Raymond to Three Forks (which they reach on April 3) by way of Wyoming's Bighorn Basin.

April 12, 1810 Two of Menard and Henry's men are killed in a Blackfoot attack, with three others missing and presumed dead.

April 22, 1810 Colter and two companions carry letters eastward, reaching St. Louis at the end of May.

May 1810 Drouillard and two others are killed in another Blackfoot attack.

Ca. June 1810 Henry's party, which includes Hoback, Reznor, and Robinson, travels south, apparently by way of Wyoming's Shoshone and Wind Rivers, and establishes Henry's Fort north of present Rexburg, Idaho.

June 9, 1810 Crooks arrives in St. Louis and soon heads north to Mackinac.

June 23, 1810 Formal papers are signed in New York to organize Astor's Pacific Fur Company; partners include Alexander McKay, Donald McKenzie, Duncan McDougall, David Stuart, Wilson Price Hunt, Ramsay Crooks, Robert McClellan, and Joseph Miller; Robert Stuart becomes a partner in September.

July 7, 1810 Clark arrives in St. Louis after a nine-month trip to the East.

Mid-July 1810 Menard's group, including Pierre Dorion and his family, arrives in St. Louis.

July 17, 1810 McKenzie, Hunt, and others arrive at Mackinac Island to recruit hands for the overland journey to the Pacific; Crooks arrives about two weeks later.

July 23, 1810 Pierre Dorion Sr. dies at about seventy years of age.

Mid-August Astorians leave Mackinac Island, reaching St. Louis in early September.

September 6, 1810 *Tonquin* sails from New York harbor.

October 21, 1810 Hunt's group departs St. Louis to winter at mouth of Nodaway River.

November 16, 1810 Hunt reaches winter camp; McClellan's group arrives about the same time, after being robbed by Sioux Indians.

December 1810 David Thompson receives word that an "officer [apparently McClallen] and 8 soldiers" have been killed by Blackfoot Indians in the area between Three Forks and Great Falls.

Late December 1810 *Tonquin* doubles Cape Horn.

January 20, 1811 Hunt and a few others return to St. Louis.

March 1, 1811 *Tonquin* leaves Sandwich Islands.

March 12, 1811 Hunt's group, which includes Pierre and Marie Dorion and their sons, sets out from St. Louis.

March 22, 1811 *Tonquin* reaches mouth of Columbia River; eight men drown in two separate incidents over the next few days.

April 2, 1811 Lisa's party, including Charbonneau and Sacagawea, leaves St. Charles, pushing hard to catch Hunt.

Mid-April 1811 Astorians from *Tonquin* begin clearing land to build Fort Astoria.

April 17, 1811 Hunt's group reaches camp at Nodaway River, joins with McClellan, Miller, and others.

May 26, 1811 Hunt's group meets Hoback, Reznor, and Robinson, who have made their way east from Fort Henry; they agree to guide Hunt west.

Early June 1811 Lisa catches Hunt; bloodshed between Lisa and several different members of Hunt's party narrowly avoided.

Ca. mid-June 1811 Virtually entire crew of *Tonquin*, as well as approximately two hundred Indians, killed when crew members ignite powder magazine after Indian attack.

July 18, 1811 Hunt, McKenzie, Crooks, McClellan, Miller, and Reed, accompanied by fifty-six men, one woman, and two children, with eighty-two pack horses, depart Arikara villages in present South Dakota and follow the Grand River west.

Late August 1811 Hunt crosses into present northeastern Wyoming; within days, Edward Rose, now leaving the party, and Crow Indians help Hunt find his way out of the Bighorn Mountains.

September 1811 Henry and several men arrive at Mandan villages with forty packs of beaver; he and Lisa reach St. Louis late in October.

September 9, 1811 Hunt begins traveling along the Wind River.

September 27, 1811 Hunt reaches confluence of the Snake and Hoback Rivers.

October 8, 1811 Hunt arrives at Henry's Fort; the group descends Henry's Fork in canoes on October 19.

October 28, 1811 Clappin drowns and many goods are lost when Crooks's canoe capsizes just west of present Burley, Idaho.

Ca. November 1811 After trapping the Bear River, Miller, Hoback, Reznor, Robinson, and Cass are robbed by Indians; they winter in southern Wyoming or northern Colorado.

November 2, 1811 McKenzie and McClellan each lead a group of men on scouting missions; Reed does the same on October 31.

November 4, 1811 Crooks returns after aborted attempt to travel back to Henry's Fort.

November 7, 1811 William Henry Harrison's troops repulse a force of Indians led by Tenskwatawa ("the Prophet') at the Battle of Tippecanoe, a key event leading to the War of 1812.

November 9, 1811 Hunt and Crooks lead groups along the north and south banks of the Snake River, respectively; both groups are soon on the verge of starvation.

December 11, 1811 Provost, one of Crooks's party, drowns after capsizing a canoe; Hunt leaves a supply of meat with Crooks, who is too sick to travel.

December 21, 1811 Hunt reunites with Crooks's men, except Dubreuil, John Day, and Crooks himself, who have stayed behind; Hunt crosses the Snake River two days later and travels into northeastern Oregon.

December 28, 1811 Marie Dorion gives birth to a baby, which dies ten days later.

January 8, 1812 Hunt's group is assisted by a band of prosperous Indians near the Umatilla River.

January 18, 1812 McKenzie, McClellan, Reed, and eight others reach Astoria by way of the Snake and Columbia Rivers.

February 15, 1812 Hunt and thirty-three others, including the Dorion family, reach Astoria.

Ca. mid-February Crooks and Day slowly make their way toward the Columbia River.

Late March 1812 McClellan saves Reed's life during an Indian attack at Celilo Falls; the two and four others abandon plans to travel to St. Louis and New York.

Spring 1812 After being robbed again by Indians, Miller, Hoback, Reznor, and Robinson travel to Bighorn Range, then cross into present Idaho; Cass either deserts or is killed by Indians.

Ca. late April 1812 Returning to Astoria from Fort Okanogan, McClellan and companions meet Crooks and Day, who have been robbed by Indians.

May 7, 1812 Death of John Colter in Missouri Territory, at about age thirty-eight.

May 11, 1812 Crooks and Day arrive at Astoria with McClellan and several others.

June 18, 1812 US declares war on Great Britain.

June 29, 1812 Stuart leaves Astoria with Crooks, McClellan, Day, Jones, Vallé, and Le Clerc.

July 3, 1812 Because of Day's "insanity," Stuart hires local Indians to escort him back to Astoria.

August 1, 1812 Following the Umatilla River, Stuart reaches the area near present Pendleton, Oregon.

August 20, 1812 Stuart's group meets Miller, Hoback, Reznor, and Robinson near the site of present Grandview, Idaho.

August 30, 1812 Hoback, Reznor, and Robinson elect to stay and trap; Miller continues on with Stuart.

Ca. September 1812 Retrieving goods from a cache near the spot where Clappin drowned, Reed meets Hoback, Reznor, and Robinson; he also finds St. Michel, Carson, Delaunay, Dubreuil, La Chappelle, Landry, and Turcotte, all of whom have been robbed by Indians, and takes them to Astoria.

September 19, 1812 Stuart's horses stolen by Crow Indians near present site of Alpine, Wyoming; the men descend the south fork of the Snake River on rafts.

October 1, 1812 Stuart reaches Pierre's Hole, stopping temporarily because Crooks is too sick to continue.

October 21, 1812 Stuart crosses the Continental Divide at South Pass and heads east.

November 1812 Madison is reelected U.S. president.

December 20, 1812 Death of Sacajawea at Fort Manuel (in present South Dakota) at about age twenty-four, from typhus fever.

December 31, 1812 Stuart's group makes winter camp near present Torrington, Wyoming.

March 8, 1813 Stuart's group resumes their eastbound journey, following the North Platte and Platte Rivers.

April 18, 1813 Stuart reaches the Missouri River.

April 30, 1813 Stuart, Crooks, McClellan, Miller, Jones, Vallé, and Le Clerc arrive in St. Louis.

June 1813 William Clark is appointed governor of Missouri Territory.

June 23, 1813 Stuart, who had left St. Louis on May 16, reaches New York and gives Astor year-old news of events in Astoria.

July 1813 John Reed departs Astoria, leading the following individuals on a trapping expedition: André La Chappelle, Giles Le Clerc, Pierre Delaunay, Pierre and Marie Dorion and their two sons, Francois Landry, and Jean Baptiste Turcotte.

Mid-August 1813 Reed's party reaches the Snake River.

Late summer 1813 Crooks, who left St. Louis early in July, reaches New York and joins Astor in Great Lakes fur trade.

Late September 1813 Hoback, Reznor, and Robinson join Reed's group.

October 16, 1813 Astoria is sold to North West Company.

Late 1813 Three members of Reed's party die—Landry, after falling from a horse; Turcotte, from an illness; and Delaunay, after deserting and apparently being killed by Indians.

Ca. January 10, 1814 Reed's party is attacked by Dog-rib tribe of Shoshone Indians; Reed, Hoback, and Robinson killed at one camp and Reznor, Dorion, La Chappelle, and Le Clerc at another; Marie Dorion and her sons, Baptiste and Paul, survive.

Early February 1814 Marie and her sons make a winter camp in Blue Mountains of present northeastern Oregon.

March 23, 1814 Nicholas Biddle informs William Clark by letter that *The History of the Expedition under the Commands of Captains Lewis and Clark* has been published and is selling well.

Late March 1814 Marie and her sons travel north and are saved by Walla Walla Indians.

April 17, 1814 Near the mouth of the Walla Walla River, Marie and her sons meet a large group of Astorians en route to Montreal.

Appendix A

Biographical Directory

John Jacob Astor (1763–1848)

Born: July 17, 1763, in Waldorf, Germany, to Johann Jakob Astor and Maria Magdalena Volfelder.

Married: Sarah Todd on September 19, 1785.

Children: Magdalen, John Jacob II, William Blackhouse, Dorothea, Eliza.

General: Arrived in the United States in 1784 and soon became interested in the fur trade. Began trading with Canadian companies in the 1790s. Founded the American Fur Company in 1808 and the Pacific Fur Company in 1810. After the War of 1812, the American Fur Company dominated the Great Lakes fur trade. The Western Department of the American Fur Company launched operations in the Plains and Rocky Mountains in the 1820s. Retired from fur business in 1834 and spent the rest of his life investing in real estate and funding the arts and other causes. Became America's first multimillionaire and was the wealthiest person in America at the time of his death.

Died: March 28, 1848, in New York.

Sources: Madsen, *John Jacob Astor*; Porter, *John Jacob Astor*; Lamar, *Encyclopedia of the West*, 65–66.

Alexander Carson (ca. 1775–1836?)

Born: About 1775, possibly in Mississippi, to Alexander Carson Sr.; mother's name unknown.

General: Likely went up the Missouri River with Chouteau in 1809 as a hunter; likely at Three Forks with Menard and Henry in the spring of 1810. Spent the winter of 1810–1811 at Arikara villages with Benjamin Jones. Joined Hunt on May 22, 1811. "Left party in September, 1811, at Mad River, to trap beaver; robbed by Crows; picked up by John Reed and taken to Astoria by McKenzie January 16, 1813; arrived at Fort George from the

169

Willamette March 20, 1814; joined the North West Company, but left Fort George for Montreal, April 4, 1814." (Porter, "Roll of Overland Astorians," 105.) "He was one of the earliest settlers at Chemaway, Oregon, and is recorded as having been at Fort George and Fort Vancouver in the Hudson's Bay Company account books of 1820–1821." (Clarke, *Men of the Expedition*, 68.)

Died: Murdered in April or May of 1836 in a town later called Alec's Butte, about six miles north of Lafayette, Yam Hill County, Oregon. According to a letter from T. J. Hubbard to James W. Nesmith written in 1858, Carson was sick and was traveling with an Indian by the name of Boney, who had been employed by Carson for several years. For some unknown reason, Boney compelled his twelve- or fourteen-year-old son to shoot Carson while the latter was sleeping in a tent. Boney and his son both died soon afterwards (cause of death unknown).

Controversy: Charles G. Clarke concludes that Carson was likely a member of the Lewis and Clark Expedition for the first leg of the journey (from St. Louis to Fort Mandan, in 1804). Clarke first speculates that the man William Clark listed as "E. Cann" or "Carrn" was actually Carson. (Clark's journal entries, July 4, 1804, and August 13, 1804, Moulton, *Journals*, 2:347, and 2:477, respectively.) He then quotes a letter from Hubbard to Nesmith (discussed above) that states: "Carson came out to the Mountains with Lewis and Clark and after returning to the States, engaged with Hunt in1811 and returned to this country [Oregon], and remained here." (Clarke, *Men of the Expedition*, 28.) Hubbard does not give the source of his information about Carson serving with Lewis and Clark. Donald Jackson effectively argues that the case is not solid enough: "I find no evidence that [Carson] was ever with Lewis and Clark. . . . The name appears as 'Carrn' and Thwaites adds '[Carson?–Ed.].' I have checked the word in the manuscript journals, and like Thwaites I get nothing from it but 'Carrn.' But I still believe that Carson, had he been with the expedition, would have been mentioned in the rosters and journal entries." (Jackson, *Letters*, 373.)

Additional Sources: Irving, *Astoria*, 169-70, 70n8; Bradbury, *Travels*, 93, 93n58, 178; Jones, *Annals of Astoria*, 72, 73.

John Colter (ca. 1774–1812)

Born: About 1774, birthplace and parents' names unknown.

Married: A woman named Sarah, maiden name unknown, in about 1811.

Children: Hiram and Evelina, birth dates unknown (although there is circumstantial evidence that Hiram was born before the Lewis and Clark Expedition, meaning that Colter was likely married, divorced, or widowed when he departed with the captains).

General: The first mention of him in the historical record came on December 30, 1803, when William Clark wrote, "Colter Kill a Deer & a turkey." Clark later recorded that Colter had enlisted with the Lewis and Clark

Expedition on October 15, 1803. Although he was disciplined at the Wood River camp during the winter of 1803–1804, Colter proved to be a reliable hunter and scout during the expedition, so much so that he was granted permission to leave the Corps of Discovery in August of 1806—at the Mandan villages—and stay in the West to trap with Dickson and Hancock. By the summer of 1807, Colter had enlisted with Lisa, and over the next three years had several notable adventures, including an amazing escape from Blackfoot Indians and the first known exploration of parts of present Yellowstone Park by a European American. He returned to St. Louis in May of 1810, eventually becoming the only member of the Lewis and Clark Expedition to become better known for his exploits after the trek than during it. However, no first-person account of Colter's fascinating experiences has been discovered.

Died: May 7, 1812, at about age thirty-eight, apparently from a disease or condition that caused jaundice. Immediately prior to his death, he had served with Nathan Boone's rangers in the War of 1812.

Controversy: Although the claim has frequently been made that Colter was born near Stuarts Draft, Virginia, no solid facts concerning his birth have been documented—not the place or date, nor his parents' names. Likewise, the claim that he served with Simon Kenton in the Indian wars and joined Lewis and Clark at Maysville, Kentucky, cannot be substantiated. Nor is there persuasive evidence that Colter crossed Teton Pass and explored Pierre's Hole in Idaho (leading scholars now to believe he traveled from Brooks Lake to Yellowstone Lake before winding back to Fort Raymond) or that he labored for the mysterious John McClallen in western Montana (Colter's service with Lisa or the Missouri Fur Company from 1807 to 1810 is reasonably well documented). Again, although many secondary works have maintained that Colter died in November of 1813, government records clearly recorded his death on May 7, 1812.

Sources: James, *Three Years,* 29; Moulton, *Journals,* 2:142; Jackson, *Letters,* 2:378; Colter-Frick, *Courageous Colter*; Harris, *John Colter.*

Ramsay Crooks (1787–1859)

Born: January 2, 1787, in Greeenock, Scotland, to William Crooks and Margaret Ramsay, who was widowed in 1796 and emigrated to Canada with her children in 1803.

Married: Marianne Pelagie Emile Pratte, on March 10, 1825.

Children: Emily, Virginia, Marguerite, Ramsey, Bernard, William, Sylvestre, Charles, Julia.

General: Worked as a clerk for the fur trader Robert Dickson. Likely went up the Missouri for the first time in 1805. Formed a partnership with Robert McClellan during the winter of 1806–1807. Became a founding partner of the Pacific Fur Company in June 1810. Went west with Hunt's group in 1811; remained in Idaho with John Day during the winter of 1811–1812 because of illness; arrived in Astoria on May 11, 1812. Resigned from the

Pacific Fur Company and returned east with Stuart, arriving in St. Louis on April 30, 1813; within months traveled to New York and accepted an offer from Astor for a one-third interest in a Great Lakes trading venture. Over the next thirty years he became one of the leading figures in the American fur trade, including a tenure as president of the Northern Department of the American Fur Company, which he and others purchased from Astor in 1834. He was well respected as a competitive but highly ethical businessman and a tireless worker, despite chronic health problems. Changing markets and fickle government regulations brought the company to a crisis in 1842, but "by long, careful, adroit maneuvering Crooks paid off every cent. In 1845 he opened a small commission house in New York, dealing in pelts of all kinds. He lived very quietly. His principal pleasure was meeting friends from the wilderness and talking over old times." (Lavender, *Fist in the Wilderness*, 419.)

Died: June 6, 1859 in New York City.

Additional Sources: Irving, *Astoria*, 129–30n10; Ancestry.com; Dictionary of Canadian Biography Online; Lavender, "Ramsay Crooks's Early Ventures."

John Day (ca. 1770–1820)

Born: About 1770 in Culpepper County, Virginia, to Ambrose and Winifred Day.

General: Arrived in present-day Missouri by 1798, obtained a land grant from the Spanish government and farmed, trapped, and mined salt. Went up the Missouri River with Crooks and McClellan in 1807 and worked with them for the next three years. Joined with Overland Astorians by December 26, 1810. Spent the winter of 1811–1812 with Crooks in present-day Idaho; reached Astoria on May 11, 1812. Started back to St. Louis with Stuart in June of 1812 but could not continue because of his "insanity," with Stuart claiming that Day attempted suicide several times. The Indian hired to escort Day back to Astoria did not do so, but a friendly Chinook by the name of Calpo took Day to Astoria on August 9, five weeks after Stuart had left him near the Willamette River. Over the next fourteen months Day lived a normal life at Astoria and frequently made successful hunting excursions. He joined with the North West Company and spent the last years of his life in Oregon, where a river and a town are named for him.

Died: February 16, 1820, in present-day central Idaho, after signing a will the previous day stating the he was "sound in mind but infirm of body." He named Donald McKenzie, who was with him at the time, as sole executor of his estate.

Controversy: The first question concerns Day's state of mind when Stuart felt compelled to leave him behind. Duncan McDougall, supervising partner at Astoria, reported that Day—who said he feigned madness because he could no longer bear McClellan's shameful treatment—arrived in good health and showed no signs of insanity. Moreover, there is no record of Day ever acting irrationally in subsequent years. As Robert F. Jones has ntoed, "John Day's conduct on this occasion cannot be fully explained. What seems likely, however, is that, as he approached the area where he had spent the winter with Ramsay Crooks, he found himself unwilling to continue. . . . Possibly the fear of facing something like that again drove Day into a temporary state of insanity or he feigned it in order to be sent back." (*Annals of Astoria*, 113n58.) Second, historians differ on whether Day was among the Montreal-bound Astorians who discovered Marie Dorion in April 1814. The "Joshua Day" listed by Alexander Henry in his journal is presumed to be John Day because no other man named Day was known to be among the Astorians. The argument that Henry simply misheard or misrecorded Day's first name does not hold up because he noted the name "John Day" in an earlier journal entry.

Additional Sources: Elliott, "Last Will and Testament of John Day"; Ancestry.com; Irving, *Astoria*, 138–39n14 (note by Edgeley W. Todd); Porter, "Roll of Overland Astorians," 106; Coues, *Journals of Henry and Thompson*, 857, 875; Drumm, "More About Astorians," 352–57; Jones, *Annals of Astoria*, 113, 115–16, 118–31,137, 189, 196, 217, 218, 220, 221.

Jean Baptiste Dorion (ca. 1807–ca. 1850)

Born: About 1807 to Pierre and Marie Dorion. (Other dates have been given for his birth, but 1807 is most likely; see the entry for Marie Dorion for more information.)

Married: Josephine Walla Walla in 1845.

Children: Denise, Pierre, Genevieve, David, Philomene, Joseph, Marianne.

General: In 1834, the naturalist John K. Townsend was traveling near the Walla Walla River and wrote that he was "accompanied by a young half breed named Baptiste Dorion, who acts as guide, groom, interpreter, &c." (Townsend, *Narrative*, 347.) According to Gordon Speck, Baptiste "and his half-breed friend McKay acted as guides and interpreters for McLoughlin and his guests; in 1844 'Baptiste Doria' paid a tax of 85¢ on horses valued at $280; and once he emerges as interpreter-guide in the 'Reminiscences of Hugh Cosgrove,' a well-to-do businessman trying to locate somewhere in Oregon about 1847." (Speck, *Breeds and Half-Breeds*, 199.) "He also served as a lieutenant with the Oregon Rifles in the Cayuse Wars of 1847." (Hardee, "Ordeal," 49.)

Died: Reportedly in 1849 or 1850, details not known.

Controversy: Doane Robinson reported that Baptiste was adopted by a Walla Walla chief and that soon after that Marie and Paul returned to the South Dakota area. Neither of these claims can be substantiated. Also, Baptiste should not be confused (but often is) with his uncle of the same name, son of Pierre Sr. and brother of Pierre Jr., a trader and interpreter on the

Missouri River who served at Fort Pierre and was called "Old Dorion" by Maximilian.

Additional Source: Peltier, *Madame Dorion*, 27–29.

Marie Dorion (ca. 1791–1850)

Born: Around 1791, among the Iowa Nation, birthplace and parents' names unknown.

Married: Pierre Dorion Jr. around 1806 (he was killed by Indians in 1814); Louis Venier, of the North West Company, around 1818 (he was reportedly killed by Indians); Jean Baptiste Toupin, an interpreter at Fort Nez Percés, in the early 1820s.

Children: Jean Baptiste, Paul, and unnamed infant who died several days after birth (by Dorion); Marguerite, born around 1819 (by Venier); Francois, born in 1825, and Marianne, born in 1827 (by Toupin).

General: After meeting the Astorians in 1814, Marie and Baptiste and Paul remained at Fort Okanogan, by then an important post owned by the North West Company. Marie and Venier likely met and lived at Fort Okanogan. Her next known residence was Fort Nez Percés, later called Fort Walla Walla, founded in 1818 near the mouth of the Walla Walla River, where Marie had met the Astorians. (This fort is now known as "Old Fort Walla Walla" and should not be confused with the "Fort Walla Walla" founded in 1858 at the site of present-day Walla Walla, Washington.) The Reverend Jason Lee and Narcissa Whitman both mentioned seeing Marie in 1838. "The water was high in the streams," wrote Lee. "I took a girl in my arms and started across, and to my astonishment was followed by the females [a Mrs. Pamburn and her daughters and Marie and her daughter, Marguerite] with larger loads than I should have probably have ventured with, consisting of children, saddles, blankets, saddle bags, dogs &c., and all came safe over." ("Diary of Reverend Jason Lee–III," 417.) In 1841 Toupin moved the family to the Willamette Valley and filed land claims about three miles east of present Salem, Oregon. Marie was a devout Catholic; she became widely respected and was known as Madame Dorion. She was so revered that she was buried inside the church. The church burned down in 1880, however, and any records identifying her burial spot were lost. The new church, built in the same general vicinity, is now the best marker of her grave. (See also the entry for Pierre Dorion.)

Death: In 1850, on September 3 (according to land office records) or September 5 (according to Catholic Church records).

Controversy: Historians generally accept the assumption made here and throughout this volume that Baptiste and Paul were born around 1807 and 1809, respectively, but such an assumption remains speculative. Hunt noted that Marie was accompanied by *two children* when the Astorians left the Arikara villages in July of 1811. Irving, also not identifying the gender of either child, says the children were two and four years old in November of

1811. Marie gave birth to a third child on December 30, 1811, but the baby (again, gender not identified) died eight days later. Gabriel Franchere, one of the Astorians who met Marie in 1814, reported that her two children were both boys and implied that neither was an infant, making it quite reasonable to conclude that these boys were the same children mentioned by Hunt and Irving and were now around six and four years old. In July 1841, near present-day Salem, Oregon, Father F. N. Blanchet validated the previous marriage between Marie and Toupin and also legitimized the two children (Francois and Marianne) born to that union. Two children from Marie's previous marriages—Baptiste Dorion and Marguerite Venier—were also acknowledged in the Catholic records at that time. Baptiste is listed as Dorion's son, but the birth date given is 1816, a date which is not possible since Dorion died in January of 1814, making 1814 the latest year that a child of Pierre Dorion could have been born. Paul is not mentioned in the Catholic record at all. One secondary source reports that "and after thinking [a] while, [Marie] said there was another one, a little man with a wide mouth that stretched nearly from ear to ear and who had odd eyes. She said that he had run away with some Indians when he grew up and she did not know where he was or even if he was alive. She gave his name as Paul." (Peltier, *Madame Dorion*, 28.) This report, however, cannot be corroborated, leaving us with no primary document positively identifying Paul as the son of Pierre and Marie Dorion. Further confusing the matter, Doane Robinson reported that Marie and Paul "returned to her Dakota home near Yankton, the transcontinental trip being one of great hardship. Soon after, she married the father of Chief Struck by the Ree, and lived until about 1860 when she died at the Yankton Agency." (Robinson, "Our First Family," 67.) This report is based on an interview with a Paul Dorion II conducted by E. E. Morford in 1926, but identities have clearly been confused. Marie's life and death in Oregon are well documented. The South Dakota woman was someone other than Marie Dorion—just as the Wyoming woman was someone other than Sacagawea. A Paul Dorion in South Dakota in the early twentieth century could have been the descendent of one of Pierre Dorion Sr.'s other sons. (See also the entry for Sacagawea.) Another controversy centers on the name "Holy Rainbow." While William Clark reported (in his journal entry of September 1, 1806) that Pierre Jr. had a Yankton Sioux wife, he did not mention her name. Gordon Speck claims that wife's name was Holy Rainbow but provides no source. (*Breeds and Half Breeds*, 165n.) Various genealogists have subsequently taken a variety of issues on this matter, with some agreeing with Speck and others reporting that Holy Rainbow was actually Pierre Jr.'s mother and others saying the Indian name of Marie herself was Holy Rainbox. Thus far, however, no primary document has been found that can settle these contradictions.

Additional Sources: Barry, "Madame Dorion"; Irving, *Astoria*, 290; Hunt, "Diary," 281; Franchere, *Narrative*, 143; Harriet D. Munnick, "Pierre Dorion"; Munnick, *Catholic Church Records at St. Paul, Oregon, 1839–1989*.

Paul Dorion (ca. 1809–1889?)

Born: About 1809 to Pierre and Marie Dorion.

Married: Reportedly first to My-Horse-Comes-Out-Horse and second to Mary Atoktisau.

General: Francis Parkman wrote that in 1846, at Fort Laramie, he saw "a shriveled little figure, wrapped from head to foot in a dingy white Canadian capote" standing in a doorway. "His face was like an old piece of leather, and his mouth spread from ear to ear. . . . He welcomed me with something more cordial than the ordinary cold salute of an Indian, for we were excellent friends." Parkman added that "Paul, thinking himself well treated, had declared everywhere that the white man had a good heart. He was a Dahcotah from the Missouri, a reputed son of the half-breed interpreter Pierre Dorion, so often mentioned in Irving's *Astoria* . . . he had been to the settlements of the whites, and visited in peace and war most of the tribes within the range of a thousand miles." (Peltier, *Madame Dorion*, 29.)

Controversy: Since even Parkman acknowledged that this person was the *reputed* son of Pierre and Marie Dorion and since Paul is not identified by name in any documents associated with Pierre or Marie, we cannot say anything about him with certainty. It is possible, for example, that one of the sons with Marie in 1814 died not long after that. Doane Robinson reported that Paul and Marie returned to their home among the Yankton Sioux and that Paul had three sons—Louis, Paul II, and David—but, as noted in the entry on Marie, this is clearly a case of mistaken identity, whether intentional or not.

Died: Reportedly in 1889 on the Iowa/Sac/Fox Reservation in Doniphan County, Kansas.

Additional Sources: Robinson, "Our First Family," 67–68; Web sitewww.tradegoods.org/dorion.htm, accessed on June 20, 2012.

Pierre Dorion Jr. (ca. 1780–1814)

Born: Around 1780 to Pierre Dorion Sr.and his Yankton Sioux wife.

Married: A Yankton Sioux woman by around 1804—what became of her is not known (see the entry for Marie Dorion); Marie Dorion around 1807.

Children: Jean Baptiste, Paul, and unnamed infant who died several days after birth—with Marie.

General: Assisted Lewis and Clark in 1804 and soon because a prominent interpreter and guide. Received a government contract to go up the Missouri in 1807 with Nathaniel Pryor and escort a group of Sioux Indians back to their homeland. As a Missouri Fur Company employee in 1809, he went up the Missouri River with Chouteau and Lisa and negotiated with Yankton and Lakota Sioux. The whiskey bill he ran up at Fort Mandan became a major source of contention between him and Lisa, and Dorion signed with Hunt early in 1811. After evading an arrest warrant initiated by Lisa, Dorin and Marie and their sons started up the Missouri on March 14. The family departed the Arikara villages on July 18. Except for hunting excursions by Pierre, the family remained with Hunt for the entire journey and arrived at Astoria on February 15, 1812. For close to a year and a half, the Dorion family and the family of the Iroquois Indian Ignace Shonowane lived a peaceful life at a camp a mile or two from Astoria, along Young's Bay. Dorion proved his worth as a hunter, scout, and canoe maker. The Dorion family left Astoria with John Reed and a group of trappers in July of 1813. They reached the Snake River in mid-August and began trapping the Boise River and surrounding region.

Died: Killed by Indians in present-day Idaho in January 1814.

Sources: Porter, "Roll of Overland Astorians," 107; Munnick, "Pierre Dorion"; Speck, *Breeds and Half Breeds*, 150–86.

John Hoback (?–1814)

Children: Apparently had a son named John, who married Darcus Killen in 1811.

General: Listed as a taxpayer in Mercer County, Kentucky, in both 1790 and 1800. Served in the Kentucky Scouts and Spies under Captain James Flinn from September to December 1793. Joined Manuel Lisa's fur-trading expedition in 1807; helped construct Fort Raymond later that year. Remained at Fort Raymond or Fort Mandan, likely with Reznor and Robinson, until going to Three Forks early in 1810 with Menard and Henry. After a series of Blackfoot attacks, traveled south and west under Henry's command, wintering in present southeastern Idaho near Henry's Fork of the Snake River. Went east early in 1811, crossing present-day Wyoming and part of South Dakota before meeting Hunt's group along the South Dakota/Nebraska border on May 26, 1811. Hoback, Reznor, and Robinson apparently remained together from that time until their deaths, leading (with various levels of success) Hunt's group across South Dakota and Wyoming, crossing the Teton Range into Idaho in early October 1811. At Henry's Fort, where they had spent the previous winter, they, along with Joseph Miller and Martin Cass, left Hunt and traveled approximately two hundred miles south, to trap the Bear River area. They then went another two hundred miles due east, across the lower valley of the Green River to Wyoming's Sierra Madre Mountains, where they were robbed by Arapaho Indians. They wintered fifty miles away, either in southern Wyoming or northern Colorado. In the spring of 1812 they were again robbed by the Arapaho, after which they wandered near the headwaters of the Wind River. Cass was either killed or deserted during this trek. They made their way back across the Tetons to the Snake River and followed it west; they were discovered by Stuart's eastbound group on August 20, 1812, near the site of present-day Grandview, Idaho. Deciding to return to Kentucky, they traveled with Stuart until August 30, when they elected to trap the Snake River region for two years—although Miller continued east with Stuart. Within a month, they saw John Reed and a few companions, who had come from Astoria to collect goods from the cache east of Caldron Linn. When Reed returned with Dorion's family and a group of trappers in September 1813, he found Hoback, Reznor, and Robinson, who had again been robbed by Indians, near the mouth of the Boise River.

Died: Killed by Indians in present-day Idaho in January 1814.

Sources: Bradbury, *Travels*, 98; Rollins, *Oregon Trail*, 86; Williams, *Hoback Family's American Story*, 6–9, 68–79; Scouts and Spies, Kentucky, 1790–1794, Records of Captain James Flinn's Company, National Archives; Ancestry.com.

Wilson Price Hunt (1783–1842)

Born: March 20, 1783, in Asbury, New Jersey, to John P. Hunt and Margaret Guild.

Married: Ann L. Hunt, widow of his cousin Theodore Hunt, on April 20, 1836; she died April 12, 1879. They did not have any children.

General: Arrived in St. Louis in 1804 and started a retail business with John Hankinson, a partnership that ended in 1809. Signed as a partner with the Pacific Fur Company in June 1810. As Astor's "chief agent," he took command of the Overland Astorians, leaving the Arikara villages in July 1811 and arriving in Astoria on February 15, 1812. "When Astoria was acquired by the North West Company, Hunt returned to the United States and in 1817 took up farming in Missouri near St. Louis, where, between 1822 and 1840 he served as postmaster. In 1837 he advertised himself as a dealer in furs." (Irving, *Astoria*, 36n41 [Todd's note].) He was a slave owner who had a reputation for honesty.

Died: April 13, 1842, in St. Louis.

Additional Sources: Elliott, "Wilson Price Hunt."

Thomas James (1782–1847)

Born: In Maryland on November 4, 1782, to Joseph Austin James and Elizabeth Hosten. The family moved to Kentucky sometime before 1798.

Married: Around 1812, wife's name not known.

General: An experienced frontiersman by the time he signed a contract with the St. Louis Missouri Fur Company on March 29, 1809. He went up the river that summer with the armada commanded by Pierre Chouteau and Manuel Lisa and the next winter made his way to Fort Raymond, where he joined with Menard and Henry. Survived Blackfoot attack and returned to St. Louis with Menard, arriving in mid-July 1810. Involved in a series of lawsuits with the Missouri Fur Company over the next few years, apparently signing a note for $100 to the company but receiving nothing from them. Purchased a large supply of goods in 1818 and in 1821 teamed with John McKnight on a trade mission to Santa Fe. They were robbed by Indians and lost a good deal of money, while Becknell, who undertook a similar venture to Santa Fe about the same time, made huge profits. An 1822–1824 trading expedition by James and others to Comanche country also failed. "Bereft of fortune but not of honor, James then resigned himself to a life of poverty and to the humdrum of a more settled existence, to his family, and to payment of his debts. . . . During those long years of defeat and hardships, James's brother supported his family and provided for the education of his children; it was all James could do to pay off his debts and leave his heirs only 'a good example and an unsullied name.'" (*Three Years*, x.) Elected General of the Second Brigade, First Division, Illinois militia in 1825. Published *Three Years Among the Indians and Mexicans* in 1847. "The book was attacked immediately after publication—probably because of James's disparaging remarks about many persons still living at that time—and [Nathaniel] Niles [who had assisted with the book] gathered as many copies as he could, and destroyed them." (*Three Years*, x–xi.) The book was reprinted in 1953 and has been widely available since then.

Died: December 17, 1847, in Monroe County, Missouri.

Source: James, *Three Years*, v–xi (introduction by A. P. Nasatir).

Benjamin Jones (?–1835)

Born: Reportedly in Kanawha County, West Virginia.

Married: Margaret (maiden name unknown); she died in May of 1837.

Children: Elvira, Melinda, Ramsey Crooks, Wilson Hunt, William Arbuckle

General: Arrived in St. Louis by 1802. Likely went up the Missouri River with Chouteau in 1809 as a hunter; likely at Three Forks with Menard and Henry in the spring of 1810. Spent the winter of 1810–1811 at Arikara villages with Alexander Carson. Joined Hunt on May 22, 1811. Reached Astoria with Hunt on February 15, 1812. Left Astoria with Stuart on June 29, 1812; arrived in St. Louis with Stuart on April 30, 1813. After his return to St. Louis, he purchased a 240-acre farm just south of the mouth of the Missouri River. In 1825 he joined an expedition tasked with marking out a road from Missouri to Santa Fe. They set out from Fort Osage on July 17, 1825. On August 11, Jones, one of the hunters and called "Old Ben Jones" by the other men, discovered a spring later called the "Diamond of the Plain." Jones was gone for four years. Moved family to Carondelet, Missouri, and later to the Gravois Creek area. Had one hundred acres in cultivation when he died.

Died: In June 1835, from cholera. At the time of his death, his sons were minors and his close friend, Wilson Price Hunt, was appointed their guardian. "The inventory of Jones' estate shows that he left a considerable fortune for that day, including fourteen slaves, a library of fifty-four books, a pleasure carriage and two well matched roan horses, live stock, farming implements and considerable real estate. He requested that the slaves bequeathed to his children should never be sold by them or their heirs 'under any pretense whatever.' Jones made provision in his will for the education of his children." (Drumm, "More About Astorians," 359.)

Additional Sources: Drumm, "More About Astorians," 357–60, with copy of his will on 359–60; *The Western Journal of Agriculture*, 1851, vol. 5 (St. Louis); Irving, *Astoria*, 169–70, 70n8; Bradbury, *Travels*, 93, 93n58, 178; Jones, *Annals of Astoria*, 72, 73; Porter, "Roll of Overland Astorians."

Manuel Lisa (1772–1820)

Born: September 8, 1772, in New Orleans, to Chrisobal de Lisa and Maria Ignacia Rodriguez.

Married: Polly Charles Chew in the 1790s—they had three children together and she died in 1818; Mitain, the daughter of an Omaha chief, in 1814—they had a son and a daughter; Mary Hempstead Keeny, in 1818.

General: Active in the Mississippi River trade by the 1790s; opened a store in Vincennes, Northwest Territory, in 1796; made an unsuccessful attempt to open the Santa Fe trade in the early 1800s; partnered with Pierre Menard and Alexander Morrison in 1807 and led a group to present-day Montana that year; founded the St. Louis Missouri Fur Company with several prominent partners in 1809 and led expeditions up the Missouri in 1809, 1811, 1812, and 1814. Performed valuable service as an Indian agent during the War of 1812.

Died: August 12, 1820, of an unidentified illness.

Source: Oglesby, "Manuel Lisa," in Hafen, *Mountain Men*, 5:179–201.

Robert McClellan (1770–1815)

Born: In 1770, near Mercersburg, Pennsylvania, to Robert McClellan Sr. and wife (name not known).

General: Served in the military from 1790 to 1795 and achieved the rank of lieutenant. "McClellan's service was as a scout or spy under the command of Captain William Wells. During these five years he became well known for the many encounters with Indians from which he emerged successful because of his mental alertness and physical activity in situations calling for prompt and decisive action." (Carter, "Robert McClellan," 221–22.) Wounded in the shoulder during the Indian wars and later applied for a pension. Began trading on the Missouri River around 1802. Had several financial disputes with Lisa over the next few years. Formed a partnership with Crooks during the winter of 1807–1808. Became a partner in the Pacific Fur Company in June 1810; departed Arikara villages with Overland Astorians in July 1811; reached Astoria with McKenzie, Reed, and others on January 18, 1812. "Their success was made possible by the fact that McClellan shot a bighorn sheep at their most critical hour." (Carter, "Robert McClellan," 226.) Resigned from company on March 1, 1812; saved Reed's life in skirmish with Indians near Celilo Falls in March; departed with Stuart's group in June of 1812; reached St. Louis on April 30, 1813. Imprisoned for debt within weeks but obtained release by initiating bankruptcy proceedings. Opened a store in Cape Girardeau, Missouri, in January 1814 but had to abandon the venture in July because of sickness. "On May 24, 1815, the Indians made an attack on a detachment of soldiers from Fort Howard, killing the Captain, Lieutenant, five privates and one citizen, besides wounding a number of soldiers and two of the citizens who came to the aid of the soldiers. The report of this affair says that Robert McClellan and other citizens deserved credit for their spirited exertions." (Drumm, "More About Astorians," 350.)

Died: On November 22, 1815, in St. Louis, after a short illness; buried on William Clark's farm. A tombstone found in 1875 (and likely inscribed by Clark) reads: "To the memory of Capt. Robert McClellan. This stone is erected by a friend who knew him to be brave, honest, and sincere; an intrepid warrior, whose services deserve perpetual remembrance. A.D. 1816." (Carter, "Robert McClellan," 228.)

Sources: All mentioned above.

Joseph Miller (?–?)

Born: In Pennsylvania.

General: Served in the military from 1799 to 1805, then became a trapper and trader. Became a partner in the Pacific Fur Company in June of 1810. Went west with Hunt but in October 1811, at Henry's Fort, resigned partnership and stayed to trap with Cass, Hoback, Reznor, and Robinson. Met Stuart's eastbound party in August 1812 and returned with them, reaching St. Louis on April 30, 1813. Nothing more is known of him.

Source: Rollins, *Oregon Trail*, c–ci.

Archibald Pelton (ca. 1780–ca. 1815)

Born: Around 1780, in New England, to David Pelton and Hannah Milliken.

General: Enlisted with the Missouri Fur Company in 1809 and went up the Missouri on the same boat with Thomas James, who said that Pelton was a "jovial, popular fellow [who] greatly amused the company in coming up the river, by his songs and sermons." (*Three Years*, 44.) Present at Three Forks in the spring of 1810, surviving a grizzly bear attack as well as Blackfoot Indian attacks. Apparently traveled with Henry to present-day Idaho during the summer of 1810 and disappeared some time after that. He was not heard of for more than a year. McKenzie, McClellan, and their companions discovered him late in 1811 in the vicinity of present-day Lewiston, Idaho. "They also encountered," wrote Franchere, "a young American, who was deranged, but who sometimes recovered his reason. This young man told them, in one of his lucid intervals, that he was from Connecticut, and was named Archibald Pelton. . . . Our people took this young man with them [to Astoria]." (Cited in Barry, "Archibald Pelton," 199.) Alexander Henry described him as an "idiot," and his name became part of the Chinook language to indicate mental derangement. He was one of the fifty men who remained at Astoria, by then called Fort George, in the spring of 1814 when the large group of Astorians went up the Columbia River en route to Montreal. Pelton is believed to be the "poor half-witted American from Boston, named Judge," who, according to Franchere, was murdered by an Indian at a logging camp in a case of mistaken identity. (Cited in Barry, "Archibald Pelton," 200.)

Died: Around 1815.

Additional Sources: Pelton, *Genealogy of the Pelton Family in America*, 454; Payette, *Oregon Country*, 190.

Jacob Reznor (1768–1814)

Born: August 13, 1768, in Rostraver Township, Cumberland County, Pennsylvania, to Peter and Mary Reasoner. (*Reznor* has now become the accepted spelling for Jacob's last name, which was spelled a variety of ways in eighteenth- and nineteenth-century documents. Bradbury had *Reesoner*.)

Married: Sarah (maiden name unknown) prior to 1790; she married Basil Burket in February or March of 1804, after Jacob was presumed dead.

Children: Solomon, William, Nancy.

General: Grew to manhood and married in Pennsylvania. Took his family to Kentucky soon after 1790. Apparently abandoned family and left Kentucky in 1797. According to family tradition, he "went off west to the mountains with a party of trappers and hunters and was never heard from again." (Anderson, *The Reasoner Story*, 56.) Might be the Jacob Reznor listed in the 1807 Indiana Territory Census. Joined Manuel Lisa's fur-trading expedition in 1807; helped construct Fort Raymond late that year. Remained at Fort Raymond or Fort Mandan, likely with Hoback and Robinson, until going to Three Forks early in 1810 with Menard and Henry. After a series of Blackfoot attacks, traveled south and west under Henry's command, wintering in present-day southeastern Idaho near Henry's Fork of the Snake River. Went east early in 1811, crossing present-day Wyoming and part of South Dakota before meeting Hunt's group along the South Dakota/Nebraska border on May 26, 1811. Hoback, Reznor, and Robinson apparently remained together from that time until their deaths. (See the entry for John Hoback for more information.)

Died: Killed by Indians in present-day Idaho in January 1814.

Additional Sources: Anderson, *The Reasoner Story*, 52–56; Bradbury, *Travels*, 98;

Edward Robinson (ca. 1745–1814)

Born: Around 1745.

General: Served in the Virginia militia and was present at the Siege of Fort Henry in 1777 (near present-day Wheeling, West Virginia). "He had been one of the first settlers of Kentucky, and engaged in many of the conflicts of the Indians on 'the Bloody Ground.' In one of these battles he had been scalped, and he still wore a handkerchief to protect the part."

(Irving, *Astoria*, 176.) Appears frequently in the records of Livingston County, Kentucky, from 1801 to 1806 and apparently owned at least three hundred acres of property. Joined Manuel Lisa's fur-trading expedition in 1807; helped construct Fort Raymond later that year. Remained at Fort Raymond or Fort Mandan, likely with Hoback and Reznor, until going to Three Forks early in 1810 with Menard and Henry. After a series of Blackfoot attacks, traveled south and west under Henry's command, wintering in present southeastern Idaho near Henry's Fork of the Snake River. Went east early in 1811, crossing present-day Wyoming and part of South Dakota before meeting Hunt's group along the South Dakota/Nebraska border on May 26, 1811. Hoback, Reznor, and Robinson apparently remained together from that time until their deaths. (See the entry for John Hoback for more information.)

Died: Killed by Indians in present-day Idaho in January 1814.

Additional Sources: Bradbury, *Travels*, 98; *Preston and Virginia Papers of the Draper Collection*; Menard, "List of Notes of the 'Men' on the Missouri Belonging in Part to Pierre Menard, 1808–1810," Pierre Menard Papers, Abraham Lincoln Presidential Library; Ancestry.com; Jerome, *Livingston County, Kentucky, County Court Order Books A-B, May 1799–January 1807*.

Edward Rose (?–1832/33)

Parents: Reportedly born to a white trader and a Cherokee-African mother.

General: "At about age eighteen he made his way to New Orleans as a deck hand on a keelboat. There his penchant for robbery and his savage readiness for a fight laid the cornerstone for his later reputation as a 'celebrated outlaw.' Here, too, he may have received the severe cut across his nose that gave him the nickname Nez Coupe or Cut Nose." (Blenkinsop, "Edward Rose," 336.) Enlisted with Lisa near the mouth of the Osage River in 1807; sent out as an emissary to the Crow Indians in fall of 1807 and lived among the Crow for several years, learning the Crow language and taking a Crow wife. Earned the name "Five Scalps" after single-handedly defeating a band of enemy Hidatsa. Signed on with Missouri Fur Company in 1809 but how long he stayed with Henry is unknown. Met Hunt at the Arikara villages in 1811 and guided him through the Bighorn Mountains, making no known attempt to sabotage the mission despite Hunt's suspicions. Listed with Lisa's Missouri Fur Company expedition in 1812. "In 1823, he was one of the key figures in William H. Ashley's disastrous defeat at the hands of the Arikaras and Colonel Leavenworth's punitive military campaign." (Blenkinsop, "Edward Rose," 340–41.) Guided Jedediah Smith into Wyoming's Bighorn Basin in 1823–1824 and continued to live a life of adventure for the next decade.

Died: Killed by Arikara warriors along the Yellowstone River in present-day Montana during the winter of 1832–1833.

Additional Sources: Holmes, "Five Scalps"; Lamar, *Encyclopedia of the West*, 987.

Sacagawea (ca. 1788–1812)

Born: About 1788 among the Shoshone nation in present Lemhi County, Idaho.

Married: Toussaint Charbonneau around 1804.

Children: Jean Baptiste, born February 11, 1805, and Lisette, born about 1812.

General: Kidnapped by Hidatsa warriors in the Three Forks area around 1800 and taken to present-day North Dakota. Subsequently sold to Charbonneau. She and Charbonneau, who lived in a Hidatsa village near the mouth of the Knife River, met Lewis and Clark in the fall of 1804 and accompanied them west in April 1805, when Baptiste, a favorite of Clark's—who called him "Pomp"—was less than two months old. Sacagawea proved to be a courageous and valuable member of the party and helped guide the captains and interpreted for them in her old homeland in western Montana and eastern Idaho. Sacagawea had a memorable reunion with her brother and other family members. On the return trip in 1806, the Charbonneaus remained in North Dakota. In 1809 they accepted Clark's offer of help and traveled to St. Louis, where they remained for a year and a half, when Charbonneau apparently grew weary of city life. When he and Sacagawea went up the river with Lisa in April 1811, they left Baptiste in Clark's care. (Clark provided for the boy's lodging and education but did not adopt him, as he had promised.) Charbonneau and Sacagawea dwelled at Fort Manuel, in present-day South Dakota for the next year and a half. Sacagawea was admired by both Lewis and Clark; others who met her called her "a good creature, of a mild and gentle disposition" and "the best [woman] in the fort."

Died: December 20, 1812, of typhus fever, near present-day Kenal, Corson County, South Dakota.

Controversy: Early in the twentieth century, Professor Grace Raymond Hebard and Dr. Charles Eastman independently reached the conclusion that an elderly Shoshone woman named Porivo, who had died on Wyoming's Wind River Indian Reservation in 1884, had actually been Sacagawea. Hebard and Eastman based their conclusions on two groups of letters and affidavits (written around 1905 and 1925) that appeared to offer strong evidence that Porivo was indeed Sacagawea. The theory gained popularity, even though many scholars, citing an 1812 document from John Luttig strongly indicating Sacagawea had died in 1812, rejected it. Then, in 1955, Dale Morgan discovered a document from William Clark clearly stating that Sacagawea had died by 1825–1828. The case was then considered closed among Lewis and Clark scholars.

Source: Morris, *Fate of the Corps*, 106–17, 210–13.

Robert Stuart (1785–1848)

Born: February 18, 1785, in the parish of Callander in Scotland, to John Stuart and Mary Buchanan.

Married: Emma Sullivan on July 21, 1813; she died on September 26, 1866.

Children: Mary Elizabeth, David, Kate, John, Robert Jr., Marion, William Maynard, Celia, William Maynard (the second of this name)

General: Left Scotland in 1807 and went to Montreal; became a clerk with the North West Company. Became a partner in the Pacific Fur Company on September 5, 1810. Sailed aboard *Tonquin* on September 6, 1810 and reached the mouth of the Columbia River in March 1811. Left Astoria with Crooks, McClellan, Day, Jones, Vallé, and Le Clerc on June 29, 1812; arrived in St. Louis on April 30, 1813; arrived in New York on June 23, 1813. Was associated with Astor and Crooks in the fur trade for the next two decades. Moved to Michilimacinac, Michigan, in 1817. Served as judge of county court in 1825. Retired from the fur business in 1834. Became a zealous member of the Presbyterian Church and was installed as an elder on November 12, 1835. Served as a director of the State Bank of Michigan, state treasurer of Michigan, and federal superintendent of Indian affairs.

Died: On October 29, 1848 in Chicago after contracting a cold; his estate was valued at $78,217.93. A newspaper obituary stated: "He leaveth behind him the incense of a good name."

Source: Rollins, *Discovery of the Oregon* Trail, xxxv–liii.

Editorial note: Sufficient information was not discovered to include entries for Pierre Delaunay, Andre La Chapelle, Francois Landry, Giles Le Clerc, John Reed, and Jean Baptiste Turcotte, all of whom were in the same trapping group as Hoback, Reznor, Robinson, and Dorion and perished in the Idaho wilderness, or for Francois Le Clerc and Andre Vallé, both members of Stuart's return party.

Appendix B

Documents

1. The First Published Account of the Astorian Adventure, 1813

Editorial Note: *Robert Stuart and his six companions arrived in St. Louis on April 30, 1813, an event announced by the* Missouri Gazette *on May 8. The following article was published in the* Missouri Gazette *on May 15, apparently based on interviews with Stuart, Crooks, and McClellan.*

AMERICAN ENTERPRIZE.

We last week promised our readers, an account of the journey of the gentlemen attached to the New York Fur Company, from the Pacific ocean to this place: we now lay it before our readers as collected from the gentlemen themselves.

On the 29th of June, 1812, Mr. Robert Steuart, one of the partners of the Pacific Fur Company, with two Frenchmen, Messrs. Ramsey Crooks and Robt. M'Clellan, left the Pacific ocean with dispatches for New York.

After ascending the Columbia river 90 miles, John Day, one of the hunters, became perfectly insane and was sent back to the main establishment, under the charge of some Indians; the remaining six pursued their voyage upwards of 900 miles, when they happily met with Mr. Joseph Miller on his way to the mouth of Columbia; he had been considerably to the south and east among the nations called Blackarms and Arapahays, by the latter of whom he was robbed; in consequence of which he suffered almost every privation human nature is capable of, and was now in a state of starvation and almost nudity when the party met him.

They now had fifteen horses, and pursued the journey for the Atlantic world, without any uncommon accident until within about 200 miles of the

187

Rocky mountains, where they unfortunately met with a party of the Crow Indians, who behaved with the most unbounded insolence, and were solely prevented from cutting off the party by observing them well armed and constantly on their guard. They however pursued on their track six days and finally stole every horse belonging to the party.

Some idea of the situation of those men may be conceived, when we take into consideration that they were now on foot and had a journey of 2000 miles before them, 1500 of which entirely unknown, as they intended and prosecuted it considerably south of Messrs. Lewis and Clark's rout; the impossibility of carrying any quantity of provisions on their backs, in addition to their ammunition and bedding, will occur, at first view. The danger to be apprehended from starvation was imminent.

They however put the best face upon their prospects, and pursued their rout towards the Rocky mountains at the head waters of the Colorado or Spanish river, and stood their course. E.S.E. until they struck the head waters of the great river Platte, which they undeviatingly followed to its mouth. It may here be observed, that this river for about 300 miles is navigable for a barge; from thence to the Otto village, within 45 miles of its entrance into the Missouri, it is a mere bed of sand, without water sufficient to float a skin canoe.

From the Otto village to St. Louis the party performed their voyage in a canoe furnished them by the natives and arrived here in perfect health on the 30th of last month. Our travellers did not hear of the war with England until they came to the Ottos; these people told them that the Shawanoe Prophet had sent them a wampum, inviting them to join the war against the Americans; that they answered the messenger, that they could make more by trapping beaver than making war against the Americans.

After crossing the hills (Rocky mountains) they happily fell in with a small party of Snake Indians, from whom they purchased a horse, who relieved them from any further carriage of food, and this faithful four-footed companion performed that service to the Otto village. They wintered on the river Platte about 600 miles from its mouth.

By information received from these gentlemen, it appears that a journey across the continent of North America, might be performed with a waggon, there being no obstruction in the wheel rout than any person would dare to call a mountin, in addition to its being much the most direct and short one to go from this place to the mouth of the Columbia river. Any future party who may undertake this journey, and are tolerably acquainted with the different places, where it would be necessary to lay up a small stock of provision, would not be impeded, as in all probability they would not meet with an Indian to interrupt their progress; although on the other route more north, there are almost insurmountable barriers.

Messrs. Hunt, Crooks, Miller, M'Clellan, M'Kenzie, and about 60 men who left St. Louis in the beginning of March, 1811, for the Pacific ocean, reached the Aricoras village on the 13th day of June, where, meeting with some American hunters who had been the preceding year on the waters of the Columbia with Mr. Henry, and who giving such an account of the route by which they passed as being far preferable in point of procuring with facility an abundant supply of food at all times, as well as avoiding even the probability of seeing their enemies the Black Feet, than by the track of captains Lewis and Clark; the gentlemen of the expedition at once abandoned their former ideas of passing by the falls of the Missouri, and made the necessary arrangements for commencing their journey over land from this place.

Eighty horse were purchased and equipped by the 17th of July, and on the day following they departed from the Aricoras, sixty persons in number, all on foot except the partners of the company. In this situation they proceeded for five days, having crossed in that time two considerable streams which joined the Missouri below the Aricoras, when finding an inland tribe of Indians calling themselves Shawhays, but known among the whites by the appellations of Cheyennes, we procured from these people an accession of forty horses, which enabled the gentlemen to furnish a horse for every two men. Steering about W.S.W. they passed the small branches of Big river, the Little Missouri above its forks, and several of the tributary streams of Powder river, one of which followed up they found a band of the Absaroka or Crow nation, encamped on its banks, at the foot of the Big Horn mountain.

For ammunition and some small articles, they exchanged all their lame for sound horses with these savages; but although that this band has been allowed, by every one who knew them, to be far the best behaved of their tribe, it was only by that unalterable determination of the gentlemen to avoid jeopardizing the safety of the party without at the same moment submitting to intentional insults, that they left this camp (not possessing a greater force then the whites) without coming to blows.

The distance from the Aricoras to this mountain, about 450 miles over an extremely rugged tract, by no means furnishing a sufficient supply of water; but during the twenty-eight days they were getting to the base of the mountain, they were only in a very few instances without abundance of buffaloe meat.

Three days took them over to the plains of Mad river (the name given the Big Horn above this mountain) which following for a number of days they left it where it was reduced to thirty yards in width, and the same evening reached the banks of the Colorado or Spanish river. Finding flocks of buffaloe at the end of the third day's travel on this stream, the party passed a week in drying buffaloe meat for the residue of the voyage, and in all probability those were the last animals of the kind they would meet with. From this camp, in one day, they crossed the dividing mountain and pitched their tents on Hobsucks Fork of Mad river, where it was near 150 feet broad, and in eight days more having passed several stupendous ridges, they encamped in the vicinity of the establishment made by Mr. Henry, in the fall of 1810, on a fork about 70 yards wide, bearing the name of that gentleman; having travelled from the main Missouri about 900 miles in 54 days.

Here abandoning their horses, the party constructed canoes and descended the Snake or Ky-eye-nem river (made by the junction of Mad river, south of Henry's fork) 400 miles, in the course of which they were obliged by their intervention of impassable rapids to make a number of portages, till at length they found the river confined between gloomy precipices at least 200 feet perpendicular, whose banks for the most part were washed by this turbulent stream, which for 30 miles was a continual succession of falls, cascades and rapids. Mr. Crook's canoe had split and upset in the middle of a rapid, by which one man was drowned, named Antoine Clappin, and that gentleman saved himself only by extreme exertion in swimming. From the repeated losses by the upsetting of canoes our stock of provisions were now reduced to a bare sufficiency for five days, totally ignorant of the country where they were, and unsuccessful in meeting any of the natives from whom they could hope for information.

Unable to proceed by water, Messrs. M'Kenzie, M'Clellan and Reed, set out in different directions inclining down the river, for the purpose of finding Indians and buying horses. Mr. Crooks with a few men returned to Henry's fork for those they had left, while Mr. Hunt remained with the main body of the men in trapping beaver for their support.—Mr. C. finding the distance much greater by land than they had contemplated, returned at the end of three days, where, waiting five more expecting relief from below, the near approach of winter made them determine on depositing all superfluous articles and proceeding on foot. Accordingly on the 10th of November, Messrs. Hunt and Crooks set out each with 18 men, one party on the north and the other on the south side of the river.

Mr. Hunt was fortunate in finding Indians with abundance of salmon and some horses, but Mr. Crooks saw but few, and in general too miserably poor to afford his party much assistance; thirteen days travel brought the latter to a high range of mountains, through which the river forced a passage, and the bank being their only guide, they still, by climbing over points of rocky ridges projecting into the stream, kept as near it as possible, till to the evening of the 3rd December, impassable precipices of immense height put an end to all hopes of following the margin of this watercourse, which here was not more than 40 yards wide, ran with incredible velocity, and was withal so foamingly tumultuous, that even had the opposite bank been fit for their purpose, attempt at rafting would have been perfect madness, as they could only have the inducement of ending in a watery grave a series of hardships and privations, to which the most hardy and determined of the human race must have found himself inadequate. They attempted to climb the mountains, still bent on pushing on, but after ascending for half a day, they discovered, to their sorrow, that they were not half way to the summit, and the snow already too deep for men in their emaciated state to proceed further.

Regaining the river bank, they returned up and on the third day met with Mr. Hunt and party, with one horse proceeding downwards; a canoe was soon made of a horse hide and in it transported what meat they could spare to Mr. Crooks' starving followers, who for the first eighteen days after leaving the place of deposit had subsisted on half a meal in twenty-four hours, and in the last nine days had eaten only one beaver, a dog, a few wild cherries and old mockasin soals, having travelled during these twenty seven days at least 550 miles. For the next four days both parties continued up the river without any other support than what little rose-buds and cherries they could find, but here they luckily fell in with some Snake Indians, from whom they got five horses, giving them three guns and some other articles for the same. Starvation had bereft J. B. Provost of his senses entirely, and on seeing the horse flesh on the opposite shore, was so agitated in crossing in a skin canoe that he upset it and was unfortunately drowned. From hence Mr. Hunt went on to a camp of Shoshonies about 90 miles above, where procuring a few horses and a guide he set out for the main Columbia, across the mountains to the south west, leaving the river where it entered the range, and on it Mr. Crooks and five men unable to travel.

Mr. H. lost a Canadian, named Carriere, by starvation, before he met the Shyey-to-ga Indians in the Columbia plains; from whom getting a supply of provisions, he soon reached the main river, which he descended in canoes and arrived without further loss at Astoria, in the month of February.

Messrs. M'Kenzie, M'Clellan and Reed had united their parties on the Snake river mountain, through which they travelled twenty-one days, to the Mulpot river, subsisting on an allowance by no means adequate to the toils they underwent daily; and to the smallness of their number (which was in all eleven) they attribute their success in getting with life to where they found some wild horses; they soon after reached the fork called by capts. Lewis and Clarke, Koolkooske; went down Lewis' partly, and the Columbia wholly, by water, without any misfortune, except the upsetting, in a rapid, of Mr. M'Clellan's canoe, and although it happened on the first day of the year, yet by great exertion they clung to the canoe till the others came to their assistance. Making their escape with the loss of some rifles, they reached Astoria early in January.

Three of the five men who remained with Mr. Crooks, afraid of perishing by want, left in February on a small river, on the road by which Mr. Hunt had passed in quest of Indians, and have not since been heard of. Mr. C. had followed Mr. H.'s track in the snow for seven days, but coming to a low prairie, he lost every appearance of the trace and was compelled to pass the

remaining part of the winter in the mountains, subsisting sometimes on beaver and horse meat, and their skins, and at others on their success in finding
roots. Finally, on the last of March, the other Canadian being unable to
proceed was left with a lodge of Shoshonies, and Mr. C. with John Day,
finding the snow sufficiently diminished, undertook, from Indian information, to cross the last ridge, which they happily effected and reached the
banks of Columbia by the middle of April, where in the beginning of May,
they fell in with Messers. Steuart, having been a few days before stripped of
everything they possessed, by a band of villains near the falls. On the10th of
May, they arrived safe at Astoria, the principal establishment of the Pacific
Fur Company, within 14 miles of cape Disappointment.

LOSS OF THE SHIP TONQUIN, NEAR THE MOUTH OF THE COLUMBIA

A large ship had arrived from New York after a passage of near seven
months, with merchandise and provisions for the Company. It was here we
learnt with sorrow that the story of the Tonquin's having been cut off was too
true. The circumstances have been related in different ways by the natives, in
the environs of the establishment, but that which from their own knowledge
carries with it the greatest appearance of truth, is as follows: That vessel,
after landing the cargo intended for Astoria, departed on a trading voyage to
the coast north of Columbia river, with a company of (including officers) 23
men, and had proceeded about 400 miles along the seaboard, when they
stopped on Vancouver's island at a place called Woody Point, inhabited by a
powerful nation called Wake-a-nin-ishes. These people came on board to
barter their furs for merchandise, and conducted themselves in the most
friendly and decorous manner during the first day, but the same evening
information was brought on board by an Indian, whom the officers had as
interpreter, that the tribe where they then lay were ill-disposed, and intended
attacking the ship next day; capt. Jonathan Thorne affected to disbelieve this
piece of news, and even when the savages came next morning in great numbers, it was only at the pressing remonstrance of Mr. M'Kay, that he ordered
seven men aloft to loosen the sails. In the mean time about 50 Indians were
permitted to come on board, who traded a number of sea otters for blankets
and knives; the former they threw into their canoes as soon as received, but
secreted the knives. Every one when armed moved from the quarter deck to a
different part of the vessel, so that by the time they were ready, in such a
manner were they distributed, that at least three savages were opposite every
man of the ship, and at a signal given, they rushed on their prey, and notwithstanding the brave resistance of every individual of the whites, they were all
butchered in a few minutes. The men above, in attempting to descend, lost

two of their number, besides one mortally wounded, who, notwithstanding his weakened condition, made good his retreat with the four others to the cabin, where, finding a quantity of loaded arms they fired on their savage assailers through the skylights and companion way, which had the effect of clearing the ship in a short time, and long before night these five intrepid sons of America were again in full possession of her. Whether from want of abilities or strength, supposing themselves unable to take the vessel back to Columbia, it cannot be ascertained, this far only is known, that between the time the Indians were driven from the ship and the following morning, the four who were unhurt left her in the long boat in hopes of regaining the river, wishing to take long with them the wounded person, who refused their offer, saying, that he must die before long, and was as well in the vessel as elsewhere.

Soon after sunrise she was surrounded by an immense number of Indians in canoes, come for the express purpose of unloading her, but who from the warm reception they met with the day before, did not seem to vie with each other in boarding.

The wounded man shewed himself over the railing, made signs that he was alone and wanted their assistance, on which some embarked, who finding what he said was true, spoke to their people, who were not any longer slow in getting on board, so that in a few seconds the desk was considerably thronged, and they proceeded to undo the hatches without further ceremony.

No sooner were they completely engaged in thus finishing this most diabolical of actions, than the only survivor of the crew descended into the cabin and set fire to the magazine containing nearly 9000 lbs of gun-powder, which in an instant blew the vessel and everyone on board to atoms.

The nation acknowledge their having lost nearly one hundred warriors, besides a vast number wounded by the explosion, who were in canoes around the ship. It was impossible to tell who the person was that so completely avenged himself, but there cannot exist a single doubt that the act will teach these villains better manners, and will eventually be of immense benefit to the coasting trade.

The four men who set off in the long boat, were, two or three days after, driven ashore in a gale, and massacred by the natives.

(From White, *Plains and Rockies*, 143–49.)

2. A Letter from Ramsay Crooks on the "Celebrated South Pass," 1856

Editorial note: *In 1856, the famed explorer John Charles Frémont was nominated as the first Republican candidate for U.S. president. In their zeal to promote Frémont as an authentic hero, the Republicans dubbed him "Pathfinder," with some even proclaiming (though Frémont himself did not) that he had discovered South Pass, a gently sloping saddle of land on the high plains of Wyoming that played a crucial role in American westward expansion. Sixty-nine-year-old Ramsay Crooks responded with this letter, which was published in the* Detroit Free Press.

The Detroit *Advertiser* having asserted that Col. Fremont was the discoverer of the South Pass of the Rocky Mountains, a correspondent of the Detroit *Free Press* denies the truth of statement and the editor of that journal published the following letter from Ramsay Crooks, Esq., of New York:

"New York, June 28, 1856.

My Dear Sir:—Just as I was about closing my letter to you of yesterday's date, I received the Detroit Free Press of the 21st inst., containing a laudation of Col. John Fremont taken from the Detroit Advertiser of the previous day and which (if it had been true) is not, in my humble opinion, a very important item in making up the essentials of such a man as should become President of this glorious confederacy.

I, however, presume it is intended to exhibit him as endowed with uncommon intrepidity and daring in exploring so wide a region, surrounded by savages and grizzly bears, thereby proving great firmness of character, so very desirable, but unfortunately so very rare in the head of a great nation.

But even if the Colonel had discovered the 'South Pass,' it does not show any more fitness for the exalted station he covets than the numerous beaver hunters and traders who passed and repassed through that noted place full twenty years before Col. Fremont had attained a legal right to vote, and were fully his equals in enterprise, energy, and indomitable perserverence, with this somewhat important difference, that he was backed by the United States treasury, while other explorers had to rely on their own resources.

The perils of the 'South Pass,' therefore, confer on the Colonel no greater claim to distinction than the trapper is entitled to, and his party must be pressed very hard when they had to drag in a circumstance so very unimportant as who discovered the 'South Pass.'

Although the *Free Press* conclusively proves that the Colonel could not be the discoverer of the 'South Pass,' the details are not accurate and in order that history (if it ever gets there) may be correctly vindicated, I will tell you how it was.

Mr. David Stuart sailed from this port in 1810 for the Columbia River on board the ship 'Tonquin' with a number of Mr. Astor's associates in the 'Pacific Fur Company.' And after the breaking up of the company in 1814, he returned through the Northwest Company's territories to Montreal, far to the north of the 'South Pass,' which he never saw.

In 1811, the overland party of Mr. Astor's expedition, under the command of Mr. Wilson P. Hunt, of Trenton, New Jersey, although numbering sixty well armed men, found the Indians so very troublesome in the country of the Yellowstone River, that the party of seven persons who left Astoria toward the end of June, 1812, considering it dangerous to pass again by the rout of 1811, turned toward the southeast as soon as they had crossed the main chain of the Rocky Mountains, and, after several days' journey, came through the celebrated 'South Pass' in the month of November, 1812.

Pursuing from thence an easterly course, they fell upon the River Platte of the Missouri, where they passed the winter and reached St. Louis in April, 1813.

The seven persons forming the party were Robert McClelland of Hagerstown, who, with the celebrated Captain Wells, was captain of spies under General Wayne in his famous Indian campaign, Joseph Miller of Baltimore, for several years an officer of the U.S. army, Robert Stuart, a citizen of Detroit, Benjamin Jones, of Missouri, who acted as huntsman of the party, Francois LeClaire, a halfbreed, and André Valée, a Canadian *voyageur*, and Ramsay Crooks, who is the only survivor of this small band of adventurers.

I am very sincerely yours,

Ramsay Crooks

Anthony Dudgeon, Esq., Detroit, Michigan."

(From Dale, "Did the Returning Astorians Use the South Pass?" 50–51.)

Appendix C

A Brief History of the Oregon Trail

1804–1806	Lewis and Clark journey from St. Louis to the Pacific coast and back, traveling part of the future Oregon Trail when they follow the Columbia River along the Washington/Oregon border.
1811–1812	After crossing South Dakota and Wyoming, the westbound Astorians pick up the future Trail near the site of present American Falls, Idaho, roughly following it all the way to Astoria.
1812–1813	The eastbound Astorians travel the great majority of the future Trail, crossing South Pass on October 21, 1812.
1824	Jedediah Smith rediscovers South Pass.
1836	Dr. Marcus Whitman and his wife, Narcissa, and Reverend Henry Spalding and his wife, Eliza, follow the Trail to the present site of Walla Walla, Washington, with Narcissa and Eliza becoming the first white women to travel the Trail.
1840	Joseph L. Meek and others are the first to complete the entire journey along the Trail by wagon.
1847	Brigham Young leads a group of Mormon pioneers along the Trail through Nebraska and Wyoming and then cuts southwest to the Great Salt Lake. Close to 70,000 Mormons will cross the plains by 1868.
1849–1854	The California Gold Rush prompts huge numbers of immigrants to go West, with more than 50,000 pioneers traveling the Trail through Nebraska and Wyoming (before

cutting southwest through Utah, Nevada, and California) in both 1850 and 1852.

1860   In one of the worst disasters on the Trail, the Utter wagon train of forty-four people is attacked by Indians near present Murphy, Idaho. Eleven members of the party and approximately twenty-five Indians are killed.

1869   The completion of the transcontinental railroad marks the virtual death of the Trail.

1880s   The last wagon trains are seen along the Trail.

Notes

PROLOGUE

1. Ross, *First Settlers*, 116. See Franchere, *Narrative*, 137–80, for a description of the journey from Astoria to Montreal. One of Astor's clerks, Gabriel Franchere, was with the party and writes of his homecoming: "I hastened to the paternal roof, where the family were not less surprised than overjoyed at beholding me. Not having heard of me, since I sailed from New York [in 1810], they had believed, in accordance with the common report, that I had been murdered by the savages, with Mr. M'Kay and the crew of the *Tonquin*: and certainly, it was by the goodness of Providence that I found myself thus safe and sound, in the midst of my relations and friends, at the end of a voyage accompanied by so many perils, and in which so many of my companions had met with untimely death" (*Narrative*, 180, bracketed insertion added). The durable Franchere, who lived until 1863 and was the last surviving Astorian, identifies the two men who drowned in rapids of the Athabasca River as André Bélanger and Olivier Roy Lapensée. The latter was likely the brother of Basile and Ignace Lapensée, who both drowned at the mouth of the Columbia in March of 1811 (as related in chapter 6, herein). They were from Montreal, so one of Franchere's companions presumably delivered the sad news to their parents (*Narrative*, 55).

2. Franchere, *Narrative*, 138; Ross, *First Settlers*, 136; Franchere, *Narrative*, 142, bracketed insertion added. Ross and Cox both report that the Astorians met Marie near the mouth of the Walla Walla River; Franchere, however, says it was farther upstream, beyond the mouth of the Snake River. Thus, the two eyewitnesses who recorded Marie's rescue, Franchere and Ross, disagree on this point. (Ross, *First Settlers*, 265; Cox, *Adventures*, 94; Franchere, *Narrative*, 138–42.)

3. Although Pierre Dorion Jr.'s widow eventually became widely known as Marie, the earliest extant document mentioning that name was created on July 19, 1841, when she was baptized and accepted into the fellowship of the Roman Catholic Church, with a record at Oregon's Willamette Mission listing her as "Marie Laguivoise." *Laguivoise* was apparently a variation of *Aiaouez*—also spelled *Aieway* or *Ayauwa*—the name of her native nation, later simplified as *Iowa*. Whether Dorion or anyone else called her Marie is simply unknown because record keepers on the scene always called her "Dorion's wife" or "Dorion's squaw," never mentioning a first name. (Barry, "Madame Dorion," 275; web site http://museum.bmi.net/MARIE%20DORION%20PEOPLE/marie_laguisvoise.htm, accessed June 15, 2011.)

4. Franchere, *Narrative*, 140.

5. Franchere, *Narrative*, 139; William Clark's journal entry, October 19, 1805, Moulton, *Journals*, 5:306; Ross, *First Settlers*, 137.

6. Alexander Henry made a list of the men in the group, and Elliott Coues offered valuable annotation. See Coues, *New Light*, 870–75. Every primary source on Astoria (and secondary source, for that matter) seems to have a unique way of spelling Astorian names, most of which have several variants. I have largely followed the conventions of Robert F. Jones in *Annals of Astoria* and Kenneth W. Porter in "Rolls of Overland Astorians."

7. Irving, *Astoria*, 239.

8. Hunt, "Diary," 283, bracketed insertion added.

9. Hunt, "Diary," 288, bracketed insertions added. "Mad River" was the Snake River, and the three peaks were the Tetons.

10. See Russell, *Firearms, Traps, and Tools*, 55, 125, 182, 403–6, for details on the weapons and tools possessed by the Astorians.

11. Irving, *Astoria*, 265–66.

12. Franchere, *Narrative*, 142.

13. Lewis's journal entry, May 16, 1805, Moulton, *Journals*, 4:157; William Clark to Toussaint Charbonneau, August 20, 1806, Jackson, *Letters*, 1:315. On December 20, 1812, at a fort south of present Mobridge, South Dakota, a clerk by the name of John Luttig recorded that "this Evening the Wife of Charbonneau a Snake Squaw, died of a putrid fever she was a good and the best Women in the fort, aged about 25 years she left a fine infant girl" (Drumm, *Journal*, 106). This description fits Sacagawea to a T, but by not identifying her by name, Luttig left the door open for the argument that inevitably ensued. In the early 1900s, two researchers studied a collection of letters and affidavits, independently concluding that an elderly Indian woman called Porivo, who had died on Wyoming's Wind River Indian Reservation in 1884, was actually Sacagawea. But the documents had all been created at least twenty years after Porivo's death, and no researcher had interviewed the woman herself. (Nor did any document written while Porivo was still alive claim she was Sacagawea.) Then, in the mid-1950s, Dale Morgan discovered a William Clark document written between 1825 and 1828 clearly stating that Sacagawea was dead, convincing most Lewis and Clark scholars they had been correct in their assumption that Luttig's note referred to Sacagawea. Not everyone was convinced, however, and the debate continues to this day, with maps of Wyoming often listing "Grave of Sacajawea" near Fort Washakie. See Morris, *Fate*, 210–13, and Howard, *Sacajawea*, 175–92, for more on this fascinating controversy. As detailed in the biographical directory, there are also two incompatible versions of what happened to Marie Dorion in her later years.

14. Jefferson to Lewis, June 20, 1803, Jackson, *Letters*, 1:61–63.

15. Josephy, "Ordeal in Hell's Canyon," 73.

16. Speck, *Breeds*, 151; Clark's journal entry, September 1, 1806, Moulton, *Journals*, 338.

17. Irving, *Astoria*, 141; Speck, *Breeds*, 151.

18. Clark's journal entry, June 12, 1804, Moulton, *Journals*, 2:294–5.

19. Clark's journal entry, August 29, 1804, Moulton, *Journals*, 3:22; bracketed insertions added.

20. Franchere, *Narrative*, 143.

21. Franchere, *Narrative*, 140.

22. Irving, *Astoria*, 498.

1. "I SHALL HAVE TWO BOATS WELL MANNED AND ARMED"

1. Ordway's journal entry, September 12, 1806, Moulton, *Journals*, 9:361.

2. Ibid.

3. Irving, *Astoria*, 138. Irving never met McClellan but interviewed several men who knew him well, most notably Crooks, who knew McClellan about as well as anyone could.

4. Drumm, "More about Astorians," 345; Lavender, *Fist in the Wilderness*, 73.

5. Holmberg, *Dear Brother*, 273–74; Lavender, *Fist in the Wilderness*, 73.

6. Clark's journal entry, September 12, 1806, Moulton, *Journals*, 8:358.

7. Thomas Jefferson to the Arikaras, [April 11, 1806], Jackson, *Letters*, 1:306. There were several chiefs among the Arikara, some identified by multiple names, so fixing the identity of individual chiefs is not always easy. See Moulton, *Journals*, 3:156n5.

8. Clark's journal entry, September 12, 1806, Moulton, *Journals*, 8:357-58.

9. Clark's journal entry, September 20, 1806, Moulton, Journals, 8:367.

10. Ibid.

11. Clark's journal entry, September 20, 1806; Lewis's journal entry, August 12, 1806; Clark's journal entry, September 17, 1806, Moulton, *Journals*, 8:367, 8:157, and 8:363, respectively, bracketed insertions added. Although Clark does not identify Crooks by name, his details all match what is known about Crooks and when added to other evidence leave little doubt that the polite young Scot was indeed Crooks. See Lavender, "Ramsay Crooks's Early Ventures," 91, 97. Crooks was employed by Robert Dickson and was supervised by James Aird, who met Lewis and Clark on September 3, 1806.

12. Irving, *Astoria*, 130. Background from Carter, "Ramsay Crooks," 125–26, and Lavender, "Ramsay Crooks's Early Ventures," 91-92.

13. William Clark to Jonathan Clark, September 23, 1806; Meriwether Lewis to Thomas Jefferson, September 23, 1806, Jackson, *Letters*, 1:325–29 and 1:319–24, respectively. See Jackson, *Letters*, 329–30n for information on the publication of Clark's letter and Holmberg, *Dear Brother*, 106–7, for a discussion of how Lewis and Clark likely coauthored the letter.

14. Although Lisa preferred to have sole control of his enterprise, he found himself in serious debt and "formed a partnership—there was no other way to obtain even the minimum of capital necessary to initiate an enterprise—with Pierre Menard and William Morrison of Kaskaskia, in the Illinois country, for the purpose of sending a trading and trapping expedition to the headwaters of the Missouri River" (Oglesby, *Manuel Lisa*, 39).

15. Utley, *A Life Wild and Perilous*, 30. I believe Utley is correct in his assumption that Hoback, Reznor, and Robinson "launched their trapping careers under the tutelage of Manuel Lisa [and] . . . followed Lisa up the Missouri in 1807" (23), an opinion shared by Richard Edward Oglesby in *Manuel Lisa and the Opening of the Missouri Fur Trade*, 45n20, 113–14. Of the three, however, Robinson is the only one mentioned in the records of Lisa and his associates. (Pierre Menard, "List of Notes of the 'Men' on the Missouri Belonging in Part to Pierre Menard," Pierre Menard Papers, Business Papers, 1774–1825, Abraham Lincoln Presidential Library, Springfield, Illinois.) The key evidence that Hoback and Reznor were also with Lisa in 1807 comes from John Bradbury, who met the three men in 1811 and wrote: "They had been *several* years hunting on and beyond the Rocky Mountains" (Bradbury, *Travels*, 98, italics added). As discussed in chapter 7, herein, Reznor had apparently left his family around 1797.

16. Utley, *A Life Wild and Perilous*, 22.

17. Oglesby, *Manuel Lisa*, 40.

18. Standard fur hunter's contract, Noy, *Distant Horizon*, 44.

19. John Ordway's journal entry, August 12, 1806, Moulton, *Journals*, 9:348.

20. Oath, Bond, and License for Indian Trade, 1807, Marshall, *Papers of Frederick Bates*, 1:204–6; standard fur hunter's contract, 1809, Noy, *Distant Horizon*, 44. Congress had passed "An Act to Regulate Trade and Intercourse with the Indian Tribes, and to Preserve Peace on the Frontiers" in 1796, renewing it every two years. The act made it illegal for traders "to hunt, or in any wise destroy the game" on Indian lands. Since the act dealt specifically with Indian nations that had signed treaties with the United States, some traders may have hoped it offered them a loophole—because the Indians of the upper Missouri—such as the Sioux, Arikara, Mandan, Crow, and Blackfoot—had not signed treaties. The trading license, however, called for "the due observance of all such regulation and restrictions, as now are in force, or shall hereafter be made for the government of trade and intercourse with the Indian Tribes," obviously expecting compliance with the 1796 act.

21. Jedediah Smith's journal entry, August 7, 1826, Brooks, *Southwest Expedition*, 36-37.

22. Licences Granted, 1807, Marshall, *Papers of Frederick Bates*, 1:202–6; Chittenden, *American Fur Trade*, 1:381, 380. The license was filed in McClellan's name because he was a U.S. citizen with a previous license.

23. Robert McClellan to Meriwether Lewis, April 5, 1807, William Clark Papers, Missouri History Museum.

24. McClellan to Lewis, April 5, 1807; William Clark to Henry Dearborn, May 18 and June 1, 1807, Jackson, *Letters*, 2:411 and 2:414, respectively.

25. Clark to Dearborn, June 1, 1807, Jackson, *Letters*, 2:414.

26. McClellan to Lewis, April 5, 1807; Henry Dearborn to James Wilkinson, April 9, 1806, Jackson, *Letters*, 1:303.

27. Clark's journal entry, September 17, 1806, Moulton, *Journals*, 8:363, bracketed insertions added. Although Wilkinson had secret dealings with John McClallan, he had not attempted to hide his "official" dealings. "I have also engaged [McClallan] . . . to look at [Sante Fe] in person pending the winter," Wilkinson wrote to Henry Dearborn, stating essentially what McClallan told Lewis and Clark. "He will take his departure from the Panis [Pawnee] towns on the River Platte" (Wilkinson to Dearborn, September 8, 1805, Clarence E. Carter, *Territorial Papers*, 13:199, bracketed insertion added.)

28. Ronda, *Astoria and Empire*, 38.

29. White, "Early Days," 5, 6. Background from Baldwin, *Keelboat Age*, 44–45, and Oglesby, *Manuel Lisa*, 44.

30. Clark's journal entries, September 3 and September 7, 1806, Moulton, *Journals*, 8:346 and 8:353, respectively.

31. Clark's journal entries, June 1 and June 2, 1804, Moulton, *Journals*, 2:267 and 2:270, respectively. Reuben Holmes wrote that Rose "proceeded, in company with some hunters, to the Osage river, where he spent the winter. Becoming fond of the independent and lawless life then led by the hunters, he bargained with Manuel Lisa, in the spring of 1807, to ascend the Missouri to the mouth of the Yellow Stone river" ("Five Scalps," 9).

32. Holmes, "Five Scalps," 6–7.

33. *Missouri Gazette*, October 12, 1808, emphasis in original; affidavit of Antoine Dubreuil, Missouri History Museum, cited in Skarsten, *George Drouillard*, 271 (translated from the French by Thomas Molnar).

34. Affidavit of Dubreuil, 271; *Missouri Gazette*, October 12, 1808.

35. Affidavit of Dubreuil, in Skarsten, *George Drouillard*, 271; *Missouri Gazette*, October 12, 1808.

36. Affidavit of Dubreuil, in Skarsten, *George Drouillard*, 271–72, bracketed insertion added.

37. Ibid.

38. William Clark to Henry Dearborn, July 17, 1807, Carter, *Territorial Papers*, 14:136; McClellan to Lewis, April 5, 1807.

39. Oglesby, *Manuel Lisa*, 32–33.

40. Douglas, *Manuel Lisa*, 251.

41. William Clark to Meriwether Lewis, August 21, 1803, Jackson, *Letters*, 1:117–18.

42. Pay Roll, Scouts and Spies, Kentucky, (1790–1794), National Archives; Lavender, *Fist in the Wilderness*, 73.

43. Nathaniel Pryor to William Clark, October 16, 1807, Jackson, *Letters*, 2:433.

44. An 1810 letter written by Pierre Menard indicates that St. Louis businessmen Sylvester Labbadie and Auguste Chouteau may have financed Crooks and McClellan's expedition. See Pierre Menard to Pierre Chouteau, April 21, 1810, in Chittenden, *American Fur Trade*, 2:878–83, and Lavender, "Ramsay Crooks's Early Ventures," 98–99.

45. Woodger and Toropov, *Encyclopedia*, p. 32; Clark's journal entries, October 6 and October 10, Moulton, *Journals*, 3:147 and 3:157, respectively.

46. Charles Courtin to "Gentlemen," June 22, 1807, entry 18, Letters Received, 1801–1870, Records of the Office of the Secretary of War, Record Group 107, National Archives, College Park, MD; Dearborn to Wilkinson, April 9, 1806, Jackson, *Letters*, 1:303–5. Courtin's letter was written to government officials in St. Louis; in Meriwether Lewis's absence, territorial secretary Frederick Bates had sent the original French letter and an English translation—the document quoted here—to Secretary of War Henry Dearborn.

47. Courtin to "Gentlemen," June 22, 1807, National Archives, College Park, MD.

48. Ibid.

49. Clark's journal entry, July 21, 1804; Ordway's journal entry, July 22, 1804; Clark's journal entries, July 22 and July 21, 1804, Moulton, *Journals*, 2:402, 9:29, 2:407, and 2:403, respectively, bracketed insertion added.

50. Courtin to Gentlemen, June 22, 1807, National Archives, College Park, MD; James, *Three Years*, 29.

51. Brackenridge, *Views of Louisiana*, 90; Oglesby's assumption that Colter was made a free trapper seems quite reasonable—see *Manuel Lisa*, 46.

52. Manuel Lisa vs. John B. Bouché , May 1811, Lisa Papers, Missouri History Museum.

53. Brackenridge, *Views of Louisiana*, 141–42.

54. Court papers, Lucas Collection, Missouri History Museum, bracketed insertion added; Lavender, *Fist in the Wilderness*, 91–92.

55. William Clark to Henry Dearborn, July 17, 1807, Clarence Carter, *Territorial Papers*, 14:136–37.

56. David Lavender claims that "McClellan had won a stay in his lawsuit so that depositions could be taken from Aird [prominent trader James Aird] on his arrival [in St. Louis] in September," but offers no documentation. (Lavendar, *Fist in the Wilderness*, 95, bracketed insertions added.)

57. Pryor to Clark, October 16, 1807, Jackson, *Letters*, 2:432–33, emphasis in original, bracketed insertion added. Major Thomas Biddle wrote that Crooks and McClellan "met returning, near this place, the boat sent by the United States to carry back the Mandan chief brought into this country by Captains Lewis and Clarke. You undoubtedly recollect that this boat was attacked by the Arickaras, and compelled to make a precipitate retreat. This act of hostility discouraged Messrs. McClinnon [McClellan] and Crooks, and they thought it prudent to decline going on" (Major Thomas Biddle, Camp Missouri, Missouri River, to Colonel Henry Atkinson, October 29, 1819, American State Papers, p. 202, bracketed insertions added).

58. Pryor to Clark, October 16, 1807, Jackson, *Letters*, 2:435.

59. Ibid.

60. Pryor to Clark, Jackson, Jackson, *Letters*, 2:435; René Jusseaume to Thomas Jefferson, December 3, 1807, *Missouri Historical Society Collections* 4 (1913): 234–36. Still determined to carry out his assignment, Pryor proposed taking Sheheke and his family overland to the Mandan villages but Sheheke declined.

61. Meriwether Lewis to Henry Dearborn, January 15, 1807, Jackson, *Letters*, 1:367. While no document definitively proves that Field was one of those killed, several factors suggest that he was. First, his expedition experience and skill as a marksman—not to mention the presence of three former companions—meant that he was likely to be sought after. Second, he is known to have been in St. Louis, probably in April, to sign a petition to Congress, not only making him available but also giving him ample time to enlist, make preparations for the journey, and leave with Pryor in June. Third, his family in Louisville learned of his death by October 24, virtually the same time such notification would have come via Pryor, who reached St. Louis in mid-October. Fourth, Clark later recorded that Field died a violent rather than nonviolent death. All of these make the case persuasive but not ironclad. (Petition to the Senate and House [after March 3, 1807], Jackson, *Letters,* 2:378–80; Holmberg, *Dear Brother*, 93–95; Clark's list of expedition members [ca. 1825–28], Jackson, *Letters*, 2:638–40.)

62. Pryor to Clark, October 16, 1807, Jackson, *Letters*, 2:436; Frederick Bates to William Clark, December 1807, Frederick Bates to Dennis Fitzhugh, December 16, 1807, Marshall, *Papers of Frederick Bates*, 2:248 and 2:236–37, respectively.

63. Pryor to Clark, October 16, 1807, Jackson, *Letters*, 2:436; Bradbury, *Travels*, 74; Dr. Thomas's journal entry, July 29, 1809, Jackson, "Journey to the Mandans," 184. Although Hiram Martin Chittenden wrote that Crooks and McClellan "established themselves [in 1807] near Council Bluffs and remained there until 1809" (*American Fur Trade*, 1:161), Dr. Thomas, who saw the wintering house in 1809 (and called it Crooks and McClellan's "old hunting camp"), and John Bradbury, who saw the house in 1811, both placed it near the mouth of the Nodaway River. Chittenden apparently based his conclusion on Major Thomas Biddle's mention that Crooks and McClellan met Pryor in the Council Bluffs area (see note 57, above). However, Biddle said nothing about where Crooks and McClellan spent the winter.

64. James, *Three Years*, 18; Irving, *Astoria*, 138–39. Ayers is also mentioned by Pierre Menard. (Menard to Chouteau, April 21, 1810, in Chittenden, *American Fur Trade*, 2:882.)

65. Lavender, *Fist in the Wilderness*, 99.

2. "A POWERFUL COMPANY IS FORMING"

1. Statement signed by Dr. Bernard G. Farrar, September 11, 1816, Jackson, *Letters*, 2:620; René Jusseaume to Thomas Jefferson, December 3, 1807, in *Missouri Historical Society Collections* 4/2 (1913): 234–36.

2. Letter signed by "James Roseman[,] Lieutenant," and "Zachary Perch[,] Captain & Commanding Officer," July 10, 1807, in Majors, "McClellan in the Rockies," 600–01, emphasis added. Majors points out (616–17) that there is no record of a James Roseman or a Zachary Perch serving in the U.S. Army from its inception in 1775 to the early 1980s (when Majors wrote his article).

3. Brackenridge, *Views of Louisiana*, 91.

4. Ibid.

5. It has also been widely assumed that Colter gave Lisa a favorable report of trapping the Yellowstone but no primary document has confirmed that theory thus far. Although Clark's journey along the Yellowstone was nonvioloent, it was not without trouble—Crow Indians stole his horses.

6. Oglesby, *Manuel Lisa*, 40–41, 54.

7. Calloway, *Winter Count*, 304, 303–4. Background from *Winter Count*, 267–72.

8. Charles McKenzie's narratives, in Wood and Thiessen, *Northern Plains*, 245.

9. Brackenridge, *Views of Louisiana*, 91–92; Allen, "The Forgotten Explorers," 32–33; Heidenreich, *Smoke Signals*, 48. Countless scholars and hobbyists alike have attempted to determine Colter's exact route, but they have generally relied on the version of William Clark's map published in the 1814 Biddle edition of the Lewis and Clark journals, and as John L. Allen has pointed out, that map, engraved from Clark's manuscript by Samuel Lewis, "is replete with errors; enough so as to render it nearly useless as a source document." Based on his painstaking work in analyzing a digitally remastered version of Clark's original map, Allen has provided a new and valuable proposal for Colter's probable route: "From Lisa's post southwest across the Pryor Mountains (or through Pryor's Gap) to the Clark's Fork River, up the Clark's Fork to the canyon, south along the Absaroka/Beartoothfront, skirting Heart Mountain on its west side, to the current site of Cody, Wyoming." Then "south along the east face of the Absarokas, crossing the Owl Creek Mountains over a low pass to the Wind River," following it "to its source in Brooks Lake." Then north along the west side of Yellowstone Lake, "missing the Yellowstone Canyon but crossing Dunraven Pass to the Yellowstone Valley, crossing the Yellowstone [River] at Bannock Fork, then up the Lamar River valley following the Bannock Trail, past Soda Butte (shown on Clark's map as a boiling spring) and across Colter's Pass to the Clark's Fork which he and his Indian companions followed downstream to the Yellowstone and back down that river to Lisa's fort" ("Forgotten Explorers," 32–33.)

10. Skarsten, *George Drouillard*, 259–70; Heidenreich, *Smoke Signals*, 48; Morris, *Fate of the Corps*, 41.

11. Holmes, "Five Scalps," 8.

12. See the narratives of David Thompson and Charles McKenzie in Wood and Thiessen, *Northern Plains*, 116 and 236, respectively.

13. Clark's journal entry, August 29, 1804, Moulton, *Journals*, 3:22.

14. Licenses granted by Governor Lewis, April 1–September 30, 1808, Marshall, *Papers of Frederick Bates*, 31; Lavender, "Ramsay Crooks's Early Ventures, 100; George Hoffman to Frederick Bates, August 23, 1808, Marshall, *Papers of Frederick Bates*, 16–17, italics in original. Background on Crooks & McClellan's comings and goings during 1808 from Lavender, *Fist in the Wilderness*, 104–6.

15. *Missouri Gazette*, October 12, 1808.

16. Buckley, *Indian Diplomat*, 75.

17. Meriwether Lewis to Henry Dearborn, January 15, 1807, Jackson, *Letters*, 1:368; *Missouri Gazette*, October 12, 1808. For details on Drouillard's trial, see Skarsten, *George Drouillard*, 271–79, and Morris, *Fate of the Corps*, 49–53.

18. Lavender, *Fist in the Wilderness*, 106; *Missouri Gazette*, October 12, 1808, italics in original.

19. Thomas Jefferson to Meriwether Lewis, July 17, 1808, Jackson, *Letters*, 2:444.

3. "DISSOLVED BY MUTUAL CONSENT"

1. Irving, *The Rocky Mountains*, 1:223. According to Merrill J. Mattes, this was the first published reference to "Colter's Hell," showing that the term "was clearly not invented by Clark, Brackenridge, Thomas James, or John Bradbury, who were personally acquainted with Colter and talked with him after his mysterious journey of 1807-1808" ("Colter's Hell," 255.) Irving correctly placed Colter's Hell on the Shoshone River, not in present Yellowstone Park, as some have mistakenly done.

2. Major Thomas Biddle, Camp Missouri, Missouri River, to Colonel Henry Atkinson, October 29, 1819, American State Papers, p. 202; Morris, "Charles Courtin," 31–33.

3. James, *Three Years*, 26; Biddle to Atkinson, October 29, 1819, 202.

4. Holmes, "Five Scalps," 8–9.

5. Ibid., 9–10.

6. Ibid., 10–11.

7. *Missouri Gazette*, April 12, 1809.

8. Ronda, *Astoria and Empire*, 50–51. Background information from Elliott, "Wilson Price Hunt."

9. Lavender, *Fist in the Wilderness*, 108, 113. As James P. Ronda points out, the correspondence between Astor and Hunt has been lost, "so it is difficult to trace either Astor's intentions or Hunt's pursuits of his employer's instructions." Ronda adds: "There can be no doubt that Crooks, McClellan, and Miller—all future Astorians—made such a journey on the Missouri in 1809. But whether they did so as advance agents for Astor remains in doubt." At the same time, Ronda acknowledges that Hunt and Hankinson dissolved their partnership in June of 1809 (a possible indication that Hunt had begun working for Astor) and that in June of 1810 Charles Gratiot wrote to Astor "that Hunt had been Crooks's supplier 'last fall.'" In addition, Thomas James, who met Crooks and McClellan on the river during the summer of 1809, called Crooks Astor's agent. (*Empire*, 53, 54.)

10. Oglesby, *Manuel Lisa*, 65; Douglas, *Manuel Lisa*, 67.

11. Foley, *Wilderness Journey*, 177; Holmberg, *Dear Brother*, 198n4. Lisa's key biographers both raise interesting points about the formation of the St. Louis Missouri Fur Company, with Walter B. Douglas saying, "the scheme was a cumbersome one, and it is surprising that Lisa should have agreed to it" (*Lisa*, 258), and Richard Edward Oglesby adding that the articles of agreement "concretely delineated the aura of distrust [that] hung about this heterogeneous collection of merchants" and that "the lengths to which these men went to insure each other's honesty not only were absurd but were partly the cause of the company's failure to take full advantage of its prospects." (*Manuel Lisa*, 70.)

12. Agreement for Return of the Mandan Chief [24 February 1809], Jackson, *Letters*, 2:446–50. As for contemporaneous objections to the agreement, on April 27, 1809, Rodolphe Tillier, former factor at Belle Fontaine, wrote President James Madison and asked, "Is it proper for the public service that the U. S. officers as a Governor or a Super Intendant of Indian Affairs & U. S. Factor at St. Louis should undertake any share in Mercantile and private concerns?" (National Archives, Record Group 107, T-1809, unregistered series, cited in Jackson, *Letters*, 2:457–58n.)

13. The license that Governor Lewis issued to Lisa on June 7, 1809, allowed him to "trade with the several nations and tribes of Indians residing on the Missouri and its branches, above the entrance of the River Platte, with the exception of the Aricaree [Arikara] nation" (License, June 7, 1809, Lisa Papers, Missouri History Museum).

14. Irving, *Astoria*, 135.

15. Agreement for the Return of the Mandan Chief, Jackson, *Letters*, 2:448; Oglesby, *Manuel Lisa*, 76; Agreement for Return of the Mandan Chief, 448; Oglesby, *Manuel Lisa*, 75.

16. Background from the 1962 J. B. Lippincott Company version of *Three Years Among the Indians and Mexicans*, a faithful, unabridged printing of the 1846 edition, with an introduction by A. P. Nasatir. As Nasatir writes, "James's book, though written some twenty-five years after the events it narrates, and distorted by its author's highly critical views, is . . . one of the most fascinating first-hand records of early experiences on the Far Western frontier, and invaluable for its information regarding episodes and persons either ignored or slighted by other authors" (p. xi).

17. James, *Three Years*, 44–45.

18. Mattes, "John Dougherty," 113, 118n12.

19. James, *Three Years*, 5, 4.

20. Pierre Menard to Adrien Langlois, June 23, 1809, cited in Oglesby, *Manuel Lisa*, 77; Manuel Lisa to William Clark, July 2, 1809, Missouri History Museum.

21. Manuel Lisa to William Clark, July 10, 1809, Missouri History Museum. Clark was indeed making every effort to have deserters arrested, and on July 22, with Lisa's letter in hand, he wrote to his brother Jonathan: "The Missouri Fur Company has met with Several disertions, I have now Six men in joil [jail] who deserted from the Company 250 miles from this [place]" (William Clark to Jonathan Clark, July 22, 1809, Holmberg, *Dear Brother*, 204).

22. Lisa to Clark, July 10, 1809, Missouri History Museum.

23. Lavender, *Fist in the Wilderness*, 115.

24. Chittenden, *American Fur Trade*, 1:381.

25. James, *Three Years*, 5, 6.

26. Ibid., 6. Oglesby blames James and his crew for these difficulties, claiming they failed to realize how important it was to get up the river as fast as possible, that "they refused to ration themselves to make the supplies stretch out a month as Lisa had calculated they should, and when they did run out of pork, they were not enterprising enough to send one of their number to hunt up some fresh meat" (*Manuel Lisa*, 82).

27. James, *Three Years*, 8.

28. Jackson, "Journey to the Mandans," 185.

29. Ibid.

30. Ibid., 186.

31. Ibid.

32. Meriwether Lewis to Pierre Chouteau, June 8, 1809, Jackson, *Letters*, 2:455; Agreement for Return of the Mandan Chief, Jackson, *Letters*, 2:447.

33. Irving, *Astoria*, 141–42.

34. Meriwether Lewis to Pierre Chouteau, 2:454; James, *Three Years*, 11; Pierre Chouteau to William Eustis, December 14, 1809, Jackson, *Letters*, 2:482.

35. Jackson, "Journey to the Mandans," 189; Chouteau to Eustis, December 14, 1809, Jackson, *Letters*, 2:482; Agreement for Return of the Mandan Chief, Jackson, *Letters*, 2:447.

36. James, *Three Years*, 11; Holmes, "Five Scalps," 24–25.

37. Holmes, "Five Scalps," 23, 25.

38. Ibid., 254–26. Neither Richard Edward Oglesby nor Walter B. Douglas, Lisa's key biographers, mentions Rose joining the St. Louis Missouri Fur Company in 1809, perhaps because none of the firsthand participants left any record of it and also because Holmes does not tell when it happened. Indeed, most of Holmes's fascinating narrative, which gives every appearance of being liberally embellished, offers no dates to help readers get oriented. Nevertheless, such historians as David Lavender (*Fist in the Wilderness*, 162), Gordon Speck (*Breeds*, 209), and Willis Blenkinsop ("Edward Rose," 338) maintain that Rose worked for the company during the 1809–1810 period and was particularly associated with Andrew Henry. And while James does not identify the rider as Rose, his description of the horseman charging out at full speed to meet the Americans is surprisingly similar to Holmes's more complete account. Nor could Holmes have been influenced by James's writing because the former published his article almost twenty years before James did.

39. Jackson, "Journey to the Mandans," 190–91; Chouteau to Eustis, December 14, 1809, Jackson, *Letters*, 2:482–83; Agreement for Return of the Mandan Chief, Jackson, *Letters*, 2:448.

40. Chouteau to Eustis December 14, 1809, Jackson, *Letters*, 2:483; Majors, "John McClellan in the Rockies," 611. See also Morris, "Charles Courtin," 31–33.

41. Oglesby, *Manuel Lisa*, 85.

42. Jackson, "Journey to the Mandans," 191-92.

43. James, *Three Years*, 14.

44. Irving, *Astoria*, 142.

45. Pierre Menard to Adrien Langlois, October 7, 1809, cited in Oglesby, *Manuel Lisa*, 91, and Aarstad, "This Unfortunate Affair," 113.

46. White and Gowans, "The Rocky Mountain Fur Trade," 62.

47. William Clark to Toussaint Charbonneau, August 20, 1806, Jackson, *Letters*, 1:315. After discovering a baptismal record for Baptiste dated December 28, 1809, at St. Louis, Bob Moore theorized quite convincingly that "as [Chouteau's] expedition prepared to return downriver, it seems likely that the Charbonneaus would have sensed that the time was right to go to St. Louis. If they took passage on the return trip with Chouteau's large, well-armed corps of soldiers and trappers (he had at least 125 men), their safety would be better assured than if they attempted to make the trip alone or with a smaller party" ("Pompey's Baptism," 13).

48. Chouteau to Eustis, December 14, 1809, Jackson, *Letters*, 2:483.

49. Major Thomas Biddle, Camp Missouri, Missouri River, to Colonel Henry Atkinson, October 29, 1819, American State Papers, 202.

50. Chittenden, *American Fur Trade*, 1:161.

51. Ibid., 1:162.

52. Ibid., 2:925; Charles Gratiot to John Jacob Astor, June 10, 1810, Gratiot Collection, Missouri History Museum.

53. Pierre Chouteau to William Simmon, November 23, 1809, Pierre Chouteau Letterbook, Missouri History Museum.

54. *Missouri Gazette*, November 2, 1809. In the two centuries since Meriwether Lewis's death, controversy has raged over whether he was murdered—and, if so, whether nameless thieves, Lewis's servant, the (supposedly) absent owner of the inn, James Neelly (Lewis's traveling companion), an agent of General James Wilkinson (fearful Lewis was about to expose his grand conspiracy), or someone else was responsible—or whether he died by his own hand—and, if so, whether the root cause was hopelessness, clinical depression, bipolar disorder, syphilis, malaria, or something else. Controversy has also raged over whether exhuming the body would help solve the mystery, as well as whether the National Park Service should grant permission for an exhumation. (Lewis's grave lies within the boundaries of the Natchez Trace Parkway, a National Park Service unit.) In April of 2010, after some waffling, the Department of the Interior stated that permission would not be granted and that the decision was final. (See Mike Esterl, "Meriwether Lewis's Final Journey Remains a Mystery," *Wall Street Journal*, September 25, 2010.) For more on the compelling debate surrounding Lewis's sad death, see the following: Thomas C. Danisi and John C. Jackson, *Meriwether Lewis* (Amherst, N.Y.: Prometheus Books), 2009, especially pp. 297–325; Vardis Fisher, *Suicide or Murder: The Strange Death of Governor Meriwether Lewis* (Athens, Ohio: Swallow Press), 1962; John D. W. Guice, ed., *By His Own Hand? The Mysterious Death of Meriwether Lewis* (Norman: University of Oklahoma Press), 2006; and James Starrs and Kira Gale, *The Death of Meriwether Lewis: A Historic Crime Scene Investigation* (Omaha, Nebr.: River Junction Press), 2009.

4. "WE ALL NOW BECAME BLIND FROM THE REFLECTION OF THE SUN'S RAYS"

1. James, *Three Years*, 14–15.

2. Ibid., 14, 17.
3. Ibid., 17–18.
4. Ibid., 18.
5. Ibid.
6. See Morris, *Fate of the Corps*, 77.
7. Lamar, *Encyclopedia of the West*, 986.
8. James, *Three Years*, 19.
9. Ibid., 20.
10. Ibid., 21. For information on the Bighorn River, see William Clark's journal entry, July 26, 1806, Moulton, *Journals*, 8:229-35. Clark estimated the width of the Bighorn at 220 yards, virtually the same as the Yellowstone. The bluff is the possible but not certain site of the fort. See Wood, "Manuel Lisa's Fort Raymond" and Wegman-French and Haecker, "Finding Lisa's 1807 Fort."
11. Bradbury, *Travels*, 151. Lisa's Fort Mandan was ten or twelve miles north of Lewis and Clark's fort of the same name, which provided living quarters for the men of the expedition during the winter of 1804-5.
12. James, *Three Years*, 21, 22.
13. The Dougherty Narrative, National Archives, cited by Kelly, "The Evacuation of Three Forks," 155; Kelly, "The Evacuation of Three Forks," 155.
14. James, *Three Years*, 22, 24, 34–35.
15. Ibid., 35.
16. A copy of Colter's promissory note to Lepage's estate is included in Colter's estate papers, Franklin County Courthouse, Union, Missouri. Lepage was indebted to Lisa when he died, and in a series of events and a paper trail so typical of the period, Colter's debt to Lepage's estate was actually paid from Colter's estate to Auguste Chouteau in 1814. Nor is there any record of Lepage's family ever receiving his pay of $116.33. See Morris, *Fate of the Corps*, 77–78, and Colter-Frick, *Courageous Colter*, 142–43
17. At the end of April, 1805, Lewis and Clark entered Montana from the northeast, and the entire company followed the Missouri River all the way to Three Forks (with a portage at Great Falls) and then followed the Jefferson and Beaverhead Rivers to the Continental Divide in the southwest corner of Montana, crossing over into Idaho in mid-August. In 1806, on the return journey, Lewis and Clark entered Montana from the northwest and eventually divided the Corps of Discovery into five groups. Lewis stayed in the north and followed the Missouri into North Dakota. Clark went southeast to Three Forks, crossed Bozeman Pass, and followed the Yellowstone to its confluence with the Missouri (at the eastern edge of North Dakota). Some of Clark's group split off and were led by Sergeant Pryor. Sergeant Ordway's contingent, which included Colter, arrived with Clark's group at Three Forks, then boarded canoes and went up the Missouri. They eventually met up with Lewis and with Sergeant Gass and his men, who had split off from Lewis and three others. The Corps had entered Montana in late June of 1806 and were reunited in North Dakota in early August.
18. Kelly, "Evacuation of Three Forks," 156.
19. Ibid.
20. James, *Three Years*, 23. James said there were thirty-two men in the company, but William Clark received reports that sixty men later separated from the main group and went south with Andrew Henry. (William Clark to William Eusits, July 20, 1810, Missouri History Museum.) Richard Oglesby therefore estimated that at least eighty men departed Fort Raymond. (*Manuel Lisa*, 93.) As Mark W. Kelly notes, "The discrepancy may be attributable to the unreported or unknown men assigned to the separate posts established on the upriver ascent; the unreported number of men bound for and leaving Three Forks by divergent routes, including an unknown number accompanying Pierre Menard; and the unknown number of men killed by the Blackfoot during the company's tenure on the Three Forks" ("The Evacuation of Three Forks," 179n33).
21. James, *Three Years*, 23.
22. Account of Major Jacob Fowler, cited in Landon Jones, *William Clark*, 10.
23. William Clark to Jonathan Clark, August 18, 1794; C. B. Brown, ed., *A View of the Soil and Climate of the United States by C. F. Volney*, 382; both cited in Jones, *William Clark*, 79.

As Landon Jones points that, Wayne's army was employing the same "slash-and-burn tac-
tics . . . the Virginians had bitterly denounced as barbaric when British Colonel Banastre
Tarleton's dragoons swept through Albemarle County in 1781" (*William Clark*, 79). Military
records for John Hoback are found in the Pay Roll and Muster Roll of Captain James Flinn's
Company of Scouts under the command of General Wayne, Kentucky Scouts and Spies,
1790–1794, National Archives. Hoback served from September 24 to December 2, 1793, and a
record dated June 24, 1794 indicates he may have been serving another term at that time.

24. West Augusta, Va., commissary's account book, June 3–Sept. 17, 1777; James Booth to
Zadoc Springer, Aug. 2, 1777; both cited in *Preston and Virginia Papers*, 210.

25. John Floyd to Thomas Jefferson, April 16, 1781, cited in Jones, *William Clark*, 42.

26. C. Hale Sipe, *The Indian Wars of Pennsylvania*, 650, cited in Jones, *William Clark*, 43.

27. Amos Kendall to F. G. Flugel, May 14, 1814, cited in Robert Vincent Remini, *Henry
Clay: Statesman for the Union* (New York: W. W. Norton), 1991, 17.

28. Kelly, "Evacuation of Three Forks," 156.

29. Ibid., 156–57.

30. James, *Three Years*, 24.

31. Ibid., 24–25.

32. Ibid., 25.

33. Ibid.

34. Pierre Menard to Pierre Chouteau, April 21, 1810, reprinted in Chittenden, *The
American Fur Trade*, 2:882–83.

35. James, *Three Years*, 34.

36. Ibid., 26–27. As for the Three Forks fort itself, in 1876, an army unit involved in the
Sioux Campaign camped at Three Forks. Lieutenant James H. Bradley made a "personal search
and diligent inquiry after any possible remaining traces of it." James then made this oft-quoted
entry in his journal: "In 1870 the outlines of the fort were still intact, from which it appears that
it was a double stockade of logs set three feet deep, enclosing an area of about 300 feet square,
situated upon the tongue of land (at that point half a mile wide) between the Jefferson and
Madison rivers about two miles above the confluence, upon the south bank of a channel now
called Jefferson Slough." Jim Hardee points out, however, that while "Bradley's information
has been universally accepted" as a description of the Missouri Fur Company's fort at Three
Forks, "as many questions are raised as are answered" ("The Fort at the Forks," 102–3,104).

37. James, *Three Years*, 36.

38. Ibid.

39. Ibid., 36–38.

40. Ibid., 38–39.

41. Pierre Menard to Pierre Chouteau, April 21, 1810, "Letters from Three Forks," 120.

42. James, *Three Years*, 39–40.

43. Ibid., 41

44. Ibid.

45. Menard to Chouteau, April 21, 1810, 120; Pierre Menard to his wife, Angelique, April
21, 1810, "Letters from Three Forks," 121.

46. James, *Three Years*, 42.

47. Menard to his wife, Angelique, April 21, 1810, "Letters from Three Forks," 121; James,
Three Years, 41–42.

48. James, *Three Years*, 42; Menard to his wife, Angelique, April 21, 1810, "Letters from
Three Forks," 121.

49. James, *Three Years*, 42; *Louisiana Gazette*, July 26, 1810.

50. Reuben Lewis to Meriwether Lewis, April 21, 1810, "Letters from Three Forks," 121.

51. James, *Three Years*, 35, emphasis in original.

52. Menard to Chouteau, April 21, 1810, "Letters from Three Forks," 120; Menard to his
wife Angelique, April 21, 1810, "Letters from Three Forks," 122.

53. Reuben Lewis to Meriwether Lewis, April 21, 1810, "Letters from Three Forks,"
121–22.

54. Ibid., 122.

55. James, *Three Years*, 35–36. After his return to St. Louis, James filed suit against the St. Louis Missouri Fur Company and was in turn countersued by them. The case dragged on throughout 1811, and Colter was called as a witness in March, June, and October of that year. (St. Louis Circuit Court Historical Records Project, accessed at http://stlcourtrecords.wustl.edu/index.php, on February 20, 2012.) Colter thus had several opportunities to see James and tell of his final escape from Blackfoot Indians. The two also likely discussed James's debt to Colter. "I sued [the St. Louis Missouri Fur Company] on my contract, and was the only one who did so," wrote James. "After many delays and continuances from term to term, I was glad to get rid of the suits and them by giving my note for one hundred dollars to the Company. This, with my debt to Colter, made me a loser to the amount of three hundred dollars by one years trapping on the head waters of the Missouri" (James, *Three Years*, 55).

56. James, *Three Years*, 44.

57. Ibid., 45.

58. Ibid., 45–46. James was quite correct in calling Drouillard *the* principal hunter of the expedition. According to the journals of Lewis and Clark and their men, Drouillard made more successful hunting trips than any other member of the Corps of Discovery. Brothers Joseph and Reubin Field were right behind him. (See Arlen J. Large, "Expedition Specialists: The Talented Helpers of Lewis and Clark," *We Proceeded On* 20 [February 1994]: 4–10.)

59. Meriwether Lewis to Henry Dearborn, January 15, 1807, Jackson, *Letters*, 1:368.

60. James, *Three Years*, 46.

61. Journal of Alexander Henry, cited in Chittenden, *American Fur Trade*, 1:155–56. Henry added that he observed that some of the beaver skins taken by the Blood Indians "were marked Valley and Jummell with different numbers—8, 15, etc." This is quite possibly a reference to Francois Vallé and Michael Immell, two of the trappers present at the time of the attack.

62. *Louisiana Gazette*, July 26, 1810; James, *Three Years*, 46.

63. Ambrose, *Undaunted Courage*, 383–84.

64. James, *Three Years*, 46–47; bracketed insertion added.

65. Ibid., 47–48.

5. "WHISKEY FLOWED LIKE MILK AND HONEY IN THE LAND OF CANAAN"

1. As noted earlier, Gratiot reported Crooks's arrival to Astor. (Gratiot to Astor, June 10, 1810, in Franchere, *Narrative*, 55.)

2. Lavender, *Fist in the Wilderness*, 120, 442n1.

3. Porter, *John Jacob Astor*, 181, 182; Lavender, *Fist in the Wilderness*, 129. McKay, McKenzie, and McDougall had all signed a preliminary agreement on March 10, 1810. As Lavender points out, this agreement "put the twenty-three-year-old Crooks on the same footing as the other, older field partners" (*Fist in the Wilderness*, 129).

4. Ross, *First Settlers*, 174. Ross's account of the overland journey is secondhand because he sailed on the *Tonquin* and based his narrative on his conversations with the participants themselves.

5. Ibid., 174–75; Jean Baptiste Perrault, "Narrative of the Travels and Adventures of a Merchant Voyageur in the Savage Territories of Northern America Leaving Montreal the 28th of May 1783," in *Michigan Pioneer and Historical Collections*, ed. John Sharpless Fox, 583.

6. Ross, *First Settlers*, 176–77.

7. Perrault, "Travels and Adventures," 584; Cox, *Adventures*, 96. As to whether the Reed who was with Crooks in 1806 was the same Reed who enlisted with Hunt and McKenzie in 1810, Lavender writes: "The Kinzie account book names James Reed as crossing the Chicago portage with Crooks in 1806. If the transcription is correct, the Reeds are different men—but the difference, James to John, is too slight to be conclusive, and Kinzie's records were not always above reproach" (*Fist in the Wilderness*, 445n14).

8. Ross, *First Settlers*, 176–78. As Reuben Gold Thwaites notes, the route taken by these Astorians had been "travelled by Marquette and Jolliet in 1763 [and] was from a well-established Indian and French waterway between the Great Lakes and the Mississippi" (Ross, *First Settlers*, 178, editorial note).

9. Porter, *John Jacob Astor*, 186, 186; Ronda, *Empire*, 94–101; Ross, *First Settlers*, 44, 43.

10. James, *Three Years*, 52.

11. Ibid., 54–55.

12. Ibid., 55.

13. Andrew Henry to Francois Vallé, June 5, 1810, in "Letters from Three Forks," 122.

14. *Louisiana Gazette*, August 8, 1811; Major Thomas Biddle, Camp Missouri, Missouri River, to Colonel Henry Atkinson, October 29, 1819, American State Papers, p. 202, bracketed insertion added.

15. Wishart, *Fur Trade of the American West*, 46; Reuben Lewis to Meriwether Lewis, April 21, 1810, in "Letters from Three Forks,"122. As Jim Hardee points out, "only a handful" of Henry's men can be identified: "Dougherty, Michael Immel, Nicholas Glineau, William Weir, Archibald Pelton, P. McBride, B. Jackson, L. Cather, and that intrepid trio, Edward Robinson, John Hoback, and Jacob Reznor. Neither their exact number nor their route is clearly known" (*Pierre's Hole!*, 72–73).

16. The Dougherty Narrative, cited in Kelly, "Evacuation from Three Forks," 163, bracketed insertion included in Kelly's transcription; Biddle to Atkinson, October 29, 1819. See Kelly's article for a detailed account of the route likely taken by this group. It has long been assumed that when Henry's group fled Three Forks they ascended the Madison River, crossed into present Idaho at Raynolds Pass, and then followed Henry's Fork down into the Snake River Valley. Such an assumption was largely based on William Clark's letter to William Eustis, which reads in part: "about 70 men of the company are yet in the upper Country. 60 went by way of Madison River over to the heads of a South branch of the Columbia to hunt & trade with the Snake Indians" (William Clark to William Eustis, July 20, 1810, cited in Kelly, "Evacuation from Three Forks," 162). Clark, however, got his information from Menard, who left Three Forks before Henry's men were attacked a second time and wouldn't have known that they changed their plans. It is also possible, as Jim Hardee notes, that "Henry may have split his party sending one group [including Dougherty] with Menard to obtain needed supplies and then head for the Columbia River drainage, while Henry led the remainder on a more direct route south by way of the Madison River." While Henry's Fort lay along Henry's Fork between present Rexburg and St. Anthony, Idaho, the men also apparently camped temporarily about thirty miles west and slightly north, near present Drummond, Idaho. In 1917, local resident Hazen Hawkes discovered a stone, widely considered genuine, containing "the names of five men, a face, a cross and the year 1810. The names on the rock are A. Henry, J. Hoback, P. McBride, B. Jackson and L. Cather" (*Pierre's Hole!*, 73,78).

17. Thompson, "Narrative," 302, bracketed insertion added.

18. Majors, "McClellan in the Rockies," 611, 612. The information presented here on McClallen (sometimes spelled *McClellan*) is based on Majors' meticulous research. For an alternate view of McClallen, see John C. Jackson, *By Honor and Right: How One Man Boldly Defined the Destiny of a Nation* (Amherst, NY: Prometheus Books), 2010.

19. William Clark to William Eustis, September 12, 1810, Carter, Territorial Papers, vol. xiv; website http://museum.bmi.net/MARIE%20DORION%20PEOPLE/pierre_dorion_ii.htm, accessed March 8, 2012.

20. Clark to Eustis, September12, 1810; John Jacob Astor to Albert Gallatin, May 26, 1810, cited in Lavender, *Fist in the Wilderness*, 444n10.

21. Ronda, *Empire*, 128, 129; Clark's journal entry, August 3, 1806, Moulton, *Journals*, 8:277; Landon Jones, *William Clark*, 192; Ronda, *Empire*, 129.

22. Ronda, *Empire*, 129; letter from Wilson Price Hunt to Frederick Bates, cited in Buckley, *Indian Diplomat*, 83; Bradbury, *Travels*, 100.

23. Irving, *Astoria*, xix, 135–36; Ross, *First Settlers*, 179–80. As Edgeley W. Todd, points out, Irving had access to many documents related to Astoria that were later destroyed. He also interviewed several people who "had been engaged in [Astor's] great undertaking," including

"a principal actor in the enterprise" who provided "many personal anecdotes for the enriching of [Irving's] work." Although it is not possible to identify these individuals, "Ramsay Crooks was still alive [when Irving did his research in the mid-1830s] and was, in fact, president of the American Fur Company at the time. It is entirely possible—even probable—" that Crooks provided details of his experiences. Irving is thus an invaluable resource on the amazing history of Astor's grand experiment. As Todd concludes, "the authoritativeness of Astoria can be relied upon in all but an exceedingly small number of instances. It is at least as sound as the authorities Irving consulted. . . . As a result of his proximate adherence to primary source materials, not only is the narrative authentic, but his descriptions of routes of travel and of terrain . . . are also faithful to the setting in which the events in Astoria actually occurred" (Irving, *Astoria*, xxii, xxiii, xxxv, xxxiii).

24. Ross, *First Settlers*, 180; Irving, *Astoria*, 135n7; Porter, "Roll of Overland Astorians."
25. Reed, Journal, vol. 1, 69–71.
26. Irving, *Astoria*, 136.
27. Ross, *First Settlers*, 180.
28. Background from Lavender, *Fist in the Wilderness*, 133.
29. Ross, *First Settlers*, 181.
30. Cited in Drumm, "More About Astorians," 348.
31. Ross, *First Settlers*, 54–55.
32. Lavender, *Fist in the Wilderness*, 133.

6. "ABOUT SEVENTY ABLE BODIED MEN, NERVED TO HARDSHIP"

1. Irving, *Astoria*, 141; shortly after arriving in Astoria in 1812, Dorion proved his worth as both a hunter and a canoe maker. For examples, see Robert F. Jones, *Annals of Astoria*, 98, 102, 104, 106, 110.
2. Irving, *Astoria*, 140–41.
3. Thomas Jefferson to Meriwether Lewis, January 22, 1804, Jackson, *Letters*, 1:166; Ambrose, *Undaunted Courage*, 170; Clark, "Estimate of Eastern Indians," Moulton, *Journals*, 3:418. Based on Clark's assessment, traders going upriver naturally concluded that getting safely past the Lakota nation would be the most difficult aspect of a journey to present North Dakota or Montana. The most serious conflicts on the river, however, came with the Arikara nation, upstream from the Lakota, where several Americans were killed in 1807 and several more in 1823. (See Morris, *Fate of the Corps*, chapter 3 and chapter 13.) The Lakota proved to be much more peaceful than Clark imagined; not only that, but they gave Lewis and Clark the benefit of the doubt by depicting the meeting with the Americans favorably in their winter counts. Cloud Shield, for example, described a year during this period when "many people camped together and had many flags flying," while American Horse's summary states, "The Dakotas had a council with the whites on the Missouri River, below the Cheyenne Agency, near the mouth of Bad Creek" (Greene, *The Year the Stars Fell*, 138).
4. Clark's field notes, September 25, 1804, and Clark's journal entry, September 25, 1804, Moulton, *Journals*, 3:111 and 3:112, respectively.
5. Irving, *Astoria*, 142.
6. Bradbury, *Travels*, 36. In a letter to Meriwether Lewis on August 16, 1809, Thomas Jefferson had written, "This will be handed you [by] Mr. Bradbury, an English botanist, who proposes to take St. Louis in his botanising tour." Bradbury arrived in St. Louis with the letter in hand on December 31, 1809, but likely had heard by then that Lewis had died in Tennessee in October. In what proved to be his last letter to Lewis, Jefferson had added: "Your friends here are well, & have been long in expectation of seeing you. I shall hope in that case to possess a due portion of you at Monticello" (Jefferson to Lewis, August 16, 1809, Jackson, *Letters*, 2:458, bracketed insertion included in Jackson's transcription).
7. Irving, *Astoria*, 142.

8. Bradbury, *Travels*, 19.
9. Bradbury, *Travels*, 38–39; Irving, *Astoria*, 144.
10. Bradbury, *Travels*, 39.
11. Ibid., 39–40n10 (Bradbury's note).
12. Bradbury, *Travels*, 39–41; Irving, *Astoria*, 135. Bradbury said the voyageur who searched for Marie was named "St. Paul," but Kenneth W. Porter does not include that name in his list of Astorians. Furthermore, Porter does not include anyone with the first or last name of Paul. However, there were two Canadian voyageurs with "Saint" in their name—Joseph Saint Amant and Louis Saint Michel. (Porter, "Roll of Overland Astorians," 111.)
13. *Louisiana Gazette*, March 14, 1811.
14. Bradbury, *Travels*, 43; Jones, *William Clark*, 41. As Gary Moulton notes, "La Charette, on Charette Creek, in Warren County, [Missouri], in 1804 [was] the westernmost white settlement on the Missouri. . . . Daniel Boone moved there from Boone's settlement sometime after 1804; he died and was buried there, but in 1845 his remains and those of his wife were moved to Kentucky. The village site, near present Marthasville, has been washed away by the Missouri" (Moulton, *Journals*, 2:252–253n5).
15. Bradbury, *Travels*, 44.
16. Ibid., 44n18 (Bradbury's note). In stating that Colter traveled three thousand miles from Three Forks to St. Louis, Bradbury accurately represented William Clark's estimated mileage—which was 2953 miles (going overland from Three Forks to the Yellowstone River and following it to the Missouri). However, Clark's figures turned out to be overestimates. For example, Clark calculated the length of the Missouri from its mouth to Three Forks to be 3,096 miles, while the actual distance is 2,341 miles. Therefore, Colter traveled several hundred miles less than three thousand. Even then, the claim (of either Colter or Bradbury) that this trip was completed in thirty days is almost certainly an exaggeration. Lewis and Clark made good time on their return journey, sometimes traveling seventy or eighty miles a day, but it still took them forty days to go from the Mandan villages in present North Dakota to St. Louis, which Clark estimated to be about 1,600 miles. Colter had to go several hundred miles farther than that and apparently went from Three Forks to the Yellowstone River by way of the Gallatin, Lamar, and Clark's Fork Rivers, adding several days of overland travel to his journey. Colter thus accomplished an amazing feat even if he made the journey in thirty-nine days (the period from April 22, the earliest he could have left, since he carried letters written on April 21, to May 31, the latest he could have arrived if Bradbury's mention of May is accurate.) (See Moulton, *Journals*, 8:381 and 3:88-3:93 for Clark's estimates; the website of the Missouri River Conservation Districts Council for current mileage [accessed on March 24, 2012]; and chapter 4 herein for Colter's possible route.) As for the second installment of Dr. Thomas's article, it is presumed but not proved to have appeared in the St. Louis newspaper. As Donald Jackson notes, "Joseph Charless, publisher of the *Missouri Gazette* . . . ran the first installment [of Thomas's article] in the issue of November 30, [1809], and probably ran the second and final installment [which included the account of Colter] early in December. But the *Gazette* is one of the scarcest of American newspapers, and in the most complete file available—at the Missouri Historical Society [now the Missouri History Museum]—part of the December 7 issue and all of the December 14 issue are missing." (Jackson, "Journey to the Mandans," 179.) Luckily, Thomas's first and second installments were reprinted in the *Pittsburgh Gazette* on July 6 and July 13, 1810, respectively, and Jackson included the second installment in "Journey to the Mandans."
17. Bradbury, *Travels*, 44–46; Irving, *Astoria*, 147. There is good evidence that Colter's son, Hiram, was born before the Lewis and Clark Expedition because he bought goods at an estate sale in 1825. What became of Hiram's mother, however, is unknown. Colter had a daughter, Evelina, who married in 1830, birth date unknown. When Colter died in May of 1812, he left a widow who is called both Loucy and Sally in the probate papers. She married a man by the name of James Brown. (Colter-Frick, *Courageous Colter*, 175, 174, 160, 166.) Irving, *Astoria*, 147. In July of 1806, near Two Medicine River in present northwest Montana, Meriwether Lewis and his three companions—George Drouillard and Joseph and Reubin Field—had killed two young Blackfoot men who attempted to steal their guns and horses. James Ronda writes that after their safe escape, Lewis and the others "left behind at the Two Medicine the seed of a myth that has long shaped popular understanding of the Blackfeet fight.

That myth links the Two Medicine encounter with later Blackfeet-American hostilities . . . and appears to have its genesis in the fertile imagination of Washington Irving" (Ronda, *Lewis and Clark among the Indians*, 243).

18. *Missouri Gazette*, Apr. 18, 1811.

19. For more information on Colter's various routes and Clark's maps, see chapter 4 herein, Allen, "The Forgotten Explorers"; Allen, *Passage Through the Garden*; Cohen, *Mapping the West*; and Kelly, "Evacuation of Three Forks."

20. Bradbury, *Travels*, 48–49, bracketed insertions added.

21. Ibid., 63, 50.

22. Ibid., 50, 52.

23. Ibid., 53, 57; William Clark to Jonathan Clark, July 3, 1810, Holmberg, *Dear Brother*, 245, 247–8n6, underlining in original. Clark's matter-of-fact tone does not necessarily indicate a lack of sympathy but seems typical of his way of recording such events. On August 27, 1827, he wrote in his Indian Office logbook: "Edmund Clark (my Infant Son) died at 81/2 A.M. (10 mo. 3 days old)" (Cited in Jones, *William Clark*, 289, parentheses and underlining in original).

24. Bradbury, *Travels*, 57–59.

25. Ibid., 60–61; Irving, *Astoria*, 152.

26. Bradbury, *Travels*, 61, 62.

27. Ibid., 62–63.

28. Ibid., 63–64.

29. Ibid., 66, 67; Irving, *Astoria*, 152, 153, bracketed insertion added. As for Dorion beating Marie, while Bradbury says that Hunt merely asked Dorion why he had done so, Irving reports that Dorion inflicted his violence "before his neighbors could interfere." Sacagawea was much luckier: on at least two occasions, William Clark vigorously defended her. The first came on June 19, 1805, when Sacagawea, who had recently been quite ill, ate "a considerable quantity of the white apples . . . together with a considerable quantity of dryed fish" without Clark's knowledge. She soon "complained very much and her fever again returned. I rebuked Sahrbono severely for suffering her to indulge herself with such food" (Clark's journal entry, June 19, 1805, Moulton, *Journals*, 4:309). A few weeks later, Clark wrote: "I checked our interpreter for Strikeing his woman at their Dinner" (Clark's journal entry, August 14, 1805, Moulton, *Journals*, 5:93). As far as is known, Charbonneau did not strike her again during the expedition.

30. Brackenridge, *Journal of a Voyage*, 5, 6. Brackenridge's claim that Henry had not been heard from in more than a year was overstated because, as noted above, Menard and Henry had parted ten months earlier, in June of 1810.

31. Ibid., 7, 8–9. Hunt had actually left on March 12, exactly three weeks ahead of Lisa, who left on April 2. The newspaper gave notice of Lisa's departure, just as it had Hunt's a few weeks earlier: "A few days ago, Mr. Manuel Lisa sailed from here on a voyage to Fort Mandan. Should Mr. Lisa join Mr. Hunt's party, on the headwaters of the Missouri, they will form an army able to oppose any number of Blackfeet which may attack them. It is thought there will be upwards of 300 Americans on the Columbia River next year" (*Louisiana Gazette*, April 11, 1811).

32. Ibid., 29; Nathaniel Pryor to William Clark, Oct. 16, 1807, Jackson, *Letters*, 2:433.

33. Brackenridge, *Journal of a Voyage*, 10.

34. "On October 30, 1810, Charbonneau purchased from [William] Clark, who was then Indian agent for Louisiana Territory, a tract of land on the Mississippi River, in Saint Ferdinand Township, near St. Louis. In the spring of 1811, Charbonneau sold the land back to Clark for one hundred dollars, a transaction recorded on March 26, 1811" (Howard, *Sacajawea*, 156–57, bracketed insertion added). Clark had promised to raise Baptiste as his own child (see Clark to Toussaint Charbonneau, August 20, 1806, Jackson, *Letters*, 1:315), but that's not exactly what happened. As Landon Jones notes, "Although the boy apparently never lived in Clark's personal household, he was baptized in St. Louis and matriculated at a parochial school run by a Baptist minister" (Jones, *William Clark*, 194). As for Lisa's attempt to catch Hunt, Brackenridge wrote on April 11: "In company with [Toussaint] Charbonneau, the interpreter, I proceeded . . . to the village of Cote sans Dessein. . . . [where Dorion had first heard of the war between the Osage and the Iowa and their allies] To our eager inquiries after Mr. Hunt, we were told, that he passed here about three weeks before. Thus far we have gained about two

days upon him" (Brackenridge, *Journal of a Voyage*, 28, bracketed insertions added). As noted, however, Lisa had left three weeks after Hunt, not three weeks and two days. Hunt had reached the village on March 21, exactly three weeks earlier, so Lisa had kept pace but had not yet gained any ground.

35. Ronda, *Empire*, 111; Ross, *First Settlers*, 87. See Ronda, *Astoria*, 87–115, for a description of the horrific voyage, including a compelling account of how Robert Stuart saved several fellow Canadians (whom Thorn had deliberately left at the Falkland Islands) by pulling a pistol and threatening to kill Thorn.

36. Franchere, *Narrative*, 55; Ross, *First Settlers*, 75.

37. Ross, *First Settlers*, 76; Franchere, *Narrative*, 55. Franchere's count of five men—Fox, the Lapensée brothers, Nadeau, and Martin—is assumed to be accurate because both he and Ross report that a total of eight men drowned in the Columbia passage. (See note 38, below.)

38. Ross, *First Settlers*, 76-78.

39. Ibid., 77.

40. Franchere, *Narrative*, 55.

41. Ross, *First Settlers*, 77. What makes this story even more heartbreaking is that two days later, Thorn insisted on sending out another boat, despite rough seas. Five men boarded the boat—Job Aitkin, the rigger; Stephen Weeks, the armorer; a sailmaker named John Coles; and Harry and Peter, two Hawaiians. A second tragedy ensued—only Weeks and one of the Hawaiians survived, meaning that eight men had been lost on the bar (a number confirmed by both Ross and Franchere). "We had left New York, for the most part strangers to one another," wrote Franchere, "but arrived at the river Columbia we were all friends, and regarded each other almost as brothers. We regretted especially the two brothers Lapensée and Joseph Nadeau: these young men had been in an especial manner recommended by their respectable parents in Canada to the care of Mr. M'Kay; and had acquired by their good conduct the esteem of the captain, of the crew, and of all the passengers. The brothers Lapensée were courageous and willing, never flinching in the hour of danger, and had become as good seamen as any on board. Messrs Fox and Aikin were both highly regarded by all; the loss of Mr. Fox, above all, who was endeared to every one by his gentlemanly behavior and affability, would have been severely regretted at any time, but it was doubly so in the present conjuncture: this gentleman, who had already made a voyage to the Northwest, could have rendered important services to the captain and to the company. The preceding days had been days of apprehension and of uneasiness: this was one of sorrow and mourning" (Franchere, *Narrative*, 60–61). As noted in the prologue, note 1, Oliver Roy Lapensée, quite possible a brother of Basile and Ignace, drowned in the Athabasca River on the return to Montreal, meaning that the parents may have been informed of the loss of three sons. That task was not left to Alexander McKay (the man who recruited them), however, because he was the one partner who perished in the West.

7. "FAMILIES, PLANTATIONS, AND ALL VANISHED"

1. Bradbury, *Travels*, 68, italics in original.

2. Ibid.; Brackenridge, *Journal of a Voyage*, 70. Brackenridge also offered a brief but insightful look at two of Lisa's chief rivals: "M'Cleland was one of Wayne's runners, and is celebrated for his courage and uncommon activity. The stories related of his personal prowess, border on the marvelous. Crooks is a young Scotchman, of an enterprising character, who came to this country from the trading associations in Canada" (Brackenridge, *Journal of a Voyage*, 70–71).

3. "Among the Astor papers, deposited at Baker Library, Harvard Graduate School of Business Administration, are two journals of the overland expedition to Astoria, containing accounts of the debits of persons connected with the expedition for articles obtained from its commissary and credits due them for wages, skins, etc. The first of these books begins at La Chine, July 6, 1810, and the second and last ends at Astoria, February 20, 1812. Here we can find data in regard to the clothing, equipment, ornaments, luxuries and amusements of the Canadian voyageurs and the American hunter and trapper, together with the prices charged

them for the various articles included in the foregoing categories and the wages which were largely, and often more than totally, swallowed up in their purchases" (Porter, "Roll of Overland Astorians," 103).

4. The total number of overland Astorians (not including Marie Dorion or her children) is eighty-six, but that includes several who served for brief periods of time. From July of 1810 to February of 1812, there were regular deserters and regular recruits. (Porter, "Roll of Overland Astorians.")

5. Irving, *Astoria*, 154.

6. Bradbury, *Travels*, 70, 71, italics in original.

7. Brackenridge, *Journal of a Voyage*, 79; Irving, *Astoria*, 156.

8. Irving, *Astoria*, 156.

9. Brackenridge, *Journal of a Voyage*, 98–99.

10. Bradbury, *Travels*, 74–75, bracketed insertion added.

11. Brackenridge, *Journal of a Voyage*, 73–74. If Samuel Herrington had been hunting on the Missouri for two years (as Bradbury claims), he quite possibly went up the river in 1809, with Thomas James and scores of others. The first mention of him in John Reed's account book came on December 31, 1810, at the winter camp at the mouth of the Nodaway River (meaning that his family could have learned of his status from someone who returned to St. Louis with Hunt in January of 1811). William enlisted in St. Louis in March of 1811. The 1830 Federal Census lists a Samuel Herrington living in Merrimac, Jefferson County, Missouri, between forty and forty-nine years old, with a wife between thirty and thirty-nine, and five children under the age of twenty. The 1850 Federal Census for the same town and county lists a William Herrington, sixty-two years old, with sons twenty and twelve years old.

12. Bradbury, *Travels*, 75–86. Bradbury wrote that Blackbird "ruled over the Mahas with a sway the most despotic. He had managed in such a manner as to inspire them with the belief that he was possessed of supernatural powers: in council no chief durst oppose him—in war it was death to disobey.... He died about the time that Louisana was added to the United States; having previously made choice of a cave for his sepulchre, on the top of a hill near the Missouri, about eighteen miles below the Maha village. By his order his body was placed on the back of his favorite horse, which was driven in the cave, the mouth of which was then closed up with stones. A large heap was afterwards raised on the summit of the hill" (Bradbury, *Travels*, 85n47).

13. Ibid., 92.

14. Irving, *Astoria*, 158.

15. Ibid., 158–59; Ronda, *Empire*, 147.

16. Bradbury, *Travels*, 90–91; Clark's journal entry, September 25, 1804, Moulton, *Journals*, 3:111.

17. Clark's journal entry, September 3, 1806, Moulton, *Journals*, 8:346; Irving, *Astoria*, 160.

18. Bradbury, *Travels*, 88–89, 89n51, italics in original.

19. Ibid., 89.

20. Background on vermilion from Tubbs, *Companion*, 299, which further points out that "Captain Lewis used vermilion ... to convince three wary Shoshone women he meant no harm on August 13, 1805: 'I now painted their tawny cheeks with vermilion which with this nation is emblematic of peace,' information he had obtained from Sacagawea."

21. Ronda, *Empire*, 148; Woodger and Toropov, *Encyclopedia*, 316, bracketed insertion added.

22. Bradbury, *Travels*, 91, 92, 93. Concerning Floyd's death, William Clark wrote: "Passed two Islands on the S. S. And at first Bluff on the S S. Serj.' Floyd Died with a great deel of Composure, before his death he Said to me, 'I am going away" [']I want you to write me a letter'—We buried him on the top of the bluff ½ Miles below a Small river to which we Gave his name, he was buried with the Honors of War much lamented." (Clark's journal entry, August 20, 1804, Moulton, *Journals*, 2:495.)

23. Bradbury, *Travels*, 93.

24. Carson is thought by some to have been with Lewis and Clark during the first leg of their journey, but the evidence is quite tentative. See the Biographical Directory for more information on both Jones and Carson.

25. Bradbury, *Travels*, 96–97

26. Brackenridge, *Journal of a Voyage*, 58, 59–60.

27. Ibid., 72–73.

28. Ibid., 85, 89.

29. Ibid., 89–90, 90–91, bracketed insertions added; Lavender, *Fist in the Wilderness*, 154.

30. Bradbury, *Travels*, 97; Irving, *Astoria*, 173. Charbonneau and his companion arrived at Lisa's camp at dawn on May 26. Brackenridge wrote: "They bring us the pleasing information, that Hunt, in consequence of our request, has agreed to wait for us, at the Poncas village" (Brackenridge, *Journal of a Voyage*, 102).

31. Bradbury, *Travels*, 97. The two deserters were Joseph La Gemonier and Louis Rivard. (Porter, "Overland Astorians," 108, 111).

32. Bradbury, *Travels*, 98, italics in original.

33. Bradbury does not say whether Hoback, Reznor, and Robinson were informed that Hunt and other members of the party had talked with Colter ten weeks earlier.

34. Anderson, *Reasoner Story*, 52–56; Randolph County, Indiana, Census, 1807.

35. Irving, *Astoria*, 176–77.

36. Ibid., 98.

37. John Long, *Voyages and Travels of an Indian Interpreter and Trader*, cited in Irving, *Astoria*, 176n5. One history of Wheeling, West Virginia, offers this description of the fighting at Fort Henry: "After the successful ambuscade the entire body of the enemy, said to number nearly four hundred, advanced, and under protection of the neighboring cabins laid siege to the fort. The fighting continued throughout the day, and traditional accounts have related many incidents such as have marked the heroic defense of many western frontier posts. Women and children assisted in the work of reloading the guns, moulding bullets and watching every move of the enemy. The garrison was outnumbered nearly ten to one, but every assault on the stockade was repelled. Such a fortification as that at Wheeling was practically impregnable to Indian attack. Unless cannon were used to breach the walls, or the structure could be set on fire, the defenders could shoot down their assailants with little danger to themselves" (Charles A. Wingerter, *History of Greater Wheeling and Vicinity* [Chicago: Lewis Publishing], 1912, http://wheeling.weirton.lib.wv.us/history/landmark/historic/fthenry.htm, accessed on April 21, 2012). The account book of Francis Duke, deputy commissary for Ohio County, for the period of June 3-September 17, 1777, lists Robinson and several other men stationed at Fort Henry, including Captains Samuel Mason and Joseph Ogle. (Draper Manuscripts, Virginia Papers, 7ZZ8-22.) After August 30, entries in the account book were made in a different hand—because Duke was killed that day. (William Hintzen, *The Border Wars of the Upper Ohio Valley, 1769–1794: Conflicts and Resolutions* [Manchester, Conn.: Precision Shooting, Inc.], 1999.)

38. Brackenridge, *Views of Louisiana*, 164.

39. *Louisiana Gazette*, October 26, 1811; Major Thomas Biddle, Camp Missouri, Missouri River, to Colonel Henry Atkinson, October 29, 1819, American State Papers, p. 202.

40. Bradbury, *Travels*, 99–100; Irving, *Astoria*, 178.

41. Bradbury, *Travels*, 103.

42. Ibid., 103–4, bracketed insertions added.

43. Ibid., 104–5, bracketed insertion added.

44. Ibid., 105–6.

45. Ibid., 106–9, bracketed insertion added.

46. Ibid., 110, 117.

47. Brackenridge, *Journal of a Voyage*, 115; Bradbury, *Travels*, 119; Brackenridge, *Journal of a Voyage*, 128.

48. Bradbury, *Travels*, 119, bracketed insertion added.

49. Ibid., 121; Irving, *Astoria*, 189; Bradbury, *Travels*, 122.

50. Ibid., 121; Irving, *Astoria*, 189; Brackenridge, *Journal of a Voyage*, 128.

51. Bradbury, *Travels*, 122.

52. Ibid.

53. Brackenridge, *Journal of a Voyage*, 129–30.
54. Ibid., 135.
55. Ibid., 135–36.
56. Ibid., 138, 139.
57. Irving, *Astoria*, 214; Chittenden, *American Fur Trade*, 2:685.
58. Reed Journal, July 8, July 15-17, August 29, 1811; Brackenridge, *Journal of a Voyage*, 166, 167.
59. Brackenridge, *Journal of a Voyage*, 149.
60. Bradbury, *Travels*, 168, 182, 183.

8. "A VERY SAD RECOLLECTION"

1. Hunt, "Diary," 281. Hunt's diary is no longer extant; the earliest available document is the French translation, which begins with a curious mix of both first- and third-person accounts and is reprinted in Rollins, *Discovery of the Oregon Trail*, 281–308. (See Rollins, *Discovery of the Oregon Trail*, lxvi, cxvii, cxviii, and cxiv for more information.) The partners, hunters, and voyagers in the overland party were as follows: Charles Boucher, Bazile Brazeau, Piere Brugere, William Cannon, Michel Carriere, Alexander Carson, Martin H. Cass, Antoine Clappin, George Cone, Joseph Cotte, Ramsay Crooks, John Day, Joseph Delaunay, Pierre Delaunay, Jean Baptiste Delorme, Pierre Detaye, Louis Dinnelle, Pierre Dorion, Jean Baptiste Dubreuil, Francois Duchouquette, Andre Dufrene, Presque Felix, Francois Fripagne, Jean Baptiste Gardapie, John Hoback, William Francois Hodgens, Wilson Price Hunt, Charles Jacquette, Joseph Jerve, Benjamin Jones, Jean Baptiste La Bonte, Louis La Bonte, Andre La Chapelle, Louis La Liberte, Francois Landry, Joseph Landry, Michel Lanson, Louis La Valle, Francois Le Clerc, Alexie LeCompt, Guillaume Le Roux, Etienne Lucier, Robert McClellan, Donald McKenzie, Francois Marcial, Joseph Miller, Jean Baptiste Ouvre, Antoine Papin, Jean Baptiste Pillon, Antoine Plante, Jean Baptiste Provost, John Reed, Jacob Reznor, Francois Robert, Edward Robinson, Edward Rose, Joseph St. Amant, Louis St. Michel, Jean Baptiste Turcotte, and Andre Valle. (Porter, "Roll of Overland Astorians.") Fourteen of the men never returned home, and most of those were killed by Indians. The woman and children, of course, were Marie, Baptiste, and Paul Dorion.
2. Hunt, "Diary," 281.
3. Irving, *Astoria*, 218.
4. Hunt, "Diary," 281.
5. Ibid., 282; Irving, *Astoria*, 227.
6. Irving, *Astoria*, 228.
7. Ibid., 229, 230. Hunt had actually crossed the Little Missouri River itself, not one of its branches. Thomas James and his two companions had crossed the same river, farther downstream, on their way to Fort Raymond late in the winter of 1809-10.
8. Hunt, "Diary," 282–83.
9. Hunt, "Diary," 284–85.
10. Ibid., 285.
11. Ibid.
12. Irving, *Astoria*, 255–56.
13. Hunt, "Diary," 286. For an interesting discussion of the naming of these mountains— and how the name *Tetons* has stuck, despite efforts to change it—see Hardee, *Pierre's Hole!*, 10–14.
14. Hunt, "Diary," 286-87.
15. Ibid., 287–88.
16. Irving, *Astoria*, 216.
17. Ibid., 264.
18. Ibid., 265.
19. Hunt, "Diary," 289.

20. Irving writes that Miller was "troubled with a bodily malady that rendered travelling on horseback extremely irksome to him," (*Astoria*, 266) but gives no further details. Hunt does not mention Miller's physical ailment or his insisting on going by canoe.

21. Hunt, "Diary," 289; Irving, *Astoria*, 267.

22. Hunt, "Diary," 289. Jim Hardee believes the Astorians most likely took Mosquito Pass, which was heavily traveled by Indians. This trail goes up Moose Creek to Mesquite Creek and then Coal Creek before crossing to Mail Cabin Creek, over Mosquito Pass, and down that stream. (Hardee, *Pierre's Hole!*, 88, 10.) Mosquito Pass lies a few miles south of Teton Pass, now traversed by Wyoming Highway 22 (which becomes Idaho Highway 33 to the west).

23. The hot springs, just east of present Newdale, Idaho, and about four miles south of the Teton River, are now part of Green Canyon Hot Springs. As Jim Hardee points out, "the hot springs are actually twelve miles to the southwest of where Birch Creek flows into the Teton River. This leads to the supposition that a transcriber may have misread northwest for Hunt's southwest" (*Pierre's Hole!*, 91). The resort is above the site of an earthen dam constructed on the Teton River, which collapsed on June 5, 1976, flooding the towns of Wilford, Sugar City, and Rexburg and the surrounding Snake River Plain and killing eleven people.

24. Hunt, "Diary," 289. "Fort Henry, built in 1810 and vacated the following spring, was the first American post built on the western side of the Continental Divide. The Tetons could be seen to the East. Located on the future site of Eagle's Nest Ford, the fort was on the south side of Henry's Fork of the Snake River, about three miles west of present St. Anthony, Idaho" (Hardee, *Pierre's Hole!*, 75).

25. Irving, *Astoria*, 269.

26. Ibid.; Hunt, "Diary," 290. Reed's account book reveals a long list of supplies issued to Miller, including a rifle, beaver traps, cloth, awls, blue beads, a variety of knives, flint and steel, two blankets, needles and thread, fish hooks, powder and lead, a half-axe, a copper kettle, a tomahawk, and a good supply of tobacco. Hoback, Reznor, and Robinson had stocked up with similar supplies on September 30 and picked up just a few items before their departure from Henry's Fort. (Reed Journal, 152, 139–42.)

27. Hunt, "Diary," 291.

28. Ibid.

29. Ibid.; the Fremont quote is cited in Julie Fanselow, *Traveling the Oregon Trail* (Guilford, Conn.: The Globe Pequot Press), 2001, 141.

30. Hunt, "Diary," 291.

31. Ibid., 292.

32. *Louisiana Gazette*, October 26, 1811; Hardee, *Pierre's Hole!*, 81.

33. Irving, *Astoria*, 276.

34. Ibid.; Stuart, "Narratives," 112, bracketed insertion in original. Caldron Linn lies west of Burley, Idaho, between Milner Dam and the Murtaugh Bridge. Carrying out his duty with businesslike precision even in the midst of tragedy, John Reed noted that three men charged tobacco to their accounts and another a knife on October 28. (Reed Journal, 161.) Reed was sent out to explore on October 31 and did not see Hunt again until they met at Astoria. Entries in Reed's journal, however, continued to be made for those traveling with Hunt, apparently in the same handwriting as before Reed's departure, raising the possibility that Reed filled in those entries at Astoria based on notes taken by Hunt.

35. Hunt, "Diary," 292; Irving, *Astoria*, 279. As Philip Ashton Rollins points out, "Hunt, during this journey, actually passed Shoshone Falls (212 feet high) and Twin Falls (182 feet high) . . . . His marked underestimate of height was due to the fact that, from his vantage spot on the rim of the canyon, he could have seen no more than the crests of these particular falls, which descended into a deep rift in the floor of the main canyon" (*Discovery of the Oregon Trail*, 319-20n180).

36. Hunt, "Diary," 292–93.

37. Irving, *Astoria*, 280; Hunt, "Diary," 293. Starting with the sixty-five people who left the Arikara village, Rollins deducts those who left, departed on other missions, or died. "The remainder of six consisted, accordingly, of Crooks and his five companions" (Rollins, *Discovery of the Oregon Trail*, 320n184). Irving, who perhaps made his own calculations, agrees that Crooks left with five others. (Irving, *Astoria*, 280.)

38. Irving, *Astoria*, 282; Hunt, "Diary," 293.

39. Hunt, "Diary," 293.

40. Ibid., 294, 295.

41. Ibid., 295; Irving, *Astoria*, 290.

42. Hunt, "Diary," 296.

43. Ibid.; *Missouri Gazette*, May 15, 1813.

44. Hunt, "Diary," 296–97.

45. Ibid., 297. Hunt had obviously obtained additional horses from the Indians, but his journal gives no indication when that happened.

46. Ibid., 297; *Missouri Gazette*, May 15, 1813; Hunt, "Diary," 298, bracketed insertion added.

47. Hunt, "Diary," 298, bracketed insertion added. Hunt made the right decision because he had reached the edge of Hell's Canyon, "the deepest gorge on the North American continent (7,900 feet deep at its maximum)—and to this day one of the least accessible in the United States. No white man had yet been through this awesome mountain trench, which now forms part of the border between Oregon and Idaho, and no one who had known its extent of more than 100 miles would have tried forcing it in winter" (Josephy, "Ordeal in Hell's Canyon," 74.) While it's true that McClellan, McKenzie, and Reed and their men pushed down the river, their exact route is not known. And, as Irving notes, they were "picked men," "in better condition, and more fitted to contend with the difficulties of the country" (Irving, *Astoria*, 296.) They were also lucky enough to find more provisions than Hunt or Crooks, and to happen upon a herd of wild horses. They reached Astoria on January 18, almost a month before Hunt.

48. Hunt, "Diary," 298, 299.

49. Ibid., 299; Irving, *Astoria*, 297.

50. Irving, *Astoria*, 300-301.

51. Ibid., 301.

52. Ibid., 301–2.

53. Hunt, "Diary," 299, 300.

54. Ibid., 300.

55. Irving, *Astoria*, 307; Hunt, "Diary," 301, 302.

56. Ronda, *Empire*, 192–93.

57. Hunt, "Diary," 302.

58. Ibid., 302–3.

59. Ibid., 305.

60. Ibid., 305, 307.

61. Ronda, *Empire*, 236, 237.

62. Hunt, "Diary," 308. For general background in this chapter, I have relied on the fine work of James P. Ronda, *Astoria and Empire*; Philip Ashton Rollins, *The Discovery of the Oregon Trail*; and J. Neilson Barry, "The Trail of the Astorians."

9. "THE INSCRUTABLE WAYS OF PROVIDENCE"

1. Jones, *Annals of Astoria*, 68.

2. Irving, *Astoria*, 322.

3. Ibid., 323.

4. Ibid., 323; Franchere, *Narrative*, 85. The men apparently wandered away from the Snake River at some point. Otherwise, they would have realized that Lewis River and the Snake were one and the same.

5. "Pelton continues as for several days past," McDougall wrote on June 16, 1812; "that he is in reality insane there is now little doubt and has become an object of compassion" (Jones, *Annals of Astoria*, 97).

6. Franchere, *Narrative*, 85.

7. Ross, *First Settlers*, 187.

8. Ibid., 188.

9. Ibid., 188–89.
10. Ibid., 189–90.
11. Ibid., 190.
12. Ibid., 190, 191–92.
13. Ibid., 192–93.
14. Ibid., 193. Dubreuil had been too weak to accompany Crooks and Day and had remained among the Shoshone. Luckily, he would be heard from again.
15. Stuart's Narratives, 3.
16. Ibid., 29, 31. Day told quite a different story to McDougall after arriving back in Astoria, saying he had essentially feigned insanity because he had a conflict with McClellan that he found unbearable. (Jones, *Annals of Astoria*, 115–16.)
17. Stuart's Narratives, 61.
18. Ibid., 83–84. Rollins speculates that "Alexis" and "Michel" could have been references to Alexander Carson and Louis St. Michel, both of whom had broken off from Hunt's group and could have been in the area. But "Makan" bore no obvious relationship to the names of the other men possibly in the region. (Rollins, *Discovery of the Oregon Trail*, 101n150.)
19. Stuart's Narratives, 84.
20. Ibid., 85–86.
21. Ibid., 86. Later in 1812, John Reed traveled from Astoria to retrieve goods from Hunt's cache near Caldron Linn and met Edward Robinson, who reportedly told Reed that Cass had been killed by Indians. "This discrepancy," wrote Irving, "concurred with other circumstances and dark surmises as to the real fate of Cass; but as no substantial grounds were ever adduced for them, we forbear to throw any deeper shades into this story of sufferings in the wilderness" (*Astoria*, 440). Porter interpreted this to mean that Cass's companions "were suspected of having killed and eaten him" ("Roll of Overland Astorians," 105).
22. Stuart's Narratives, 107–8.
23. Ibid., 112, 113.
24. Ibid., 113.
25. Ibid., 129; quotes concerning Soda Springs cited in Fanselow, *Traveling the Oregon Trail*, 129.
26. Stuart's Narratives, 131, 132, 133.
27. Ibid., 133, 134, bracketed insertions and italics in original.
28. Ibid, 135. As Rollins points out, "True, it was not more than 30 miles to where, on Hoback River, Stuart was to camp on October 9; but apparently there was no reason for him to know this fact, and the montane pocket which then encircled him granted no views of distant landmarks." (*Discovery of the Oregon Trail*, 147n85).
29. Stuart's Narratives, 150, 151.
30. Ibid., 151.
31. Ibid., 152.
32. Ibid., 152, 153, 154–55.
33. Ibid., 156.
34. Ibid., 157. This story of the Canadian's grotesque proposal may well have helped start the rumor that Cass's companions had killed and eaten him. See note 21, above.
35. Ibid., 163.
36. Ronda, *Empire*, 323. As Edgeley W. Todd explains, "[The Astorians] were now at the western approach to South Pass, which looks more like a long, sloping hill than like a lofty mountain, in spite of its elevation of 7,550 feet at the summit. The broad recess forming South Pass is bounded on the north by the tapering-off remnants of the southern extremity of the Wind River Mountains, and on the south by the comparatively much lower Antelope Hills. It was toward the Antelope Hills that Stuart was now heading." (Irving, *Astoria*, 406n10).
37. Stuart's Narratives, 239; *Missouri Gazette*, May 8, 1813. See Appendix B for the complete text of the article on the Astorians published in the May 15, 1813, *Missouri Gazette*.
38. The following item ran in the May 29, 1813, *Missouri Gazette*: "TAKE NOTICE. My creditors are hereby notified, that on Monday the 7th day of June 1813, I shall apply to Wm. Christy Esqr. or in his absence, to some other judge of the court of Common Pleas of the country of St. Louis; to take the benefit of the several acts of the Territory, concerning insolvent

debtors, and to be released from my imprisonment, when and where you may attend if you think proper. Robt. M'Clelan. St. Louis jail; May 18th, 1813."

EPILOGUE

1. Ross, *First Settlers*, 266; Franchere, *Journal of a Voyage*, 153n5. Historians have differed on two points: who died of scrofula and what that affliction actually was. A note in Franchere's manuscript reads: "This man died in the month of November, of scrofula." Lamb interprets this as a reference to Turcotte, although Hoyt C. Franchere had argued earlier that it was actually a reference to Landry. Franchere, *Journal of a Voyage*, 153n4; Franchere, *Adventure at Astoria*, 133n3. In addition, most commentators believe scrofula was tuberculosis, but some say syphilis.

2. Franchere, *Journal of a Voyage*, 153n5; Ross, *First Settlers*, 266. See Moulton, *Journals*, 8:351 and 8:352n4 for Lewis and Clark's possible sighting of Delaunay.

3. Ross, *First Settlers*, 266; Cox, *Adventures*, 94.

4. Ross, *First Settlers*, 266, 266–67.

5. Cox, *Adventures*, 94; Ross, *First Settlers*, 267.

6. Ross, *First Settlers*, 267; Cox, *Adventures*, 95.

7. Ross, *First Settlers*, 267.

8. Ross, *First Settlers*, 267; Cox, *Adventures*, 95. Wilson Price Hunt, leader of the westbound Astorians, made it clear that Marie had two children with her in July of 1811 and that one of them was two years old at the end of 1811. Rollins, *Oregon Trail*, 281, 301. Washington Irving, who interviewed a number of Astorians, identified both children as boys and said they were two and four years old at the end of 1811. *Astoria*, 290. Assuming that both boys survived for the next two years—and there is no evidence they didn't—they would have been four and six years old when their father and Reed's other men were killed. I believe this evidence trumps the claim by Cox, who was not an eyewitness of Marie's meeting with the Astorians, that the boys were three years and four months old. *Adventures*, 95. Moreover, it is quite unlikely that Marie could have put both boys on a horse and led them if they had been that young. None of the key sources—Bradbury, Franchere, Ross, Cox, or Irving—actually names the boys. Other nineteenth-century sources, however, identify Baptiste as one of the sons, but some of those sources also muddy the waters by claiming he was born around 1816, not 1807. Barry, "Madame Dorian," 275–78. I have not found any nineteenth-century documents identifying Paul as Pierre and Marie's son, but modern genealogists have done so. (See, for example, http://museum.bmi.net/MARIE%20DORION%20PEOPLE/marie_laguisvoise.htm and http://www.tradegoods.org/dorion.htm, both accessed on June 17, 2009.) Therefore, while I agree with David A. White (*News of the Plains and Rockies*, 1:135) that the boys were named Baptiste and Paul and were four and two years old, respectively, in 1811; the case is hardly rock solid.

9. Cox, *Adventures*, 95.

10. Ross, *First Settlers*, 267.

11. Ibid.

12. Ibid., 268.

13. Ibid.

14. Ibid., 268–69.

15. Ibid., 269–70, italics in original. The ship *Lark* was carrying a number of Astorians when it foundered near the Sandwich Islands in August 1813. See Ronda, *Empire*, 286, 291, 297, for more information.

16. John Jacob Astor to Ramsay Crooks, September 14, 1814, cited in Ronda, *Empire*, 301.

Works Cited

Aarstad, Rich. "'This Unfortunate Affair . . .': An 1810 Letter from the Three Forks of the Missouri." *Selected Papers*. Ed. Jim Hardee. Three Forks: Three Forks Historical Society, 2011. 112–18.

Allen, John L. "The Forgotten Explorers." *Selected Papers*. Ed. Jim Hardee. Three Forks: Three Forks Historical Society, 2011. 26–39.

———. *Passage Through the Garden: Lewis and Clark and the Image of the American Northwest*. Urbana: University of Illinois Press, 1975.

American State Papers, Senate, 16th Congress, 1st Session. Indians Affairs. Vol. 2. Washington, DC: Gales and Seaton, 1832–1861.

Anderson, Marie and Donald. *The Reasoner Story, 1665–1990*. Privately printed in Salt Lake City, 1990. (Copy available at the Family History Library, Salt Lake City.)

Astor, John Jacob. Papers of John Jacob Astor. Baker Library, Harvard University Graduate School of Business Administration, Boston, Mass.

Baldwin, Leland D. *The Keelboat Age on Western Waters*. Pittsburgh: University of Pittsburgh Press, 1941.

Barry, J. Neilson. "Archibald Pelton, the First Follower of Lewis and Clark." *Washington Historical Quarterly* 19 (1928): 199–201.

———. "Madame Dorion of the Astorians." *Oregon Historical Quarterly* 30 (1929): 272–78.

———. "The Trail of the Astorians." *Oregon Historical Quarterly* 13 (1912): 227–39.

Blenkinsop, Willis. "Edward Rose." *Mountain Men*. Ed. LeRoy R. Hafen. Vol. 9. Glendale: A. H. Clark Co., 1965–1972. 335–45.

Brackenridge, Henry Marie. *Journal of a Voyage Up the River Missouri; Performed in Eighteen Hundred and Eleven*. Baltimore: Coale and Maxwell, 1816.

————. *Views of Louisiana: Containing Geographical, Statistical and Historical Notices of That Vast and Important Portion of America.* Baltimore: Schaeffer & Maund, 1817.

Bradbury, John. *Travels in the Interior of America, 2nd ed.*, 1819; reprinted in *Early Western Travels, 1748–1846.* Ed. Reuben Gold Thwaites. Vol. 5. Cleveland: A. H. Clark, 1904–1907.

Brooks, George R. *The Southwest Expedition of Jedediah S. Smith.* 1977. Lincoln: University of Nebraska Press, 1989.

Buckley, Jay A. *William Clark: Indian Diplomat.* Norman: University of Oklahoma Press, 2008.

Calloway, Colin G. *One Vast Winter Count.* Lincoln: University of Nebraska Press, 2003.

Carter, Clarence E., comp. and ed. *The Territorial Papers of the United States.* 25 vols. Washington DC: Government Printing Office, 1943–1960.

Carter, Harvey L. "Ramsay Crooks." *The Mountain Men and the Fur Trade of the Far West.* Ed. LeRoy R. Hafen. Vol. 9. Glendale: A. H. Clark Co., 1965–1972. 125–31.

Carter, Harvey L. "William McClellan." *The Mountain Men and the Fur Trade of the Far West.* Ed. LeRoy R. Hafen. Vol. 7. Glendale: A. H. Clark Co., 1965–1972. 221–28.

Cartwright, Peter. *The Backwoods Preacher: Being the Autobiography of Peter Cartwright, the Oldest American Methodist Traveling Preacher.* London: Daldy, Isbister & Co., 1878.

Chittenden, Hiram M. *The American Fur Trade of the Far West.* 2 vols. 1935. Lincoln: University of Nebraska Press, 1986.

Clarke, Charles G. *Men of the Lewis and Clark Expedition.* 1970. Lincoln: University of Nebraska Press, 2002.

————. "A Roster of the Lewis and Clark Expedition." *Daughters of the American Revolution Magazine* Nov 1965: 878–82,921.

Cohen, Paul E. *Mapping the West: America's Westward Movement, 1524–1890.* New York: Rizzoli, 2002.

Colter-Frick, L. R. *Courageous Colter and Companions.* Washington, Mo.: Privately printed, 1997.

Coues, Elliott, ed. *The History of the Lewis and Clark Expedition.* 3 vols. 1893. New York: Dover Publications, 1979.

————, ed. *New Light on the Early History of the Greater Northwest: The Manuscript Journals of Alexander Henry and David Thompson.* 3 vols. 1897. Minneapolis: Ross and Haines, 1965.

Cox, Ross. *Adventures on the Columbia River*, 1832. Santa Barbara: The Narrative Press, 2004.

Dale, Harrison C. "Did the Returning Astorians Use the South Pass?" *Oregon Historical Quarterly* 17 (1916): 47–51.

Dary, David. *The Oregon Trail: An American Saga*. New York: Oxford University Press, 2004.

"Diary of Reverend Jason Lee-III." *Oregon Historical Quarterly* 17 (1916): 397–430.

Douglas, Walter B. *Manuel Lisa*. New York: Argosy-Antiquarian Ltd., 1964.

Drumm, Stella M., ed. [John Luttig's] *Journal of a Fur-Trading Expedition on the Upper Missouri, 1812–1813*. St. Louis: Missouri Historical Society, 1920.

———. "More About Astorians." *Oregon Historical Quarterly* 24 (1923): 335–60.

Elliott, T. C. "Last Will and Testament of John Day." *Oregon Historical Quarterly* 17 (1916): 373–79.

———. "Wilson Price Hunt, 1783–1842." *Oregon Historical Quarterly* 32 (June 1931): 130–34.

Fanselow, Julie. *Traveling the Oregon Trail*. Guilford: Falcon, 2001.

Foley, William E. *Wilderness Journey: The Life of William Clark*. Columbia: University of Missouri Press, 2004.

Fox, John Sharpless. "Narrative of Jean Baptiste Perrault." *Michigan Pioneer and Historical Collections* 37 (1909–1910): 508–619.

Franchere, Gabriel. *Journal of a Voyage on the North West Coast of North America during the Years 1811, 1812, 1813, and 1814*. Edited by W. Kaye Lamb. Toronto: Champlain Society, 1969.

———. *Narrative of a Voyage to the Northwest Coast of America in the Years 1811, 1812, 1813, and 1814*. Trans. and ed. J. V. Huntington, 1854. Charleston: Bibliobazaar, 2007.

Ghent, William. "Sketch of John Colter." *Annals of Wyoming* 10 (July 1938): 111–116.

Greene, Candace S. and Russell Thornton. *The Year the Stars Fell: Lakota Winter Counts at the Smithsonian*. Lincoln: University of Nebraska Press, 2007.

Hafen, LeRoy R. *The Mountain Men and the Fur Trade of the Far West*. 10 vols. Glendale: A. H. Clark Co., 1965–72.

Hardee, Jim. *Pierre's Hole! The Fur Trade History of Teton Valley, Idaho*. Pinedale: Sublette County Historical Society, 2010.

———, ed. *Selected Papers of the 2010 Fur Trade Symposium at the Three Forks*. Three Forks: Three Forks Historical Society, 2011. 98–111.

———. "The Fort at the Forks: 'A Good State of Defense." *Selected Papers*. Three Forks: Three Forks Historical Society, 2011. 98–111.

———. "The Ordeal of Marie Dorion." *True West*, October 1991: 46–49.

Harris, Burton. *John Colter: His Years in the Rockies*. 1952. Lincoln: University of Nebraska Press, 1993.

Heidenreich, C. Adrian. *Smoke Signals in Crow (Apsáalooke) Country: Beyond the Capture of Horses from the Lewis and Clark Expedition.* Billings: Author, 2006.

Heitman, Francis. *Historical Register and Dictionary of the United States Army from its Organization, September 28, 1789, to March 2, 1903.* 2 vols. Washington DC: Government Printing Office. 1903. Urbana: University of Illinois Press, 1965.

Holmberg, James J. *Dear Brother: Letters of William Clark to Jonathan Clark.* New Haven: Yale University Press, 2002.

Holmes, Reuben. "The Five Scalps." *Missouri Historical Society Glimpses of the Past* 5 (January–March 1938): 1–54.

Howard, Harold. *Sacajawea.* Norman: University of Oklahoma Press, 1971.

Hunt, Wilson Price. "Wilson Price Hunt's Diary of his Overland Trip Westward to Astoria in 1811–12." *Discovery of the Oregon Trail.* Trans. for *Nouvelles Annales des Voyages*, Paris, 1821. Ed. Philip Ashton Rollins. New York: Charles Scribner's Sons, 1935. 281–328.

Irving, Washington. *Astoria.* 1836. Ed. Edgley W. Todd. Norman: University of Oklahoma Press, 1964.

Irving, Washington. *The Rocky Mountains: or, Scenes Incidents, and Adventures in the Far West; Digested from the Journal of Capt. B. L. E. Bonneville.* 2 vols. Philadelphia: Carey, Lea, and Blanchard, 1837.

Jackson, Donald. "Journey to the Mandans, 1809; the Lost Narrative of Dr. Thomas." *Bulletin of the Missouri Historical Society* 20 (April 1964): 179–192.

———, ed. *Letters of the Lewis and Clark Expedition with Related Documents.* 2 vols. 1963. Urbana: University of Illinois Press, 1978.

James, Thomas. *Three Years Among the Indians and Mexicans.* Philadelphia: J. B. Lippincott Company, 1962.

Jones, Landon Y. *William Clark and the Shaping of the West.* New York: Hill and Wang, 2004.

Jones, Robert F., ed. *Annals of Astoria. The Headquarters Log of the Pacific Fur Company on the Columbia River, 1811–1813.* New York: Fordham University Press, 1999.

———, ed. *Astorian Adventure. The Journal of Alfred Seton, 1811–1815.* New York: Fordham University Press, 1993.

Josephy, Alvin M. "Ordeal in Hell's Canyon." *American Heritage* 18 (December 1966): 73–95.

Kelly, Mark W. "The Evacuation of the Three Forks–per the Doughterty Map." *Selected Papers.* Ed. Jim Hardee. Three Forks: Three Forks Historical Society, 2011. 149–82.

Lamar, Howard R. *The New Encyclopedia of the American West.* New Haven: Yale University Press, 1998.

Lavender, David. "Ramsay Crooks's Early Ventures on the Missouri River: A Series of Conjectures." *Bulletin of the Missouri Historical Society* 20 (July 1964): 91–106.

———. *The Fist in the Wilderness*. 1964. Lincoln: University of Nebraska Press, 1998.

"Letters from Three Forks." *Selected Papers*. Ed. Jim Hardee. Three Forks: Three Forks Historical Society, 2011. 119–32.

Madsen, Axel. *John Jacob Astor: America's First Multimillionaire*. New York: John Wiley and Sons, 2001.

Majors, Harry M. "John McClellan in the Montana Rockies, 1807: The First Americans after Lewis and Clark." *Northwest Discovery* 2 (November–December 1981): 554–630.

Marshall, Thomas Maitland, ed. *The Life and Papers of Frederick Bates*. St. Louis: Missouri Historical Society, 1926.

Mattes, Merrill J. "Behind the Legend of Colter's Hell: The Early Exploration of Yellowstone Park." *Mississippi Valley Historical Review* 36 (September 1949): 151–82.

———. "John Dougherty." *Mountain Men*. Ed. LeRoy R. Hafen. Vol. 8. Glendale: A. H. Clark Co., 1965–72. 113–42.

Moore, Bob. "Pompey's Baptism." *We Proceeded On* 26 (February 2000): 11–17.

Morris, Larry E. "After the Expedition." *American History* (March–April, 2003): 44–56, 58, 60.

———. "Dependable John Ordway." *We Proceeded On* 27 (May 2001): 28–33.

———. *The Fate of the Corps: What Became of the Lewis and Clark Explorers After the Expedition*. New Haven: Yale University Press, 2004.

———. "The Life of John Colter. *We Proceeded On* 34 (November 2008): 6–15.

———. "The Mysterious Charles Courtin and the Early Missouri Fur Trade." *Missouri Historical Review* 104 (October 2009): 21–39.

Moulton, Gary, ed. *The Journals of the Lewis and Clark Expedition*. 13 vols. Lincoln: University of Nebraska Press, 1986–97.

Munnick, Harriet D. *Catholic Church Records of the Pacific Northwest: St. Paul, Oregon 1839–1989*. Oregon City: Binford & Mort Pubs, 1980.

———. "Pierre Dorion." *Mountain Men*. Ed. LeRoy R. Hafen. Vol 8. Glendale: A. H. Clark Co., 1965–1972. 107–12.

Noy, Gary. *Distant Horizon: Documents from the Nineteenth-Century American West*. Lincoln: University of Nebraska Press, 1999.

Oglesby, Richard E. "Manuel Lisa." *Mountain Men*. Ed. LeRoy R. Hafen. Vol. 5. Glendale: A. H. Clark Co., 1965–1972. 179–201.

———. *Manuel Lisa and the Opening of the Missouri Fur Trade*. Norman: University of Oklahoma Press, 1963.

Payette, B. C. *The Oregon Country Under the Union Jack*. Postscript Edition. Montreal, Canada: Payette Radio Limited, 1962.

Peltier, Jerome. *Madame Dorion*. Fairfield, WA: Ye Galleon Press, 1980.

Pelton, J. M. *Genealogy of the Pelton Family in America*. Albany: Joel Munsell's Sons, 1892.

Perrault, Jean Baptiste. "Narrative of the Travels and Adventures of a Merchant Voyageur in the Savage Territories of Northern America Leaving Montreal the 28th of May 1783." *Michigan Pioneer and Historical Collections*. Ed. John Sharpless Fox. Vol. 37. 1909–1910. 508–619.

Porter, Kenneth W. *John Jacob Astor, Business Man*. 2 vols. Cambridge: Harvard University Press, 1931.

———. "Roll of Overland Astorians, 1810–1812." *Oregon Historical Quarterly* 34 (June 1933): 103–12.

The Preston and Virginia Papers of the Draper Collection of Manuscripts. Madison: State Historical Society of Wisconsin, 1915.

Reed, John. Journal of John Reed. Baker Library, Harvard University Graduate School of Business Administration, Boston, Mass.

Robinson, Doane. "Our First Family." *South Dakota Historical Collections* 13 (1926): 46–68.

Rollins, Philip Ashton, ed. *The Discovery of the Oregon Trail*. New York: Charles Scribner's Sons, 1935.

Ronda, James P. *Astoria and Empire*. Lincoln: University of Nebraska Press, 1990.

———. *Lewis and Clark among the Indians*. Lincoln: University of Nebraska Press, 1984.

Ross, Alexander. *Adventures of the First Settlers on the Columbia River, 1810–1813*. 1904. Oregon State University Press: Corvallis, 2000.

Russell, Carl P. *Firearms, Traps, and Tools of the Mountain Men*. New York: Knopf, 1967.

Skarsten, M. O. *George Drouillard: Hunter and Interpreter for Lewis and Clark and Fur Trader, 1807–1810*. 1964. University of Nebraska Press: Lincoln, 2005.

Speck, Gordon. *Breeds and Half-Breeds*. New York: Clarkson N. Potter, 1969.

Stuart, Robert. "Robert Stuart's Narratives of His Overland Trip Eastward from Astoria in 1812–13." *Discovery of the Oregon Trail*. Ed. Philip Ashton Rollins. New York: Charles Scribner's Sons, 1935. 3–263. [From the original manuscripts in the collection of William Robertson Coe, Esq.]

Thompson, David. "Narrative of the Expedition to the Kootanae and Flat Bow Indian Countries, on the Sources of the Columbia River, Pacific Ocean." *Oregon Historical Quarterly* 26 (March 1925): 23–49.

Thwaites, Reuben Gold. *Early Western Travels, 1748–1846*. 32 vols. Cleveland: A. H. Clark, 1904–1907.

Townsend, John K. *Narrative of a Journey Across the Rocky Mountains, to the Columbia River*. Philadelphia: Henry Perkins, 1839.

Tubbs, Stephenie Ambrose. *The Lewis and Clark Companion: An Encyclopedic Guide to the Voyage of Discovery*. New York: Henry Holt and Company, 2003.

Utley, Robert M. *A Life Wild and Perilous: Mountain Men and the Paths to the Pacific*. New York: Henry Holt and Company, 1997.

Vinton, Stallo. *John Colter, Discoverer of Yellowstone Park*. New York: E. Eberstadt, 1926.

Wegman-French, Lysa, and Charles Haecker. "Recent Historical and Archaeological Investigations Toward Finding Manuel Lisa's 1807 Fort." *Selected Papers*. Ed. Jim Hardee. Three Forks: Three Forks Historical Society, 2011. 40–53.

White, David A. *News of the Plains and Rockies, 1803–1865*. Vol 1. Spokane: Arthur H. Clark, 1996.

White, James Haley. "Early Days in St. Louis." *Missouri Historical Society Glimpses of the Past* 6 (January–March 1939): 5–13.

White, Linda Harper, and Fred R. Gowans. "Andrew Henry and the Rocky Mountain Fur Trade." *Montana: The Magazine of Western History* 43 (Winter 1993): 58–65.

Williams, Marion. *The Hoback Family's American Story*. No date, no publisher. (Copy available at the Kentucky Historical Society, Frankfort, Kentucky.)

Wishart, David J. *The Fur Trade of the American West, 1807–1840: A Geographical Synthesis*. Lincoln: University of Nebraska Press, 1979.

Wood, W. Raymond. "Manuel Lisa's Fort Raymond: First Post in the Far West, November 1807–March 1813." From the website Discovering Lewis & Clark, http://lewis-clark.org/content/content-article.asp?ArticleID=2970, accessed on March 30, 2012.

Wood, W. Raymond, and Thomas D. Thiessen, eds. *Early Fur Trade on the Northern Plains: Canadian Traders Among the Mandan and Hidatsa Indians, 1738–1818*. Norman: University of Oklahoma Press, 1985.

Woodger, Elin, and Brandon Toropov. *Encyclopedia of The Lewis and Clark Expedition*. New York: Checkmark Books, 2004.

Index

About the Author

Larry E. Morris is the author of *The Fate of the Corps*, which was named a Top Academic Title by *Choice* and a History Book Club selection. Morris has published articles on early Western history in such periodicals as *The Missouri Historical Review*, *American History*, and *We Proceeded On*. He is a senior editor with the Joseph Smith Papers Project. He and his wife, Deborah, have four children—Isaac, Courtney, Justin, and Whitney—and live in Salt Lake City.